99

99

STORIES OF THE GAME

WAYNE GRETZKY

with KIRSTIE McLELLAN DAY

VIKING

VIKING

an imprint of Penguin Canada, a division of Penguin Random House Canada Limited

Canada • USA • UK • Ireland • Australia • New Zealand • India • South Africa • China

First published 2016

www.penguinrandomhouse.ca

LIBRARY AND ARCHIVES CANADA CATALOGUING IN PUBLICATION

Gretzky, Wayne, 1961-, author
99 : stories of the game / Wayne Gretzky with Kirstie McLellan Day.

ISBN 978-0-7352-3262-4 (hardback)
ISBN 978-0-7352-3263-1 (electronic)

1. National Hockey League—History. 2. Hockey—History.
I. McLellan Day, Kirstie, author II. Title. III. Title: Ninety-nine.

GV847.8.N3G74 2016   796.962'64   C2016-902527-6

Cover design by Stephen Brayda
Cover image by Bruce Bennett/Getty Images

Printed and bound in the United States of America

10 9 8 7 6 5 4 3 2 1

Penguin
Random House
Canada

*dedicated to
all the hockey parents and grandparents,
especially my own*

CONTENTS

PROLOGUE

A lot can change in ninety-nine years. When I think of how different the world is today from the way it was when my grandparents were growing up, it seems as though just about anything that feels permanent could change beyond all recognition over all that time.

But some things really don't change. Probably the most important things. And to me, hockey is one of the most important things. I have always loved the game of hockey. I love the old stories, and the personalities that make the game great. I love the speed, and the grace and athleticism, of course. But behind every big play, there's a guy who grew up dreaming of making that big play. He's got a story, and he was inspired by someone else's.

One of the truly amazing things about coming into the NHL as a rookie is that you are pretty much guaranteed to find yourself in the dressing room with, or lining up against, a guy you grew up idolizing. For me, that was Gordie Howe—I think that is a well-known fact. But there is not a player in the league who didn't take a look around on his first day and realize that the guy he wanted to be one day is right there in front of him.

That's why these stories I've brought together here are so important to me. They're not just a list of things that have happened in hockey over the past ninety-nine years. These stories are what keep the game going. They record what the game is really about.

We talk a lot about how the game has changed over the years, from the golden age of the Original Six, through the wild violence of the 70s and the high-scoring "river hockey" of the 80s, through the defense-first 90s, and so on. We talk about how coaching and fitness and goaltending styles are different now. And we talk about how players are so much bigger and faster today. And that is all true. But none of this means that hockey itself has changed.

When we look at old photos of players from the league's early years, with their slicked-back hair and woolen sweaters, it's easy to forget that they were someone's heroes. But that is exactly who they were. Just as Pavel Datsyuk and Steve Stamkos are some kid's heroes today. They played the same game, with the same passion, and thrilled their fans in exactly the same way.

Those guys in the black-and-white photos or grainy old footage are no different from the players we see in today's NHL. Sure, guys today are bigger on average. But biggest never meant best. You don't have to look very hard to find a smaller guy among the top scorers in the league. And sure, the game is faster now than it has ever been. But faster doesn't mean better either. Or not exactly. There have always been the Guy Lafleurs and Glenn Andersons and Alex Ovechkins who could kill you with pure speed. But I can think of a couple of guys who were not the greatest skaters who scored more goals than any of those three.

As for toughness, as you'll see in the chapters that follow, some of the things that went on ninety-nine years ago would have made the Broad Street Bullies blush.

Yes, hockey is fast and rough and tough. But being faster and rougher and tougher doesn't necessarily make you better. I have been on a team that came out on top in a game even though we knew that the guys in the other room were more skilled. It happens. Some teams that look great on paper don't work out on the ice. I've been part of that side of it too.

It happens in part because no one knows exactly what makes hockey hockey. It's not just the rules. Those change. It's not the equipment. God knows, everything is a lot different today. (But it is fun to imagine Bobby Hull stepping into a slap shot with one of the composite sticks Shea Weber uses, or a speed demon like Howie Morenz wearing ultra-lightweight custom Bauers like Taylor Hall's.) What makes hockey the greatest game on the planet is something else. Something you can't quite put your finger on. Coaches and GMs would be invincible if they knew exactly what makes a team more than just names on a roster. But even the Scotty Bowmans and Pat Quinns had their share of losses. The fact is, greatness is not captured in statistics. It's captured in stories.

It seems to me that part of the secret of what makes our game so great can be found in the origins of the precursor to the NHL— the first professional league, which was started up in northern Michigan, of all places, in a town called Houghton. That's right. We always think of hockey as a Canadian sport, but the first professional hockey league was started in the United States—though it was founded by a Canadian, a dentist named Jack Gibson.

Gibson was a really good player, but he received a lifetime ban from one of the most powerful and influential hockey organizations in the country, the Ontario Hockey Association (OHA), when his team won the provincial intermediate championship and each of the players accepted a ten-dollar gold coin from the mayor of the Ontario city of Berlin, which is now called Kitchener. That was considered a violation of the spirit of amateurism. If Gibson wanted to play hockey, it was not going to be in Canada.

After dental school, Gibson moved to Houghton, a working-class town full of copper miners who loved the toughness of the game. People called Houghton "the Canada of the United States" because of the long, harsh winters. A young reporter noticed Gibson had a few articles about his hockey-playing days in a binder in his waiting room. Some businesspeople in the community got together and persuaded him to captain a professional team, the Portage Lakes. Towns around Houghton formed rival teams and together they created the International Hockey League (IHL) in 1904–1905. Even though the OHA forbade Canadian teams from playing in the IHL, a team from Sault Ste. Marie did it anyway. It was game on.

It can't have been very fun playing against the Portage Lakes. It was seven-man hockey, played sixty minutes with a ten-minute rest at halftime. There were no substitutions unless a player was knocked out cold. And slashing wasn't slashing until you hit above the knees. Goalies were not allowed to go down, but that may have been for the best, as they also didn't wear masks. That season, the Lakes piled up 258 goals for and only 49 goals against in 25 games, an average of more than 10 goals per game.

In 1904, Jack's team challenged both the 1902 Stanley Cup winner, Montreal's AAA Little Men of Iron, and the 1903 and 1904 Stanley Cup champion, the Ottawa Silver Seven. Both said no. But that same year during a Stanley Cup challenge series between Ottawa and the Montreal Wanderers, the owners of the two teams got into a fight over a tie game and the Wanderers dropped out of the playoffs. Jack Gibson jumped on the opportunity and challenged the Wanderers to a two-game "world championship." It wasn't even close. That March, the pride of a small mining town in northern Michigan smoked the Montreal Wanderers 8–4 and 9–2.

Some of the best players from Canada had been playing in the States because they were paid openly. There had always been some secret payments to get players to stay in Canada, but by 1906 professionals were allowed into the Eastern Canada Amateur Hockey Association, and that opened the door to professional hockey. The Lakes lost their goalie, Riley Hern, to the Montreal Wanderers in 1906. He would go on to win three Stanley Cups with them. As fewer and fewer Canadian players migrated to the IHL, the league found itself starved for talent and eventually folded. Jack Gibson packed up and moved his practice to Calgary in 1909.

The league hadn't lasted long, but it had captured what is so exciting about the game. It brought together a bunch of guys who wanted to see how they stacked up against the best opposition they could find. The fact that the rules against professionalism quickly changed is a pretty strong sign that the IHL was onto something. Getting paid to play hockey doesn't mean you love it any less. In fact, it may allow you to love it more.

The Portage Lakes were going out of their way to look for a challenge. They had to go knocking on doors to prove they were the best in the world. Today, there is only one route to the top of the hockey world, but it is generally considered the most grueling route to the top in any major sport—as many as twenty-eight games played at white-hot intensity. In the 2013 Stanley Cup final, Patrice Bergeron played with a broken rib, a separated shoulder, torn muscles, and a punctured lung. He wasn't earning his regular salary to do any of this, and after the last game he lined up and shook hands with the guys who had put him through all this pain.

To me, that echoes the spirit of those first pro players. They didn't love the game because they were professionals—they became professionals because they loved the game. That is what makes our game great, and I can't imagine that ever changing.

I don't think I am all that different from the kid I used to be, who was fascinated by the stories of hard-nosed guys from small towns who took on the world and made their mark. And I don't think that kid was any different from the kid down the street or across town. We all love these stories, and we are all shaped by them.

This year is the league's 99th anniversary. And 99 is a pretty special number to me. It's special not because I wore it. It's special because someone who came before me wore number 9. All I wanted to be when I was growing up was Gordie Howe. It was the same for Gordie. He idolized the guys who came before him, and I know it's the same for the guys who came after me. Without these stories, I would not have been the player I was, and the NHL wouldn't be the league that it is today. This past June we all came face-to-face with what the history of hockey means to us when one of hockey's greatest stories came to an end. People around the world paused to acknowledge what Gordie Howe had meant to them when he passed away. I was at the visitation myself, and I met people who had flown in from Russia, Finland, and even France. Gordie played at a time before hockey was truly international, and yet there at Joe Louis Arena in Detroit, I saw with my own eyes that his legacy means something wherever the game is played.

I don't think there will ever be a better ambassador for the game or anyone better suited to the name Mr. Hockey. Gordie was everything we love about this sport we play and cheer for. Our game is about grace and toughness, about unyielding courage and complete humility. That's what it is at its best, anyway. And that was Gordie. There were people at the funeral who were proud of the scars he had given them, and there were many more with stories of Mr. Hockey's legendary kindness.

For me, though, the best Gordie Howe memory I have is when I met my idol for the very first time. I was just a kid, and he was even greater than I had hoped he would be. I told all of my friends about it then, and still talk about it today. It's just like when you watch a bunch of kids playing road hockey or practicing the shoot-out moves they saw on Saturday night. Stories are as important to the game as ice and pucks.

Imagine being a hockey fan and never having heard of, say, Mario Lemieux or Bobby Orr, Jean Béliveau or Bobby Hull. It would be a bit like not knowing the game at all. They changed the game in ways we can only be grateful for. And the same goes for the guys that came before them, the guys who played our game ninety-nine years ago.

So, to the builders like Gibson and the Patrick brothers, to Howie Morenz, hockey's first star player, to all the superstars from around the world who have lit up the league, and to all the third- and fourth-line guys who played just as important a role—this book is a thank-you.

One

THE FIRST
HOCKEY STAR

When I was fourteen or fifteen years old, I'd head down to Canadian National Exhibition Stadium in Toronto, pay a buck, go to a Blue Jays game, and then walk around the Hockey Hall of Fame just staring at everything for hours. My friends used to say, "You're going to the Hall of Fame again?"

I'd say, "Yeah."

They'd say, "Same stuff there as last week."

That was the point. I'd look at Howie Morenz's stick and think, "How did he score so much with that stick?" It was so straight and heavy. On some of the old sticks you could even see the nail that joined the blade to the shaft. As a kid, I couldn't get over how different everything looked from the equipment that I was using at the time.

By the time I was playing in the NHL, I was using the best sticks in the world. But today kids look at my sticks and wonder how we ever played the game with lumber like that. Put it this way: you can pick up a goalie stick today and my wooden Titan would've been twice as heavy. The two guys with the stiffest and heaviest sticks in the league in my era were Mike Bossy and me. In fact, he and I used pretty much the same stick for a long time. We might not have had the hardest shots, but we both knew exactly where the puck was going to go. Fans will probably remember the way Bossy and Guy Lafleur would wind up and take a slap shot off the rush at full speed. I used to do the same thing. With a stick that stiff, you needed that windup to get a heavy shot.

With today's whippier sticks, guys can load up quickly and shoot off the back foot, which takes a lot less time. In my experience, the game changed considerably between 1987 and 1997 in that there was less time to get off a slap shot with a full windup. Mark Messier was one of the first guys to shoot off the back foot to catch a goalie napping. I remember Owen Nolan did the same thing in the 1997 All-Star game—though he wasn't trying to catch Dominik Hasek napping. He actually pointed at the corner he was aiming at and still beat Hasek. But those are big, strong guys. Now everyone is using a whippy stick, and using the release to fool goalies into misreading the angle. A guy like Phil Kessel uses his stick like a slingshot. The only time you see a slap shot now pretty much is when a defenseman has time to tee one up from the point. And it's no surprise that the guys with the hardest shots use the stiffest sticks. Shea Weber, Zdeno Chara, and Brent Burns use sticks that a lot of guys couldn't even bend.

In 1989, Jim Easton, who was a good friend of mine, came to me and said, "Wayne, we have this stick for you. It's a product you're going to love. We were able to make the stiffness that you like, but it's only a third of the weight." It was a two-piece stick with an aluminum shaft. I loved it. It was still very stiff—a slap shot seemed to explode off the blade. But it was so light that all the weight was in the blade, so you could feel the puck better.

I thought, "Okay. That sounds good." Because, believe it or not, as a kid I always used a light stick. My dad always said, "You gotta have a light stick."

The other thing I did with my wooden sticks was round the shaft so it was more like a lacrosse stick. Paul Coffey did the same thing. It made it easier to roll your hands down the stick and it was much more comfortable. So Easton made me this stick that was stiff and had a rounded shaft but was much lighter. The first time I used it I thought, "Wow! Where has this been all my life?"

In L.A. our equipment manager Peter Millar taped my sticks. A lot of people have a tape knob, but I liked a pre-cut knob on top. Every stick was dated. So if you think you've got one of my game sticks, have a look at the end of the stick and there'll be a date on it written with a Sharpie. By then I was using the Easton aluminum two-piece so Peter would tape up the blade, heat it up, put it in the shaft, and then add the knob and mark the date.

Very few guys used an aluminum two-piece at the time, so when I started using the Easton it kind of changed hockey for a while, because everybody followed. I never used the composite one-piece, but players today swear by it. These days if you showed them an aluminum two-piece, they would look at you and say, "What the heck is that?" And I don't blame them because that's the way I felt back when I was looking at Howie Morenz's sticks when I was a kid.

Obviously, Howie Morenz was before my time. He was before Gordie Howe's time. In fact, when Maurice Richard started tearing up the league, Morenz was the guy fans compared him to. But while I had never seen him play, looking at his stick, I had some sense of what the game would have been like when he played. I could easily imagine how the puck would feel on the blade of a heavy stick like that. The sticks guys used back then were a lot shorter, so I could see that they would have had to play with their hands closer together. You would have the puck on a string with a short stick like that, and a wrist shot would be tough for a goalie to read coming off the blade. But you would really have to keep your head up.

You can see how just looking at those old sticks would fire up a kid's imagination. Peering through the glass of the Hall of Fame, I could see how the game was played. It would have been incredibly tough, but it would also have been an elegant game built around puck control and shrewdly and spontaneously exploiting opportunities. That's how Howie Morenz played the game anyway.

In 1950, the Canadian Press polled sportswriters across the country. They named Morenz the greatest hockey player of the first half of the century. Because so few of us have seen him play, it's not easy to understand what an achievement that is. But put it this way—look at the guys who would top anyone's list of the best players of the *second* half of the century. Howe, Richard, Hull, Orr, Lafleur, Lemieux. To be the best of the second half of the century, you would have to be better than all of them. Anyone who was the best of the first half is in that league.

Morenz was certainly the NHL's first superstar. Games were sold out wherever he played. For many American fans new to hockey, Morenz was the face of the game. His speed and grace defined hockey for its newest fans, and redefined it for those who loved the game. More than any who had come before him, Morenz showed that while hockey would always be a team game, true greatness could lift people out of their seats.

Howie Morenz was the youngest of six kids. He grew up playing hockey on Mill Pond, which was part of the Thames River, just a few blocks from his home in Mitchell, Ontario. After school, he'd grab a pair of old two-dollar tube skates that had already been through his two older brothers and the new stick he got for Christmas. The most popular stick at the time was a Draper and Maynard Sporting Goods stick with the tip painted red. It was made of ash and just about as strong as steel. A stick like that would last years.

Morenz played shinny with his brothers. His friends and family have said that you could always find him on the ice with a stick in his hand. He would carry a chunk of coal in his pocket to shoot on the pond. Over and over again, he'd whack it down the ice. But sometimes it would jump the tree trunk he used as a goalie, so he had to skate as fast as he could to try to catch it before it went too far. If you've ever skated on a frozen pond, you know it's full of rocks and frozen twigs and branches. Perth County is also a migratory path for diver birds. That meant more than a million ducks flew overhead during peak migration. Morenz had to learn to pivot fast or he'd trip over the frozen duck droppings on the ice.

I know kids don't play outdoors as much as they used to. But for me it has always been part of the game. I first skated on the Nith River, which ran behind my grandparents' backyard, so I know a little what it must have felt like for Morenz. My father used to take me to the park in Brantford before he built our first backyard rink. Even when I was with the Oilers, if we had some time off between a Saturday night and a midweek game, Kevin Lowe, Marty McSorley, Paul Coffey, and I would sometimes grab our sticks and gloves and head down to the pond to play with the kids who would be shooting a tennis ball around. I remember that our skates didn't have to be as sharp as they would be on indoor ice, as they didn't have to bite as deep. Like Morenz, we had to watch out for cracks in the ice—and make sure our shots were on net. Otherwise we would be hunting for the ball or puck in the snow.

Morenz got better and better, working his way up to junior in the OHA. He was fast, but he didn't think he was good enough to play professionally. He had a temper on the ice and got into a few fights, but off the ice he was an easygoing guy. The family then moved to Stratford. He loved living there and hanging out with his buddies. When he was done school, he played amateur hockey with the Grand Trunk Railway team.

In 1923, when Morenz was twenty, Léo Dandurand was the managing partner of the Montreal Canadiens. Dandurand and his friends, one of the Canadiens' first goaltenders, Joe Cattarinich, along with businessman Louis Letourneau, had owned the team since 1921.

They bought it at auction. Dandurand called his friend Cecil Hart to represent them. They were competing against the Mount Royal Arena Company and NHL president Frank Calder. The bid was up to $10,000 when Hart called Dandurand and asked him what to do. Dandurand said to go to the limit. Hart came back into the room and offered $11,000 and won the bid. That was a lot of money back then. A labor job paid about fifty-five cents per hour. Less than four dollars a day. It would have taken most guys ten years to earn $11,000. But the investment was worth it. The Canadiens made $20,000 net that first year.

Dandurand, Cattarinich, and Hart wanted Morenz to join the Canadiens. But Morenz's parents, William and his wife, Rosina, were born in Germany, which was suffering from the terrible after-effects of the First World War. Their families back in the old country were in bad financial trouble and needed help. The German mark was basically worthless, reduced to one-trillionth of its value. It took a wheelbarrow of them to buy a loaf of bread. Morenz had only two more years of apprenticeship for his machinist ticket so his father wanted him to stay and complete it.

Dandurand wasn't taking no for an answer. He called Cecil Hart again and gave him two signed blank checks. He told him to meet with Morenz and his dad and to get the kid to come to Montreal. Hart signed Morenz on July 7, 1923. The contract was for three years at $2,500 per year, with an $850 signing bonus.

Both Morenz and his father had second thoughts immediately. Morenz's mother had just died and he felt bad about leaving home. He sent the check back to the Canadiens and said he'd decided to play in the OHA instead.

Léo Dandurand sent Morenz a train ticket and told the press he knew amateurs got paid under the table and he was going to blackball Howie if he backed out of his contract. Morenz came to see him. He was upset. He had tears in his eyes when he told Dandurand he wasn't big enough or strong enough to play pro hockey and that moving to Montreal would ruin his life. But Dandurand wouldn't budge. Finally, reluctantly, the league's first star committed to the Canadiens.

Georges Vezina was the goalie. Vezina had signed with the team thirteen years earlier. He had the best goals-against average in the league, 1.97. He allowed just 48 goals in 24 games that season. To give you an idea of just how good that is, Henrik Lundqvist from the Rangers has a 2.28 career GAA, Jonathan Quick from the Kings has a career 2.27 GAA and Canadiens' Carey Price, who might be the best in the world right now, has a career 2.43. In others words, Montreal had one of the best goalies of all time in net.

On March 22, 1924, the Canadiens played the Calgary Tigers of the Western Canada Hockey League in the first game of a best-of-three Stanley Cup final that began at Montreal's Mount Royal Arena.

The Mount Royal Arena was four years old and it used natural ice. The problem with natural ice is you're at the mercy of the weather. And the weather in Montreal that March was so warm the ice was melting. In 1990, when I was with the Kings, we played exhibition games in Miami and St. Petersburg in slush and it is really tough. Your leg muscles ache from trying to push through it. The puck won't lie flat. Of course, both teams have to play on the same bad ice, so it's no use complaining about it. Still, you never want to see a game decided by the ice conditions.

Bad ice definitely works against a guy like Morenz, whose game was speed and puck control. He was a rookie and had defenses looking for him, the same way Connor McDavid does today. And yet somehow he still managed to make the end-to-end rushes he'd become famous for. The series was so exciting that Charles Adams, a Boston hockey fan who owned a chain of grocery stores, was inspired to buy the city's first NHL franchise, the Boston Bruins. More about that later.

In the first game, Calgary lost 6–1. The ice had become unplayable so Game Two was moved to the Ottawa Auditorium, which had artificial ice.

It was a rough game. Any team handed a lopsided loss is going to respond with a new level of intensity, and that often means a very physical game. True champions are the teams that have an answer for that. Morenz kept the first-period shots on goal even and scored one for the Canadiens. The Tigers stormed back. Calgary's captain, Herb Gardiner, who had thirty pounds on Howie, caught him in the middle of the ice with an elbows-up check. I saw Marty McSorley do the same thing to Doug Gilmour sixty-nine years later when we played in the 1993 Cup semifinal against the Leafs, and it turned the series around.

Morenz came off with his arm dangling at his side and a cut on the head. He was on his way to the hospital by the start of the third period. On the other side of the ledger, Montreal enforcer Sprague Cleghorn got a stick up on Calgary's Bernie Morris in the first period and sent him to the dressing room. Morris played the rest of the game with his head wrapped in bandages. During his career, Cleghorn sent fifty "stretcher jobs" to the hospital. Two years later, Cleghorn was traded to the newly formed Boston Bruins, where he'd end up mentoring a young defenseman named Eddie Shore.

In the last four minutes, the Tigers pulled their goalie to go with six attackers. But Vezina had a hot hand. The final score was 3–0 Canadiens.

By 1932–33, Morenz had won the Cup three times. He had also won three Hart trophies as the league's most valuable player. The New York Americans' goaltender, Roy Worters, called him "that s.o.b. seven seventy-seven" because when Howie started down for the rush, he moved so fast it looked like he had three sevens instead of just one on his sweater.

The NHL is unique among the major sports in that players shake hands after a hard-fought playoff series, but Morenz took sportsmanship even further. After a loss, he would go into the winning dressing room to shake hands. He was a great sportsman, but inside, he took losses hard. Sometimes he'd walk the streets all night just to cool off. He might end up at a teammate's door before the sun came up to talk about what went wrong in the game.

Everywhere he played, he became a marked man. That's the way it works with every superstar. He was sticked and hacked and whacked every time he stepped on the ice. He would pick himself up and come back just as hard. That's the other part of being a star. Think of Paul Kariya scraping himself off the ice after getting run over by Scott Stevens in 2003, then coming back to put an absolute laser over Martin Brodeur's shoulder. If a guy like Morenz was going to play in the NHL, that was the way he would have to play.

His whole line played that way. His left-winger, Aurel "Little Giant" Joliat, was only 5'7" and 136 pounds, but he didn't back down from anyone. Joliat played in the Habs' very first game in the Forum when it opened in 1924, scoring twice in a 7–1 win over Toronto. And he delighted the crowd one last time in 1984 when he did a couple of laps and scored a goal on Jacques Plante. He was eighty-three years old. He had played sixteen seasons with the Canadiens and is still the second-highest scoring left-winger in Montreal history, behind Steve Shutt.

Joliat would often tell a story about Morenz. In a game against the Montreal Maroons, he was rushing in on goal when two defensemen locked their sticks in front of him. Going full tilt, he ran into the sticks, did a somersault up in the air, and landed on his head. After the game, his teammates asked him, "You okay, kid?" Morenz answered, "Never felt better in my life."

In 1937, when Morenz was only thirty-four years old, he was ready to retire. He decided he would finish the season and then that was it. The Canadiens were at the top of their division by the end of January when last-place Chicago came into the Forum. It was supposed to be an easy win.

Howie wore a small skate. A lot of guys do. Paul Coffey was the best skater in the league in our era. He wore a customized skate two sizes smaller than his shoe. He took his skates to a leather-worker to have extra stitching put into the ankles to make them stiffer. The stiffer a skate is, the more power is transferred to the blade. Soon a lot of guys were doing it. Paul and I also used to wear new skates into the hot tub to break them down and mold them to our feet. I would then take the extra step of shipping the skates to my best friend, John Mowat, who was playing NCAA hockey at Ohio State at the time. His feet were the same size as mine, and college players practice a lot compared to players in major junior. So John would wear my skates in practice for six to eight weeks, then ship them back. Still, they were really tight. Watch footage of Paul Coffey and me in Edmonton going down the tunnel before warm-up—we can hardly walk.

Joliat thought Howie's small skates had something to do with what happened next. Howie was speeding around the net when he tripped and slid into the boards with his feet in the air. Clarence Campbell, who became the president of the NHL from 1946 to 1977, was refereeing that game. He said that when Morenz kicked out to stop himself, the force of his weight made his blades stick into the boards, like knives thrown against wood.

The Hawks defenseman Earl Seibert was following Morenz into the corner. Seibert was built the way coaches like defensemen— 6'2", 200 pounds. He fell over Howie's left leg and fractured it in four places. Even though it was an accident, Siebert was booed whenever he went into Montreal for the rest of his career.

While Morenz was in the hospital with his leg packed in ice and up in traction, his team and most of the guys on the other teams would visit. They would bring whiskey and beer and the boys would sit around and play cards for hours.

At first Morenz would smoke his pipe and talk about his comeback, but after more than a month in bed, he became depressed. Even though it looked like his leg was healing nicely, he told his linemate Joliat that he would be watching him in the playoffs from "up there," and pointed to heaven.

He started to get sicker and sicker and spent more and more time in bed. Lying down for long periods of time can cause blood clots. On the morning of Monday, March 8, 1937, the team doctor found some in Howie's legs and set up surgery to remove them the next morning. Morenz had chest pains all that day. After a light supper and a nap, he got out of bed, fell down, and died.

The next night, before opening faceoff between the Canadiens and the Maroons, the Forum was quiet while a bugler played that lonely solo that they play for fallen soldiers. It's called the Last Post. You could hear it echo off the ice. The only other sound you could hear was people crying.

On Thursday Howie's body was taken to the Montreal Forum and placed at center ice. Fifty thousand people filed past his open casket prior to the service. Joliat told the press, "Hockey was Howie's life. When he realized he would never play again, he couldn't live with it. I think Howie died of a broken heart."

The Canadiens lost in the first round of the playoffs that year. Morenz's rookie teammate Toe Blake said, "We didn't have much heart for hockey after he died."

But of course, that was not entirely the case. As much as Morenz meant to the Habs, a team is more than a group of individual players. Though Morenz was never forgotten, the Montreal Canadiens certainly regained their heart for hockey. In fact, they went on to become by far the most successful team in the league over its ninety-nine years and far and away its most storied. The Habs have more than their fair share of legends in Hockey Hall of Fame, Toe Blake among them. That was the case when I was a kid, and many have followed since then. The league would not be the same without the Habs, and the Habs would not be the same without Howie Morenz.

Two

IN THE BEGINNING

The Montreal Canadiens are the only NHL team that existed before the league itself. They started up in 1909–10 with the new National Hockey Association (NHA), an elite professional hockey league in Eastern Canada. The old prejudice against professional sports still existed. People thought of amateurs as gentlemen and pros as thugs. The NHA wanted to do two things: change the perception and make money.

The original teams were the Renfrew Creamery Kings, Cobalt Silver Kings, Haileybury Comets, and Montreal Wanderers. The Ottawa Senators and Montreal Shamrocks joined the league later, in mid-January 1910. Obviously, Montreal was a hotbed of hockey even before the NHL arrived, with three teams in the new league.

Interestingly, Montreal's Jubilee Arena was home to two rival teams—the Wanderers, who represented the city's English-speakers, and the Canadiens, who appealed to the francophones. Montreal businessman J. Ambrose O'Brien formed the Montreal Canadiens and hired a great defensive playmaker, Jack "Speed Merchant"

Laviolette, as the team's first player captain and coach and general manager. Jack liked to drive fast and in 1918, just two years after he led the Canadiens to their first Stanley Cup, his car struck a pole and his right leg was crushed so badly, he had to have it amputated below the knee. He loved the game so much, he had an artificial foot designed for a skate and stayed with the league as a referee.

Before the NHA came along, games were played in two thirty-minute halves. But the NHA owners noticed that a lot of their revenue came from food and drink at the arenas, so they changed the rules to three twenty-minute periods. That way fans could visit the concession stands one more time. Years later, when Harold Ballard was part owner of the Toronto Maple Leafs, he'd turn off the water fountains so the public would buy more drinks.

The NHA made other changes. The puck was now dropped instead of being placed on the ice. Assists were recorded, rather than just goals. Players were fined for penalties. The biggest change to the game was probably the end of the position called "rover." The rover was a seventh player, usually the best player on the team. He patrolled the whole ice and joined the defense or forwards, wherever he was needed. There was a lot of controversy about moving to a six-man team. *Toronto Star* editor W.A. Hewitt (Foster Hewitt's father) said it was like watching baseball without the shortstop. The six-man game made hockey more of an individual effort. But fans loved it because as the ice opened up, guys had the space to hold on to the puck and rush it.

In 1912, a new team called the Toronto Hockey Club joined the league. They'd soon be renamed the Toronto Blueshirts because of their blue sweaters with a large white letter *T* for Toronto on the front. Their first game was at the Arena Gardens in Toronto on Christmas Day 1912 against the Canadiens in front of 4,500 fans.

The Arena was the third rink in the country to have indoor ice. The fans found it a lot more comfortable than sitting outside in the freezing cold. But by today's standards it was like a big barn. The seats were made of long planks of unpolished wood.

The Montreal Gazette reported on Toronto's first game. Two defensemen brought the puck up. One moved back and four attackers camped out in front of the net. Georges Vezina was fined five dollars for lying on the ice in front of his net and Canadiens right-winger Didier Pitre was fined seven dollars for two majors.

In a sense, the Blueshirts were an expansion team—seven of them had never played pro before—and the result was what you might expect from a game between the Habs and an expansion team: Montreal won 9–5. But the Blueshirts went on to win the Stanley Cup in their second season (1913–14) under player-coach Jack Marshall. So Toronto and Montreal were rivals even before the NHL came along.

Eddie Livingstone bought the Toronto Blueshirts from Frank Robinson in 1915. But he and the other NHA owners didn't get along. They were always fighting and threatening to sue each other. They especially didn't like the fact that Eddie hired some muscle guys who hung around when they tried to negotiate with him.

By the start of the final NHA season, 1916–17, there were six teams in the league: Montreal Wanderers, Montreal Canadiens, Ottawa Senators, Quebec Bulldogs, Toronto Blueshirts—and because so many players were enlisting to fight overseas in World War I, the league invited the 228th Battalion team to join.

They called themselves the Northern Fusiliers—and people loved them. There were six Stanley Cup winners on the team: center Sam "Goldie" Prodgers won with the 1912 Quebec Bulldogs and again in 1916 with the Canadiens; Howard McNamara, the captain, won a Cup in 1916 with the Canadiens along with Amos Arbour; Howard's brother George McNamara won the Cup with the Blueshirts in 1914; Eddie Oatman won with Quebec in 1912; and Lieutenant "Roxy" Rocque Beaudro won the Cup in 1907 with the Kenora Thistles. Imagine six Stanley Cup winners enlisting in a single unit today. They would be the most popular team in the league.

For many years when I was playing, especially in Canada, our relationship to war went back to our parents and grandparents who experienced the world wars. It wasn't until the 90s that war was something we thought about much. We just took for granted the sacrifices that people made for us. After that, from Florida to Vancouver, whenever anyone from the military was introduced, they would get a louder ovation than the players, and they deserved it. Just imagine the reception they would get if they were actually playing.

The Fusiliers dressed in khaki uniforms and the fans went crazy when they skated out. They were leading the league in goals when they were called overseas on February 1917, before the end of the season. Thankfully, none of them died in combat. But they did what they shipped out to do. Their big defenseman, Art Duncan, received the Military Cross for shooting down eleven enemy planes as a member of the Royal Flying Corps.

With the Fusiliers gone, the NHA owners—minus Eddie Livingstone—secretly met at the Windsor Hotel in Montreal and planned to form a new league before the start of the next season. They wanted to get rid of Livingstone, so they decided to suspend the NHA at the start of the 1917–18 season and start up a new league called the National Hockey League. It was formed under president Frank Calder. The teams were the Wanderers, Canadiens, Senators, and a temporary Toronto franchise called the Toronto

Arenas. It was operated by the Toronto Arena Company that also owned the Montreal Arena. Not surprisingly, the team was made up mostly of guys who had played for the Blueshirts the year before.

The Arenas won the Stanley Cup in that first season, 1917–18. Livingston was furious to have lost his team and his league, and he sued. But to no effect. The new league was here to stay, as were Toronto and Montreal, two teams whose rivalry would become legendary. In 1919 the Arenas would become the Toronto St. Pats. Eight years later they would change their name to the Toronto Maple Leafs.

Three

TEX'S RANGERS
AND THE LEAFS

I
f you want to stand out in New York, you need to think big.
New Yorkers aren't sitting around, waiting for something interesting to happen. Things are happening there all the time. If
you want people to pay attention, you need to be as exciting as the
most exciting city in the world.

That was just as true in the 1920s as it is today. Yankee Stadium
had just been built. The New York Giants football team had just
come into existence. And colorful promoters like Tex Rickard were
creating sports heroes through big events.

In July 1921, Rickard put together the first million-dollar
sports contest, a boxing match between the world heavyweight
champion, Jack Dempsey, and Georges Carpentier, who was the
world lightweight champion and a decorated French World War I
pilot. Rickard billed it the fight of the century, though Dempsey
outweighed the Frenchman by thirty pounds.

Rickard borrowed a quarter of a million dollars to build a
venue for the fight in Jersey City, just across the Hudson River
from Manhattan. The arena took only nine weeks to build, though

it was big enough to hold 91,612 people. Rickard sold it out, and there were a few times during the fight when the stands swayed quite a bit. Dempsey knocked Carpentier out in the fourth round and Rickard grossed $1,789,238.

Rickard also ran Madison Square Garden. In 1926, when he saw Howie Morenz and the Canadiens skate against his tenants, the New York Americans, he got so excited by the game that he and his partner, Colonel John Hammond, petitioned the NHL for another New York team and won the franchise.

Rickard wanted to come out guns blazing so he hired a guy named Conn Smythe as general manager for $10,000 and asked him to put the team together. Today, the annual trophy for playoff MVP—as well as the division both the Kings and Oilers played in when I was in the league—is named after Smythe, which gives some sense of his importance to the game. But even if he had never taken a job with the NHL, he would still be an impressive figure. He was a varsity athlete in both hockey and football who interrupted his engineering studies to enlist as an artillery officer in the First World War, where he was awarded the Military Cross for stopping a German counterattack with only his revolver. He then joined the Royal Flying Corps, was shot down, and ended the war as a POW. (He enlisted again in the Second World War and was wounded in France.) He was a remarkable man.

When the First World War ended, he returned to the University of Toronto and ended up coaching his old hockey team. The Blues, as they were called, used to travel to Boston to play, which is where Smythe met Charles Adams, who later recommended him to Rickard and Hammond. As he began building the team, sportswriters started calling it "Tex's Rangers" and the name stuck. They're still the Rangers today. And I was lucky enough to wear their iconic sweater.

Like a lot of GMs, Smythe built from the blue line out. He recruited 6'2", 210-pound veteran defenseman Ivan "Ching" Johnson from Winnipeg, Manitoba. Then he went after Clarence "Taffy" Abel, who was a nimble 225. They were two of the biggest guys in hockey. No one likes going into the corner with a defenseman who outweighs you by forty pounds.

Puck possession was not as critical as it is today. Back then, you could let someone have possession and still contain them. When I played with the Oilers, before Marty McSorley moved back to defense full-time, he was on a line with Kevin McClelland and Dave Semenko. They might not have touched the puck for a whole minute and a half, but the other team never got out of their own zone. That's what it would have been like playing against Johnson and Abel.

Smythe had a hard time pinning the two big defensemen to a contract. He said that every time he and Johnson reached a deal, Johnson would have to call to check with his wife and she'd change the deal so they'd have to start all over again. After a few hours of this, Smythe sweetened the pot and made a final offer on one condition: Johnson had to sign it before calling home.

Abel, who was born at the turn of the century in Sault Ste. Marie, Michigan, was the first American player to establish himself in the NHL. He was an even tougher guy to sign. He kept backing off. So Smythe asked to meet in his stateroom on the train. When Abel got there, Smythe locked the door and told him he couldn't leave until he signed. When the train started to move, Abel signed the contract, opened the door, and jumped off onto the platform.

Smythe looked for players in the Western Hockey League (WHL). The WHL was good hockey. In 1925–26 it had six teams: Saskatoon Sheiks, Calgary Tigers, Edmonton Eskimos, Portland

Rosebuds, Vancouver Maroons, and Victoria Cougars. It was the last league outside the NHL to compete for the Stanley Cup. In fact, a year earlier, the Victoria Cougars had beaten the Canadiens in the finals. But the WHL teams were losing the ability to be financially competitive with the NHL.

Frank Patrick, along with his brother Lester, had been in charge of professional hockey in the west for fifteen seasons. When they came to the conclusion that the league could not survive, they arranged the sale of WHL players to NHL teams in May 1926, with the proceeds divided among the WHL owners. Obviously, that was a very different time when it came to labor relations. Up until the late 60s, players were just employees, not partners. Players today would shake their heads at the idea of their contracts being sold from one league to another, but that's the way it was back then. Nobody knew any better.

The Patrick brothers are thought of as two of the biggest influences in the formation of the game we play today. Raised in Montreal, Lester, who was the oldest of eight children, was best known as a high-scoring defenseman who won two Stanley Cups with the Montreal Wanderers in 1906 and 1907. Their dad Joe sold his lumber business and the Patricks formed the Pacific Coast Hockey Association (PCHA) in 1911. They invested in the $350,000 Denman Arena, home to the Vancouver Millionaires. And it was the Patricks who came up with a way to make artificial ice that is still used today. One of their franchises, the Seattle Metropolitans of the PCHA, was the first American team to win the Stanley Cup, in 1917. With Lester as coach and manager, the Victoria Cougars won the Cup in 1925. These guys had hockey in their blood.

The brothers came up with a lot of the rules and innovations that fans will find very familiar today, including the playoff system, penalty shots, the blue line, the forward pass, numbers on sweaters, programs, letting goalies leave their feet to make a save, on-the-fly line changes, and farm teams. And that's not all. The Patrick family will definitely be part of the story later on.

In any case, Smythe was far from done assembling the Rangers' roster. He managed to get two of the best players in the western league, brothers Bill and Bun Cook from Saskatoon. On their recommendation, he then signed a guy who would go on to become one of the greatest New York Rangers of all time—though Smythe immediately regretted adding him to the team. Frank Boucher was a former RCMP officer and a truly special hockey player. (In Game Two of the 1924 Stanley Cup semifinal, his Vancouver Maroons had lost 2–1 to the Montreal Canadiens; Boucher scored the lone Vancouver goal, and both Montreal goals were scored by his brother Bill.) But he was small—5'9" and about 135 pounds. When Smythe met his new star at the train, he exclaimed, "I paid fifteen thousand dollars for you? Bill Cook must be crazy."

Bill Cook ended up looking pretty smart. Boucher played center on the famous Bread Line between the Cook brothers. They won the Stanley Cup in 1928 and 1933, and Boucher was with the Rangers until he retired in 1938. He then came back as a coach, leading the Rangers to another Cup in 1940. And when the New York roster was depleted by the Second World War, he came out of retirement to play one more season. Perhaps the most amazing thing about Boucher was that New York did not win a Cup without Frank Boucher until Mark Messier was the captain in 1994. Or perhaps the most surprising thing is that Conn Smythe didn't want him around.

One of them was going to have to go, and in the end it turned out to be Smythe. He built a strong team at an economical price of $32,000. But he found himself out of a job before the Rangers' first season even began after he locked horns with Rickard and his partner. He refused to sign a guy named Babe Dye. Smythe wanted team players and he thought Dye was too much of an individual. His bosses disagreed. Dye had scored 175 goals in 172 games in his first seven NHL seasons, mostly in Toronto. Meanwhile, the Rangers won the Stanley Cup in their second year of operation. Frank Boucher scored the series-winning goal in Game Five.

The Rangers wanted to make a big splash for their inaugural game on November 16, 1926. Lou Marsh was the referee and was told to use a dinner bell instead of a whistle. It was a short-lived idea. The Rangers' publicist, Johnny Bruno, came up with the scheme that they should kidnap their top scorer and captain, Bill Cook, three days before opener and then "find" him just before the game. That was another short-lived idea.

A good GM is never out of work for long. After being fired, Smythe moved back to Toronto. Jack Bickell, one of the owners of the St. Pats, planned to move his franchise to Philadelphia for $200,000. When he saw the Rangers go to the top of their division that first year, he figured Smythe must have known what he was doing and offered him control of his team.

Smythe said he would do it, but only if the team stayed in Toronto—and if he could buy a piece. Bickell told him to find investors to match Philadelphia's offer and agreed to invest $40,000 himself. Smythe put down $10,000. He then found the other $150,000 and renamed the team the Maple Leafs in honor of the emblem on the 1924 Olympic team sweaters and the insignia on the uniform he'd worn as a Canadian soldier during the war. And he changed the team color from green to white.

Smythe's history and the Leafs have been bound together ever since. Maple Leaf Gardens, the team's home for decades, was known as "the house that Smythe built." Quite literally, there would not be a team called the Maple Leafs today if it weren't for Smythe, and hockey history, along with generations of kids' dreams, would look very different. So it's strange to think that if he had been a bit more of a showman, he would have stayed in New York, in the Rangers' front office. And the Leafs would never have been.

Four

THE BRUINS

s a player, I have to admit that I never loved playing at the Boston Garden. I doubt anyone loved playing there, apart from the Bruins. Most rinks are 200 feet by 85, but the Garden was 191 by 83—nine feet shorter and two feet narrower. That may not sound like a lot, but it makes a real difference.

Anyone who has watched hockey on an Olympic-sized sheet, which is wider than an NHL rink, knows how different that game is. Those few feet of extra width make it nearly impossible for the defensive team to close the gap on the attackers. A smart passing team should be able to control the puck around the perimeter almost indefinitely, and an attacker coming in with speed has all kinds of room to step around a defenseman to the outside. North Americans find the adjustment to playing defense on the big ice a huge obstacle, and even some incredibly skilled Europeans never get the hang of the North American game. With less ice to defend, NHL defensemen learn to step up at the blue line, which can be a pretty unpleasant welcome to the North American game to a player who thinks he has room on the outside.

In any case, even a slightly smaller ice surface means you have less time and space to maneuver before someone closes the gap on you and separates you from the puck. No team knows that better than the Bruins. Back then they played half their games on small ice, and they have always been built to separate the visiting teams from the puck. When you play the Bruins on their home ice, you have no choice but to play their game.

And they are good at their game. Just think of some of the guys who became heroes in Boston over the years: Derek Sanderson, John Wensink, Terry O'Reilly, Stan Jonathan, and Peter McNab. And more recently, guys like Shawn Thornton, Milan Lucic, and Brad Marchand have been able to continue the tradition on the standard-sized ice surface of the TD Garden. I doubt anyone ever enjoyed playing against these guys.

There weren't a whole lot of rinks that we were intimidated going into, but the Garden was rough and tumble and the Bruins had the team to go with it. Mark Messier used to say playing at the Garden was like being in a game of pinball. There was just no time and space to play the free-flowing game we loved. When we went to Boston, we knew we would be mucking it up with one of the toughest teams in the league. It wasn't until the 1988 playoffs against the Bruins that we figured out what to do. I'll talk about that in a bit.

Boston Garden also made it easier for one of their forwards, Steve Kasper, to stay in my back pocket. Steve would literally follow me around on every shift to try to keep the puck away from me. Steve was a good player and played the game hard—and the small ice made it that much easier for him to shadow me. That tactic happened more in my era. You don't see it much anymore. Eventually, I figured out how to handle it. I'd shadow one of their players, which would take out two of their guys and open up ice for the rest of our guys.

Of course, the other thing the Bruins always seemed to have more than their fair share of was elite defensemen. It is almost unfair that the same team has had Bobby Orr, Brad Park, Ray Bourque, and Zdeno Chara. I remember playing against Bourque in the Garden. The neutral zone there is so shallow that if Bourque came out of the zone with any speed, he was at the red line before you knew it and could either tee up a slap shot or blow by a flat-footed backchecker.

The size of the ice at the Garden seems to have been ideal for counterattacking defensemen, and Eddie Shore was possibly the most exciting defenseman in the world before the rink was even built.

On October 1, 1924, it was announced that Boston would have the first American NHL team under the leadership of club president Charles (C.F.) Adams, the founder of the First National grocery store chain. Adams first heard about the game of hockey from his young son, Weston, over breakfast one morning. C.F. Adams started going to games in Montreal and, after watching the 1924 Stanley Cup playoffs between the Canadiens and the Calgary Tigers, he decided to bring a team to Boston. The Bruins and the Canadiens have one of the deepest rivalries in the game, but the fact is that if Weston Adams hadn't fallen in love with the game in Montreal, there might never have been an NHL team in Boston.

One of the first things Adams did was hire Art Ross, a Stanley Cup winner with the Kenora Thistles in 1907 and the Montreal Wanderers in 1908. Ross had coached at McGill University and then refereed in the NHL. He would become one of the great men of hockey. In fact, the annual trophy for the player who leads the league in points is named after him. But when he was twenty-two, he was just another hockey player. Ross moved to Montreal to play with the Wanderers and became good friends with other players in the league including Frank and Lester Patrick. And so when the WHL folded, the Patricks gave Ross the heads-up about a twenty-three-year-old farm boy from Saskatchewan—a tough, fast defenseman with the Edmonton Eskimos named Eddie Shore. Adams bought the rights to Shore and six other players (one of them was Frank Boucher—soon traded to the Rangers) for $50,000.

Like Bobby Orr and Paul Coffey, Shore changed the game by rushing the puck. Teams just didn't have an answer for that kind of offensive threat coming from the back end. But Shore was more like Orr in that he was very physical and loved to mix it up. Paul was a player who would pick you apart with his skating. He found holes and would accelerate past guys, but Shore earned some of his open ice by making guys think twice about taking any liberties with him.

In fact, Shore is still in the record books. He is the only defenseman to win the Hart Trophy four times, but he also holds the unofficial record for most fighting majors in a single game—five. He was absolutely fearless, and more than a little mean. He hit like a freight train but also skated the puck through the middle of the ice, inviting guys to hit him. Usually, they would bounce right off, but still, when you play that way, you are pretty much taking on the whole league. Everyone wanted a shot at Shore. He ended his career with nearly 1,000 stitches, fourteen broken noses, and five broken jaws. Like most top-pairing defensemen of his time, he would also play over fifty minutes a game—at least double what an elite defenseman plays today.

Shore wasn't just indestructible—he was absolutely electrifying on the ice. Like Bobby Orr and Paul Coffey, he could open up the ice for his teammates by drawing the defense to him, and he had the vision to go with it. If you were open, the puck was coming. And like Orr and Coffey, he had a stride that others just couldn't match. It was like those guys were gliding. You see guys really working when they skate, digging into the ice. But somehow the truly gifted skaters seem to stay on top of the ice like it takes no effort at all. Everybody else was always a step or two behind. Shore is credited with inventing what was called the "power play" back then. Today it means that you're outnumbering your opponent when they're penalized. But when Shore was on the ice, it meant playing as though the other team was outnumbered, because Shore was such an efficient skater that it was like he was at both ends of the ice.

It would be hard to exaggerate how important Shore was to the game. He was named to the first All-Star team just about every year he played. *The Hockey News* ranked him among the top ten ever to play the game. But even that doesn't capture the effect he had on the league. Remember that the NHL had just expanded into the United States. When the league expanded again years later, there were franchises that didn't make it. A team like the Penguins might not have survived if it weren't for Mario Lemieux coming along. It was the same way with Shore. When the league needed a star, there he was.

Fans crowded into the tiny Boston Arena to see Shore. It became clear right away that the Bruins needed a bigger rink. So Tex Rickard, who had just built Madison Square Garden, figured he would do in Boston what he had done in New York. Boston Garden opened in 1928. Because Rickard was a boxing promoter, the rink was designed to bring the fans as close to the action as possible. People would call it "the house that Eddie Shore built." Interestingly, the Arena is the only original NHL rink still standing and still in use. It was home ice for the New England Whalers for a season, and today it's the home of the Northeastern Huskies.

The first time I saw the Garden, I was still playing in the World Hockey Association (WHA). A friend of mine from the Oilers, Garnet "Ace" Bailey took me to see a Bruins game, and I could not believe an NHL team could play in a rink so small. It looked like a Junior B rink. There was just no room to move. Then I looked at the bench and saw the Big Bad Bruins. My next thought was, "Guy Lafleur must be more incredible than I imagined." Even with those guys trying to stop him, he always managed to play great hockey out there.

The thing is, Boston was such a tough place to play that it brought out the best in some players. We had to respect the Bruins and their building. And there was more than a little fear of being embarrassed on national television. That's probably true of all the great rinks, but none was as intimidating as that one. Personally, I never saw a team focus better than the 1988 Oilers going into Boston for Game Three.

On the other side of the coin, the visitors' dressing room was notoriously small and uncomfortable. But we really didn't care. The only thing we complained about was that it was like a sauna down there. We'd plug in a few fans and that helped a bit.

I understand why so many of those old rinks were replaced—Boston Garden, the Forum, Maple Leaf Gardens. And I can certainly see the appeal of the modern NHL dressing rooms, with their chefs and other amenities. But I was lucky to have had the thrill of using the ice and the dressing rooms that guys like Eddie Shore once used.

Five

THE HAWKS

═══════════════

I will never forget my first game in the NHL. You grow up imagining it, then there you are, walking out the tunnel to the ice surface. So many things are just the way you imagined them, while other things are exactly like a hundred other rinks you've played in. Ice has a special smell wherever you go. But we were at the old Chicago Stadium, which was unlike any other arena. There were more fans than I was used to at WHA games, and the organ was just blasting. My heart was pounding with excitement.

I was even more excited when I lined up against Stan Mikita for the first draw of my NHL career. Mikita was one of my heroes and possibly the best center in the league for a decade. But he wasn't a big guy, and as I put my stick down at the faceoff dot, I visualized winning the draw. It wasn't even close. It was a while before I started beating legends.

Chicago was always a loud rink, and the fans there had a tradition of singing through the anthems. But it was never louder than the night we played the All-Star game there in 1991. The coalition bombing that started off Operation Desert Storm had begun two days earlier, and the crowd was in a patriotic mood. When the announcer expressed the NHL's and the NHLPA's support for the troops, the crowd's roar started to build. There was a moment of silence, when people were encouraged to think about the men and women in the Persian Gulf. The cheering started to grow again as singer Wayne Messmer approached the end of "O Canada," then exploded as he began "The Star-Spangled Banner." The building was shaking with the cheers. I had a cousin in the United States Marine Corps at the time, so when I was standing there at center ice, taking in all that emotion, I was also feeling it myself.

In 1994, just days before the Blackhawks' last game in their old barn, Messmer was on his way home after a Blackhawks win when he was shot in the throat by a robber while sitting in his car. He recovered eventually, but it was touch and go whether he'd sing again. Rather than replace him, the Chicago fans sang the national anthem in tribute to him and were every bit as loud singing as they had always been at cheering. It might have been the most emotional anthem ever heard in an NHL rink.

N ot many people know this, but the Chicago Blackhawks got their start in Regina, Saskatchewan. In 1921, the Regina Capitals were a great team in the Western Canadian Hockey League. Their two top players were Hockey Hall of Famers George Hay and his best buddy Dick Irvin. But the team went downhill, and by their fourth season they won only eight out of twenty-eight games. They relocated to Portland, Oregon, and were renamed the Portland Rosebuds. When the league folded the next year, the Rosebuds were sold to Major Frederic McLaughlin, who'd just won the NHL franchise in Chicago.

In civilian life, McLaughlin was the president of his family's coffee import business. He'd taken a leave of absence during the First World War to join a machine gun unit in the U.S. Army. His unit's nickname was the Blackhawks after Black Sparrow Hawk, a Sauk warrior (part of the Algonquian people) who fought on the side of the British in the War of 1812. And so that's what McLaughlin called his hockey team.

Dick Irvin moved to Chicago to play with the Black Hawks and at thirty-four years old, he managed to come in just one point behind the Rangers' Bill Cook in the league scoring race. Irvin had 18 goals and 18 assists in 43 games. Howie Morenz was third. Howie Morenz was, you know, Howie Morenz, so the fact Dick Irvin beat him in scoring tells you something.

But early the next season, Irvin suffered a fractured skull when he was hit by Mervyn "Red" Dutton, who had three inches and twenty pounds on him. He came back, but his playing days were numbered. For the final twelve games of 1928–29, he was behind the bench as the Hawks' coach. He accepted the lead coaching job full-time in 1930. That season, the team made it to the Stanley Cup final against the defending champions, the Montreal Canadiens. It was the best the Hawks had ever finished. But when Chicago lost the series, McLaughlin fired him anyway.

McLaughlin hired a constant stream of coaches—fourteen of them between 1926–27 and 1944–45. In 1933, he brought in Godfrey Matheson to coach after meeting him on a train. Matheson lasted two games. Conn Smythe called McLaughlin "the biggest nut I met in my entire life." McLaughlin also fought constantly with Red Wings owner Jim Norris.

McLaughlin was married to a Broadway actress named Irene Castle. That would be like being married to someone as famous as

Nicole Kidman today. He got her to design the team emblem. She did a nice job—a version of it is still used today.

McLaughlin was born in Chicago and he was a super patriot. He wanted to build a team with all American-born players, but there weren't many, so he scoured the country. By 1937–38, eleven out of the twenty-five guys who saw action with the Hawks were born in the U.S., including Cully Dahlstrom who won the Calder Trophy that year. McLaughlin even hired an American-born coach named Bill Stewart. Stewart's background was major league baseball. He was an umpire. It sounds incredible, but Stewart coached the team to a Stanley Cup his first year.

I think there's a real connection between hockey and baseball. At any given moment the game can turn on the measure of one guy's skill—the batter, pitcher, or fielder—but you still win as a team. It's such an exciting game. It's the only major league sport without a clock, so you are never out of it. You could be down seven runs in the bottom of the ninth and still win. And it's way harder to play professionally than anyone can imagine. Harder to hit, harder to pitch, harder to field. So when you see it played well, it's beautiful.

There are a lot of hockey players who could have played pro baseball—Eddie Mio, Marty McSorley, Theo Fleury. Jarome Iginla was the starting catcher on the Canadian National Junior team and Jamie Benn was MVP when the AAA champion Victoria Capitals won the provincial championships. Gordie Howe was scouted as a baseball player and used to practice with the Detroit Tigers just for fun. Not surprisingly, he could hit it out of the park.

In any case, the season after Chicago won the Cup in 1938 McLaughlin fired Stewart. The Black Hawks came in last the season after the 1938 Cup win and didn't rebound for years. They came in last nine times between 1947 and 1957, and then everything turned around when Bobby Hull joined the team. McLaughlin died in 1944 and took his dream of icing an all-American team with him.

I think one of the great things about hockey is the sportsmanship, and you can see it in the way the Original Six stepped up during those lean years for the Hawks. The other teams didn't want to see Chicago fail so they made a few trades with the Hawks to help out and to create some parity. In 1950 Detroit traded Al Dewsbury, Jack Stewart, Don Morrison, and Pete Babando, along with a great goaltender, Harry Lumley, for Sugar Jim Henry, Bob Goldham, Metro Prystai, and Gaye Stewart. And in 1954, the Canadiens sent Ed Litzenberger over to the Black Hawks. Litzenberger was awarded the Calder Trophy as the top rookie that year and he captained Chicago to a Stanley Cup win in 1961.

But when I think of pre–Bobby Hull Chicago, I always think of Al Rollins. In 1950–51, rookie Al Rollins split Toronto's goaltending duties with Turk Broda, who was near the end of his Hall of Fame career. Having two goalies was unusual. Most teams ran with one for the entire season. By February 1951 Rollins had lost only four out of thirty-one games. He won the Vezina that year.

When Rollins finished the regular season with shutouts in two of the Leafs' last three games, he was given the nod to start the playoffs. He injured his knee in the first period of the first game. Broda took over the series and the Leafs eliminated the Bruins to advance to the finals against Montreal. All five games in the 1951 final went into overtime. Broda played the first two games of the series, a win and a loss. Rollins' knee was better so he took over and won all three final games. The Cup-winning goal in Game Five was scored by a happy-go-lucky kid named Bill Barilko. Barilko's plane went missing on a fishing trip in Northern Ontario that summer. The Leafs didn't win another Cup until 1962, the year the wrecked plane was discovered. It became kind of a Leafs superstition.

But Rollins was with the Leafs only one more season. He started 1952–53 as a Hawk. So Rollins went from winning a Stanley Cup and a Vezina with the best team in the league to trying to win games for the worst team in the league. Despite the fact Chicago won only twelve games in 1953–54, Rollins was awarded the Hart that season in spite of Chicago's last-place finish. Three of those wins were shutouts. At one point he said he faced more breakaways in a game against Chicago than in a practice in Toronto. But playing in Chicago was really tough for him because he hated losing. It wore on him. He was a team player. Rollins, along with Brooklyn Americans' star player, "Cowboy" Tom Anderson, are the only two Hart Trophy winners prior to 2002 not in the Hall of Fame.

The hockey world is such a small one. Al's son Jerry was my teammate on the first professional team I played for, the Indianapolis Racers. Jerry was a tough defenseman. At training camp in 1978 our coach Pat "Whitey" Stapleton told Jerry, "Go out and hit Gretzky, lay it on him and see how he responds." So Jerry chased me all over the ice. Thank God he didn't catch me. Later he said, "Man, you evaporated out there. You just disappeared on me."

Six

THE WINGS

<hr/>

Pretty much everything is connected to everything else in the history of the NHL. I was lucky enough to play with guys who were in the league in the 50s and 60s—and even Gordie Howe, whose career started in the 40s. I am just one guy, and I was on the ice with players who had skated in eight different decades. Through coaches and teammates and guys on other teams I found a reason to talk to, I made connections to many more. Every player does. Recently, the sons of the guys who were in the league with me have been showing up in the NHL. That's just one more way that the stories of our game come together.

Another way we are all connected is through the buildings we played in. A lot of the old barns are gone now, of course, but I feel especially lucky that I got to play one game in the Olympia in Detroit. If the NHL and the WHA had merged a year later, I would never have had that chance. The last game at the Old Red Barn, as it was called, was in December 1979—and the Oilers were the visiting team on November 7 that year. (By coincidence, our first home game in Edmonton was against Detroit.) I was cutting it close, but I got to skate out onto the ice I had imagined when I was a kid in the backyard. I grew up pretty close to Toronto, so I had the opportunity to see a few Leafs and Marlies games at Maple Leaf Gardens, but the first time I ever saw the Olympia was the night I played there. It was kind of overpowering, getting the opportunity to play in a place I had grown up dreaming about. It's one of the things I'll never forget about my career.

It's funny how memories are so closely tied to the places where they were formed. I doubt anyone will ever forget the unique rafters inside Maple Leaf Gardens, the famous escalators at the front of the Montreal Forum, or the portrait of Queen Elizabeth that hung in the old Winnipeg Arena. For me, the Northlands Coliseum will always be a special place. But I am lucky that I got to play at the Olympia, where those Red Wings teams I dreamt about as a kid won all those Stanley Cups. By the way, the Wings beat us 5–3.

The Red Wings go all the way back to the Victoria Cougars of the WHL. Their roster was sold to a group of Detroit investors who won the franchise in the spring of 1926. The Victoria Cougars were a great team. They won the Stanley Cup in 1925 and lost to the Montreal Maroons in the 1926 finals.

Their biggest star was Frank Foyston. Frank was one of the first players that Lester and Frank Patrick went after to captain the Seattle Metropolitans when they added the team to their Pacific Coast Hockey Association (PCHA) in 1915–16. When the Metropolitans were just two years old in 1916–17, they played the Montreal Canadiens in a best-of-five series final. Foyston led the Metropolitans to the first Stanley Cup win for an American team. But by the time Frank came to Detroit, he was thirty-five years old and he was winding down.

Detroit finished last its first season and ended up more than $80,000 in debt. Frank Calder recommended Jack Adams as general manager and coach to the owners.

Jack Adams was the son of a railroader from Fort William, now part of Thunder Bay, Ontario. He was a rugged, physical player who could also put the puck in the net. In fact, he led the PCHA in scoring with Vancouver in 1921–22, and led the Toronto St. Pats playing on a line with Babe Dye (the guy Conn Smythe didn't want in New York). He would win two Stanley Cups, and he retired from playing after winning with the Ottawa Senators in 1927. That year was the first time players were awarded Stanley Cup rings. Their rings were made of eighteen-carat gold with fourteen diamonds in the shape of an *O*. But it was as a coach and GM that Adams is best known. He was with the Wings for thirty-five seasons. Today, the annual trophy for the league's best coach is named after him.

Adams turned the team around. In the first home game of 1927–28, Detroit's second NHL season, when the new Olympia Stadium opened, more than 14,000 people turned out to watch the Detroit Cougars play the Ottawa Senators. The *Detroit Times* wrote that hockey "is football set to lightning." Adams took the team into their first playoffs the next season.

After Major McLaughlin beat out Jim Norris Sr. for the hockey franchise in Chicago, the two of them never got along. Things got worse when the NHL forced McLaughlin to make Chicago Stadium the Hawks' home ice. Norris had controlling ownership in the building. He had invested in it when he thought he was going to win a Chicago franchise. McLaughlin and Norris Sr. fought over the leasing arrangements for years.

Norris Sr. was quite a character. Because his son had the same name, his friends called him "Big Jim." He made millions owning

Great Lakes steamers and a successful grain brokerage firm. Norris wanted an NHL franchise, so he bought Olympia Stadium in Detroit along with the Cougars (who had by then become the Falcons), and renamed the team the Red Wings after the logo of the Montreal Athletic Club, whose amateur hockey team won the first two Stanley Cups. He paid off their debts and invested in player acquisition, farm team development, and scouting. He also kept Jack Adams on with the club.

The first year, Adams was on a very short leash, always in fear of losing his job. He had to call Norris after every game to report what happened. The next year Norris reportedly eliminated Adams' contract and, on a handshake, told him to consider himself on probation until further notice. He was on probation for twenty-nine seasons, until 1962.

He was hard-nosed. Red Kelly told me how Adams would come into the locker room and stand right in front of the player that he was haranguing. He was a little pigeon-toed so he had to watch it or he'd trip. On every team the coach will pick on a guy just to get everyone's attention. In Detroit in the early 1950s, one of the guys Adams liked to pick on was Benny Woit.

Adams sat right behind the bench. Sometimes his glasses would fog over and so he couldn't really see who was on the ice. He used to insist that one defenseman stay back in front of the net at all times and if that defenseman moved out of position, Adams would yell at him after the game. He always seemed to assume it was Woit. Often he was wrong, but Woit never said anything. That was the way it was.

Adams would get on Woit so much that during one game after the second period, Woit got into the locker room fast, ahead of Adams, and grabbed an orange. He dropped the peels down right in front of his stall.

Adams came into the room all excited, ran up to Woit and started going off on him, but as he moved around his feet started to slip on the peels and he almost fell. It threw him off so much he forgot what he was yelling about and stormed out of the room.

Woit and Red Kelly played together on defense. Woit was strong, a really solid hitter, but not the greatest skater in the world. Red loved to carry the puck so Woit would clear the way. They had great chemistry as a pair. Red went on to win eight Stanley Cups, four with the Wings, four with the Leafs.

Bill Quackenbush was a big happy guy who liked to talk and break out into song. He helped out the younger defensemen like Red Kelly, who learned a lot from him his first year. Quackenbush was a good communicator. He'd yell, "Go get 'em Red!" Defensemen still do that today. One guy will yell, "Take 'em!" meaning "Don't worry about this guy—you can commit to your man." If you're indecisive, guys will have the time and space to pick you apart. The key ingredient is communication. You've got to talk to each other.

Quackenbush got into trouble with Jack Adams in the playoffs. The Toronto Maple Leafs became the first NHL team to win three Cups in a row in 1949 when they swept Detroit four games to none for the second straight year. The Leafs outshot the Wings 31–15 in the last game and Adams was furious. The *Ottawa Citizen* called Detroit "leg-weary." Adams waved the paper around looking for someone to blame. A little while later when he found out that Bill Quackenbush had gone golfing the day before the game, he traded him to Boston before the next season started.

When Tommy Ivan was the coach in Detroit from 1947 to 1954, he was the buffer between Adams and the players. Tommy Ivan was a smaller guy, only about 5'5", and a really good dresser. He didn't like to yell at the guys. He treated them with respect.

One of the first things Ivan did was to make Sid Abel the centerman between nineteen-year-old Gordie Howe and twenty-two-year-old Ted Lindsay. They were called the Production Line. Abel was the veteran, but his two wingers were best friends on and off the ice so they had a tendency to look for each other and forget about their centerman. But if Abel was open and they didn't pass to him, he'd call them over and start bawling them out. And they'd listen. He got them into the habit of including him in the play.

Abel was sold to Chicago in 1952 and Alex Delvecchio replaced him. Gordie and Ted Lindsay were now the veterans. They didn't need to listen to a twenty-year-old sophomore, and so they went back to passing to each other. That's why if you look at the statistics, Gordie and Lindsay are often twenty to forty points ahead of Delvecchio.

Ted Lindsay was one of the greatest Wings to ever play the game. With Adams as GM, Lindsay was a key factor to four of Detroit's Cups (1950, 1952, 1954, and 1955). In the mid-50s, Lindsay was the highest-scoring left-winger in NHL history. He was tough and he scared guys. Lindsay said you only found men in the corners, never chickens. He had seven hundred stitches in his head to prove it.

Lindsay would take on anyone—including his boss. And the whole league reaped the benefits. At the beginning of this book, I mentioned I'd like to thank the guys who played before me. Ted Lindsay is one of those at the top of that list. His unselfishness made a huge difference for all of us.

Lindsay was a hockey star and so he was financially comfortable, but he knew not many players made more than $10,000 a year. These were guys from small towns in Canada who often left school early to play hockey.

In 1956–57, the year he had eighty-five points, the most in his career, Lindsay formed a players' association—the first step toward a union—along with other guys throughout the league, like Chicago's Gus Mortson, Boston's Fernie Flaman, New York's Bill Gadsby, Toronto's Jim Thomson and Tod Sloan, and Montreal's Dollard St. Laurent. Doug Harvey, the best defenseman in Canadiens history, was one of the key organizers behind the association and Montreal traded him away as punishment a few seasons later. Harvey responded by winning another Norris Trophy that year.

Jack Adams pulled the *C* off Ted Lindsay's jersey in 1956. The next season, after thirteen years with the Wings, Lindsay was traded to the Hawks. The fact that the owners were willing to make examples of future Hall of Famers like Harvey and Lindsay shows how seriously they took the threat to their power. Ultimately, the association failed. But it was only a matter of time before the players started to earn their fare share. The NHLPA finally got off the ground almost ten years later, in 1967.

Lindsay played three seasons for the Hawks. They made the playoffs the last two seasons he was with the team. But his heart wasn't in it. He always said, "I still had a Red Wing on my forehead, on my backside and over my heart. I was existing. Nothing more." Lindsay came out of retirement when he was thirty-nine years old to play one last year with Detroit so he could retire a Red Wing.

A lot of guys have worn other teams' sweaters, but they are forever with their original team. I'm not sure people even remember Bobby Orr played a few games in two seasons with Chicago. Bobby Hull will always be a Black Hawk despite eight years with the Winnipeg Jets. Brian Leetch ended his career with the Bruins, but he will always be a New York Ranger. And when Ray Bourque won the 2001 Stanley Cup with Colorado, he took it home to Boston, where he had played for twenty-one seasons, and raised it over his head at City Hall Plaza to thousands of cheering fans.

That's the kind of amazing bond a guy can build in hockey. Ray Bourque's win was their win.

Players weren't the only people Lindsay stood up for. He was inducted into the Hall of Fame in 1966, but declined to go to the ceremony because women weren't allowed into the event. He felt his wife and family were part of his career and they deserved to be there. The next year, the rules were changed and families were invited.

Ted Lindsay is a pretty good example of what toughness means to a hockey player. People sometimes get the idea that hockey players simply like violence, but that's not the case. They can be aggressive, and they don't like getting pushed around, but real toughness isn't about bullying another guy. It's usually about sticking up for someone else—or taking a hit for someone else. Lindsay was known as "Terrible" Ted because he was as tough a competitor as they come. In fact, people say that the penalty for elbowing was put in the rule book because of Lindsay. But if you needed help, he had your back.

To say that you hate playing against a guy but that you would love to have him on your team is one of the biggest compliments in our game. Ted Lindsay may be more deserving of that compliment than anyone in the history of the game.

Seven

THE ORIGINAL SIX

E very year around the draft, fans of every team debate the importance of various roles on the team. Which is more valuable—a first-line center like Sidney Crosby? A lethal winger like Alex Ovechkin? A top-pairing defenseman like Erik Karlsson? A franchise goalie like Carey Price? These guys are scarce. There are only thirty first-line centers in the NHL, only thirty number-one goalies, and so on.

Now, imagine a league in which twenty-four of those guys aren't good enough to keep their jobs. That was the Original Six.

That's how it worked. Only six guys were good enough to take each of those jobs. Or put it this way: if you took only the first lines from every team in the league today, you would still have more forwards than you would roster spots on six teams. If you took only the goalies invited to the All-Star game, you'd have enough to fill the starters' roles.

In other words, these guys were *good*.

To be fair, there were no Europeans to speak of in the league back then, and very few Americans. But still, anyone who was one of the best six players in North America at his position was a very good hockey player. With so few roster spots to go around, there were simply no weak players in the Original Six.

In 1942, at the start of the Original Six era, the league looked like this: Montreal Canadiens, Toronto Maple Leafs, Detroit Red Wings, Chicago Black Hawks, New York Rangers, and Boston Bruins. The Americans had dropped out. The Americans' veteran defenseman and coach, Red Dutton, had retired from playing to manage and coach the team. Dutton thought moving the team to Brooklyn would create more of a rivalry with the Rangers. So even though they still played at Madison Square Garden, the team name was changed to the Brooklyn Americans for the 1941–42 season, but they finished in last place and suspended operations. There had been various numbers of teams in the league over the years. But when the dust settled there were six, and it stayed that way for decades.

In the early 1940s, the Second World War began taking its toll on the NHL as players enlisted. About eighty NHLers served in the military during the war—that was roughly about half the league. Each team was allowed to dress only thirteen skaters and one goalie per game. Boston was hit hard like all of the teams. They lost the entire "Kraut Line."

We probably wouldn't give a line a nickname based on an ethnic slur today, but those were different times, and all three guys were of German ancestry. Milt Schmidt, Woody Dumart, and Bobby Bauer all grew up together in Kitchener, Ontario, and all ended up playing for the Bruins. In 1939–40, the three buddies finished 1-2-3 in the NHL scoring race. In 1942, all three then did something that shows that as important as our game is, other things are more important. They took a train to Montreal, and enlisted in the Royal Canadian Air Force.

They had time to return to Boston before reporting for duty and were back in their Bruins uniforms on February 10 for their final game as a line. Boston thumped Montreal 8–1, and the Kraut Line ended up with eleven points. They were carried off the ice like heroes. They all survived the war and were back playing for the Bruins in 1945.

Regular-season overtime was canceled during the war because trains had to run on schedule. It didn't return until the 1983–84 NHL season. Still, the schedule was hard. A team like the Montreal Canadiens would leave home after a game on a Saturday night, travel to Chicago, and get there so close to game time that a police escort would accompany them with sirens to the Chicago Stadium. After the game, they'd get back on the train and head home to Montreal. Forty-eight hours to play one hockey game. After tying a game one night, Dick Irvin said, "It's a long way to go for one point." But that's what it was like, and all the teams went through it.

Because the teams played each other so regularly and there were so few players on each team and they competed against each other fourteen times a year (seven times at home and seven times on the road), fans knew the players. They would follow their stories almost like a drama.

The biggest rivalries were just about everybody versus the Canadiens. Toe Blake, who won three Stanley Cups as a player (one with the Maroons and two with the Canadiens and eight more as coach of the Canadiens), was once asked if he liked Gordie Howe as a person when he played against him. Blake said that the only time he and Gordie spoke was on the ice and it was to tell each other off.

Nobody wanted to beat Montreal more than the Bruins. If you look at old newspapers back in the 30s and 40s, you really get a sense of what the games were like. There is an article in *The Boston Globe* from February 5, 1941 about a game the night before. It said, "It was the roughest free-swinging engagement presented at the Garden in years . . ." The referee didn't call any minor penalties for charging, slashing, or high-sticking because if he did the game would never have ended. A couple of guys were cut, another was knocked out. Montreal's coach, Dick Irvin, came out on the ice and held the game up while he argued with referee Bill Stewart. Montreal rookie Elmer Lach was taken off for stitches when his teammate Murph Chamberlain charged Milt Schmidt, sending him head over heels over the boards and into the Canadiens' bench where Lach was peacefully watching the game when Schmidt's skate sliced him open.

That same year, Lach skated around Chicago defenseman Earl Seibert, the same guy who fell over Howie Morenz's leg in 1937 and broke it. Seibert was twenty-nine and Lach was twenty-three. As he went by, Elmer said to Seibert, "You old bastard, you're too old to catch me." That was the first of seven times Elmer would have his nose broken. A few years later Elmer Lach would win the Hart Trophy playing on the Punch Line with Rocket Richard and Toe Blake. Elmer Lach died in April 2015, at ninety-seven years of age.

Conn Smythe always said hockey was war, and those Original Six teams battled hard. It wasn't about money. Most guys took home very modest salaries and had second jobs to feed their families. And it wasn't just about a hundred guys doing everything they could to keep their jobs. It was about heart.

That's just the way it works when you play against the same guys game after game. Hockey players remember everything. It's in the nature of the game that someone is going to get a stick up on you, or give you a little cross-check in the back as you look for position in the slot, or someone is going to chirp at you. Or maybe someone just beats you fair and square and you don't like it. No one likes to be beaten. You don't retaliate in the moment. You just remember the guy's number, and sort it out later, usually when the referee isn't nearby. (The one exception to this is the big hit. If guys think a hit is uncalled for or could lead to injury, someone is going to straighten it out right there and then so it doesn't happen again.) If you play the same guys fourteen times a season, plus playoffs, pretty soon every number on that team is going to mean something to you. And probably every guy on that team feels he owes you one too. It makes for an intense game.

I didn't play in the Original Six, of course, but I know exactly what it feels like to compete with another team so closely that you come to hate them. We played the Smythe Division teams eight times per season—the Edmonton Oilers, Calgary Flames, Vancouver Canucks, Winnipeg Jets, and Los Angeles Kings. Calgary was our biggest rivalry. Calgary was just a three-hour drive away, but the feeling was not neighborly.

You play eighty games in the regular season and you get into a rhythm. As an athlete, you prepare the day before the game in a certain way. You eat properly, sleep, and get ready for the game. But when a Calgary game was on the schedule, you'd start preparing days in advance because you knew it was going to be everything you could handle. Both teams had tough guys, dirty guys, skill guys, and elite goaltending. In the mid-1980s, we were the two best teams in the West. Winnipeg was close. The Cup stayed in Alberta for six of seven years. And the year it didn't, the Flames narrowly lost to Montreal in the final.

In 1986, we ended the season with 119 points. Calgary had 89 and Winnipeg had dropped to 59. In the playoffs, Calgary swept the Jets and we swept Vancouver. And then we faced each other in the Smythe Division finals. They beat us because the Flames coach, Bob "Badger" Johnson, figured out how to bottle up our offense. We'd won the last two Cups and got lax in our commitment to detail. We needed to learn a lesson. And it took a team like Calgary, who played a system-oriented game, to beat us.

I later learned that in practice Johnson put all the Flames up in the nosebleed seats of the Saddledome and had an assistant coach down on the ice with a walkie-talkie simulating Paul Coffey's breakout. Johnson was showing his players how to scrub off Paul's speed. His plan was to have his team funnel Paul up the boards to stop him from getting into open ice. It took a strategist, a real deep thinker like Bob Johnson, to come up with a game plan to neutralize us.

We were two talented teams with lots of competitive guys, so yeah, we hated one another. It wasn't so much that we hated them as people, though. We hated them as matchups. Mark Messier knew he was going to be seeing Joel Otto night after night. Dave Semenko knew he was going to be battling Tim Hunter over and over. For Jari Kurri and me, we knew the Calgary defense was going to target us physically every chance they got. One thing Glen Sather used to say was that he didn't ask fifty-goal-scorers to fight, and he didn't ask tough guys to score fifty goals. But he did make sure we all knew that if we were going to be successful, we had to be tough enough to make the play. Both teams had that mindset. You knew you were going to be physically punished, but you would do anything to score.

We wouldn't go out together after a game and party like some teams do today. We didn't even want to see their faces. An Oiler and a Flame wouldn't be caught dead with each another, even in the off-season. But that mutual dislike lasted only as long as we were playing against each other. Today, a lot of those guys would do anything for one another to help out with a charity. That's the beauty of sport. When you get two similarly stacked teams with highly competitive people, there are going to be fireworks. But that's just a form of respect.

One of the greatest things we have in our sport is our history. The trophies we have, and the great players, and the rivalries differentiate our game from everything else. You can't replace history, so I don't want to say that the rivalry between the Oilers and the Flames was the same as, for example, the one between the Canadiens and the Leafs. But from the first day of every season, we knew that the road to the Stanley Cup went through Calgary, and I'm sure the Original Six teams felt the same way about one another. Knowing our opponents that well and wanting to beat them that badly made us better teams. And I think that spirit was something that was passed down by the Original Six.

Eight

THE STANLEY CUP

H ockey is a team game. So when you win the Stanley Cup you share the win. Throughout the season and the play-offs you've also shared some of the heartaches and dis-appointments and you've come through it all together. If you ask anybody who's won a Stanley Cup, he will tell you it's the ultimate team accomplishment. Everybody has to participate. It's not like other sports where some of the best players play three-quarters of the game. Every guy on the team has to play his heart out to win the Stanley Cup.

When I was four years old I won the Stanley Cup every night, because every night was April 14, 1955, Game Seven, Detroit versus Montreal. And I was Gordie Howe scoring the Cup-winning goal. I'd do everything Gordie did, come in on my picnic table net, look over to one side, flick my wrist as if I were going to pass it, and then shoot. I'd even switch hands like Gordie did, and I got pretty good at skating with one hand on the stick. I tried to comb my hair like Gordie's and go out onto our backyard rink without my helmet on, because Gordie Howe didn't wear a helmet. When my dad got home from work he'd come out and make me put one on—"You gotta wear a helmet, Wayne." And so I'd be Gordie Howe—with a helmet.

I'll never forget the excitement of watching the Red Wings play the Leafs on Saturday nights. NHL games came on at eight-thirty so I'd have to go to bed after the second period, but if the Red Wings were playing, my dad would let me stay up and watch the whole game.

Lord Stanley of Preston, who became the governor general of Canada in 1888, saw his first hockey game at the 1889 Montreal Winter Carnival. Not long after, his thirteen-year-old daughter Isobel played shinny in the first recorded game of female hockey. His sons, twenty-three-year-old Edward, nineteen-year-old Arthur, and fourteen-year-old Algernon, loved hockey too. They joined the Ottawa "Rideau Rebels," and in 1890 Arthur came up with the idea for the Ontario Hockey Association, which was formed by teams from Ottawa, Kingston, Toronto, and London.

Lord Stanley would go to watch his sons and Isobel play. He was the original hockey dad. He wrote a letter that was read at the 1892 Ottawa Amateur Athletic Association dinner, where they were celebrating the club's third winning season. The letter said, "It would be a good thing if there were a challenge cup, which would be held from year to year by the leading hockey club in Canada. . . . I am willing to give a cup which shall be held annually by the winning club." That fall, a 7½" by 11½" sterling silver punch bowl arrived from England. One side said, "Dominion Hockey Challenge Cup," and the other said, "From Stanley of Preston."

When Lord Stanley donated the cup, he laid out some rules. The Cup had to be returned in good shape and on time. Each winner could have its team name and the year engraved on it. The Cup would never belong to any one team no matter how many times they won it and the trustees would have final say. He donated it to the Amateur Hockey Association of Canada.

Lord Stanley's brother died before the end of the regular season the year Stanley donated the Cup, so he returned to England to become the 16th Earl of Derby and never saw the Cup presented.

They don't say it's the hardest sports trophy in the world to win for nothing. There are sixteen teams in the playoffs. They line up to play best-of-seven series. The winners move on to play other winners in another best-of-seven series. Those winners move on again until there are just two teams left. To take home the Cup, you have to play up to twenty-eight games, about one every other night.

It is probably not fair to judge a guy's legacy by whether or not he won a Cup. There is no player in the world that can carry a team through four rounds. That's another way of saying that no team that counts on one or two guys game in and game out is going to win the Cup. It's just not going to happen. You look at the way Alex Ovechkin played in the 2016 playoffs, and there is no way you can say it's his fault the Capitals fell short. It's a team game, and Washington lost as a team.

And yet, you look at guys like Mike Keane, who seemed to win a Cup wherever he played. That's no coincidence. Or you look at other guys who seem to have a knack for scoring game-winning goals in the playoffs. And it's almost never the team's superstar. It's true that playoff hockey is different, and some guys just have another gear when the regular season is over. The year we won our fourth Cup, Kevin Lowe broke his wrist in the first round and played the rest of that spring in a cast. Every team has a player like that. At the end of the day, the prize is too big not to give that kind of effort.

In big games, the stars are bigger targets than ever. One reason third-line guys often end up being the heroes is that the first-line guys have been shut down by smart coaching and stifling defense. In my mind, what makes a star player a superstar is the ability to play through that in big games. To me, that's Mark Messier. The bigger the game, the better he played. Whether it was a Canada Cup final or a Game Seven, he could bring the energy and the passion to a whole new level.

Just about the biggest compliment I can offer to a hockey player is to compare him to Gordie Howe, and to me Mark is the closest I've ever seen. He was a big, strong guy—as a center, he could bull guys right off the faceoff dot. Or he could just grind the other team down over the course of a game. I've taken many faceoffs against Mark Messier, and I can't see how anyone would describe it as fun. Like Gordie, Mark could create space for himself with the liberal use of his stick. And if someone took issue with that, he was more than happy to settle the dispute with his gloves off. If you're playing in the NHL, you're probably not an easy person to intimidate. But Mark could scare guys.

But also like Gordie, Messier became more of a finesse player as his career went on. It's hard to go from being a pure power forward to playing a finesse game. But those two guys did it. They were among the best passers and playmakers in the game. That just comes down to a tremendous hockey sense, which is another of the best compliments you can pay a guy. It's a pretty impressive thing to win a one-on-one battle in the NHL with pure skill or speed or strength. But it's even harder to slow things down and beat a whole team just by seeing the ice better. Those two could do that.

Mark's leadership skills are no secret. He won the Conn Smythe in 1984, so it's pretty clear what he meant to the Oilers. But I think that was magnified when he was with the Rangers. Today it's common for players to guarantee a win, but nobody did that in 1994. When the Rangers fell behind 3–2 in their Eastern Conference series against New Jersey, however, Mark told the media that his team wasn't done. Then he came out and played the game of his life. Remember, the Rangers were trailing going into the third period. Their season was almost over. Then Mark took a pass as he was heading up the middle, powered in on the backhand, and found the net behind Marty Brodeur. He went on to score two more to complete the hat trick, but that backhand goal defined his career—power, finesse, and the ability to come through when he had to.

Some people thought that his comment to the media was cocky or selfish, but that wasn't Mark at all. He was just the opposite. He was putting all the pressure on himself and letting the other guys just play their game. If he hadn't made that prediction, the whole team would have felt like chokers. After he made it, it was all on him. Every New Jersey player wanted more than ever to shut him down. Every reporter would have mocked him if the Rangers had lost. He knew that. And he knew that would be good for the team. That's real leadership. Standing up and yelling in the dressing room before the game doesn't make you a leader. Being unselfish does.

I wasn't on that 1994 Rangers team, of course. But I've seen his unselfishness firsthand over the years. If I had a three-goal game with the Oilers, Mark was as happy as if he'd scored those goals himself. He was genuinely pleased for a teammate who had a good game. We are still good friends, and we shake our heads when we read about teammates who don't get along or who ask to be traded because of poison in the dressing room.

For us it was the opposite. We made each other better. Glen Sather used to play our lines against each other in practice. How could I not become a better hockey player lining up against one of the best of all time almost every day? I consider myself lucky to have played with him. I know we wouldn't have won the 1984 Canada Cup without him, and in my mind he is the definition of what it takes to win a Stanley Cup.

As a hockey player, the thing you remember most is your first Stanley Cup. It's a feeling you wish every guy in the NHL could experience at some point. But the fact that not everybody gets that chance is part of what makes it so special. There are some pretty special players who never got to lift the Cup. You think of really well-respected guys like Marcel Dionne and Darryl Sittler. Everyone would love to see Jarome Iginla finally win one after coming so close. And it was almost a relief when Ray Bourque finally did.

The Cup has gone missing a few times. In 1905, on the way to a party, the Ottawa Silver Seven placed some bets on how far it could slide and drop-kicked it onto the frozen Rideau Canal. In 1923, King Clancy took it home to show his father, but the following season the Senators forgot he had it and drove themselves crazy looking for it.

In 1924, the Canadiens were on their way over to owner Léo Dandurand's home with the Cup when they got a flat tire. They placed the Cup on the sidewalk while they changed the flat and accidentally left it behind when they drove off.

In 1970, the original collar beneath the bowl was stolen from the Hockey Hall of Fame and then found seven years later in the back of a Toronto store.

In 1987, when we won the Cup against Philadelphia, we didn't have a formal after-party. We'd won three Cups in four years so we celebrated at the rink and then we all went to a nightclub called Barry T's in the south end of Edmonton. We were having a great time. The whole team was there. About two hours into the night, we looked over and the Stanley Cup was just sitting at the end of the bar. No players were around it, just the odd fan who would come up and take a picture with it.

Later on, our goalie Andy Moog and his wife decided to head home. Andy picked up the Cup from the end of the bar and held it over his head while the guys cheered and slapped him on the back. Then the party went on.

Andy carried the Cup out the door, put it in his trunk, and drove home. Three hours later, he got up and drove his little daughter Alyssa to school. He got out, opened his trunk, grabbed the Cup, and carried it in. He put it on the office counter and said, "I'll be back after school," and went home to bed.

Around lunchtime, the Oilers public relations director Bill Tuele called up. He'd been calling the whole team and finally he got to number 35. He said, "Andy, do you know where the Cup is?" When Andy said, "Yeah, it's at my daughter's school," he made Bill's day. No one wants to be the guy who loses the Cup.

The next year, in September 1988, the NHL hired Phil Pritchard, the Keeper of the Cup, and it hasn't been lost since.

Nine

THE VEZINA

══════════════

T he Stanley Cup meant so much to Georges Vezina that on March 30, 1916, the night the Canadiens won their first Cup and the night his second son was born and only a few hours old, Georges named the baby Marcel Stanley. His older son, Jean-Jules, had been the first baby to have his picture taken while sitting in the Cup. Today, just about every guy with a baby does it. I might have done it too if I'd thought of it.

Vezina grew up in Chicoutimi, a small, very beautiful French-Canadian town of about 6,000 people, two hours straight north of Quebec City in the middle of the northern wilderness. It's very close to the town of Péribonka, where my 1984 Canada Cup line-mate Michel Goulet grew up.

In February 1910, the Canadiens were on the road and stopped at Chicoutimi to play a group of locals from the Price Brothers Pulp Mill. Everyone thought it would be an easy win, but the Canadiens couldn't get the puck past the goalie—a guy named Georges Vezina. At twenty-three years old he wasn't a very big guy, only 5'6" and 165 pounds. And he'd been skating for only five years. He learned to play hockey in his boots.

When they returned home, Montreal's goalie, Joe Cattarinich, convinced the team to give Vezina a tryout. By December they had signed Georges for $800 a year.

Georges Vezina was the first goalie to record an NHL shutout. He did it against the Toronto Blueshirts on February 18, 1918. He led the league in wins that year.

At that time, Montreal was the unhealthiest city in Canada. More than 85 percent of the people rented their homes, many of them in sprawling slums. The only healthcare and welfare available were through religious charities. The death rate from tuberculosis alone was more than 200 per 100,000. There were about 618,500 people living in the metropolitan area. That means more than 1,200 men, women, and children died from TB each year. Somewhere along the way, Georges Vezina contracted the disease, but he kept it to himself and kept playing.

Rangers legend Frank Boucher said that Vezina was "pale" and "frail-looking" but "remarkably good with his stick." "He'd pick off more shots with it than he did with his glove. He stood upright in the net and scarcely ever left his feet. He always wore a toque—a small, knitted hat with no brim in Montreal colors—bleu, blanc et rouge." That toque was so famous that Canadiens goalie Jose Theodore wore one over his mask for the 2003 Heritage Classic as a tribute.

Goalies are all different. Vezina was one of the calm ones. Boucher remembered him "as the coolest man I ever saw." He stayed so un-ruffled in the net that the newspapers called him the "Chicoutimi Cucumber." His teammates said that before a game, he'd sit by him-self in the locker room smoking his pipe and reading the paper.

Grant Fuhr was like that. He had that same cool demeanor. If Grant said three words in a sentence it was a busy day. When he was in net, Grant didn't do much talking. Once in a while he'd bark, "Arrgh!" or holler out, "Hey!" But he was always steady and calm under fire.

A calm goalie has an incredible effect on a team. I remember, in the 1987 finals, we lost Game Six 3–2 in Philadelphia. We had two days to get ready for Game Seven. We had a light skate on the second day, then everyone went their own way. After morning skate on game day, one of the reporters asked Grant what he had done to prepare for the big game. He surprised everyone by telling the group that he had played golf.

"How many holes?" someone asked.

"Thirty-six," was his answer.

Someone asked why, suggesting that two rounds of golf was a bit much before a big game.

"Because it was getting too dark to play fifty-four," was his reply. And the guys loved it. That sense of calm was just what we needed to hear. And we weren't disappointed. He stood on his head in a 3–1 win.

That fall, I was sitting on the bench at the Canada Cup in the second game against the Soviets. It was 5–5 late in the third, and Grant was in net. The guy beside me on the bench (Dale Hawerchuk) wasn't an Oiler, so I turned to reassure him. "They've got five," I told him. "But we could play another seven periods and they wouldn't get another." And they didn't.

Grant was probably the greatest athlete I ever played with. He's the tenth winningest goalie in regular season—third in playoff wins in NHL history. If it wasn't for him, I don't think I'd have four championship rings.

In Georges Vezina's whole career, from 1910 to 1925, he never missed a game. He made 328 consecutive starts in the regular season and 39 more in the playoffs.

By November 28, 1925, Vezina had lost thirty-five pounds since training camp. The Canadiens were playing the Pittsburgh Pirates, a new team in the NHL, and that night Vezina showed up paler and more haggard-looking than usual. He stopped shots in the first period but left the ice coughing up blood. He stayed in the dressing room with only his pads off hoping he'd feel good enough to go out again. But he was having a tough time breathing, and with a temperature of 102 he could barely move. The next day he saw his doctor. Tuberculosis was the diagnosis.

Vezina came back one more time to pick up his sweater. Léo Dandurand told reporters that Vezina had "tears running down his cheeks," and so did everyone else who was there. He returned to Chicoutimi and died the next spring on March 27, 1926. It was a sad day for hockey.

At the start of the next season, the team owners, Léo Dandurand, Louis Letourneau, and Joseph Cattarinich, honored their goalie by donating the Vezina Trophy to the NHL. It is awarded to the goalie who lets in the fewest goals. (Today the league's GMs vote to select the season's best goalie.)

In 1987–88, Grant Fuhr played all nine Canada Cup games. We beat the Soviets to win the tournament, and then he played seventy-five regular-season and nineteen playoff games to win the Stanley Cup against the Bruins. That year, Grant won the Vezina.

Ten

THE LADY BYNG

======================

I t's one of the oldest tricks in the book. If you can't catch the guy you're chasing on the backcheck, it's never a bad idea to tap your stick or call for a drop pass. Every once in a while the guy will just hand you the puck without looking. Everyone has done it, and everyone has been fooled into giving away the puck at one point or another.

I say it's never a bad idea, but as with anything in hockey, eventually you're going to come face-to-face with the guy you tricked. In 1922, Ottawa rookie King Clancy called for a pass from Canadiens tough guy Sprague Cleghorn, then turned around and scored when he got the puck. As the teams were leaving the ice, Cleghorn called over in a friendly voice, "Hey, Clancy!" Clancy turned and Cleghorn knocked him out cold.

In the stands that night was Lady Evelyn Byng, wife of the governor general of Canada. Lord Byng had been in command of the 100,000 Canadian troops who fought at Vimy Ridge and finally figured out how to crack the previously impregnable German defenses. It was one of the most important battles of the First

World War, and certainly the most famous in Canadian history. After the war, Byng was knighted, and in 1921 he was appointed governor general.

When the Byngs moved to Ottawa they both became big hockey fans. The Senators were their team. Lady Byng gave her staff strict instructions not to book any events for Saturday nights, because she hated to miss the Senators' games.

Still, what Lady Byng saw often horrified her. Back then, hockey was known as "hell on ice." She hated to see fans throwing garbage and coins on the ice and stopping the game, and she cringed at some of the violence that was so common back then. If you believed in the British sense of gentlemanly fair play, you probably saw room for improvement in the NHL of the 1920s.

Sprague Cleghorn had been a key man in Ottawa's two Stanley Cup–winning teams in 1919–20 and 1920–21. He hit like a train and could move the puck. But most people thought of him as a tough guy. The Senators' owner and manager, Tommy Gorman, said that Sprague was always "ready, willing and eager to swing fists or stick any time."

Maybe he was a little too ready. Cleghorn was traded to Montreal in 1921. Whether he was bitter about the trade or just in a bad mood, Cleghorn was a one-man wrecking crew when the Habs visited the heavily favored Senators on February 1, 1922.

In the first period Cleghorn sent Ottawa's left-winger Eddie Gerard to the hospital with a stick just over his eye as he skated by. Next, he went after Senators' superstar Frank Nighbor and broke his arm. In the third period, he ran Cy Denneny into the boards from behind and sent him off on a stretcher. All three players missed the next two games. Because of how Gerard was cut, Cleghorn was accused of playing with a nail on his stick. The Ottawa police wanted to arrest him but nobody could prove it.

Like the rest of the crowd that night who booed every time Cleghorn came on for a shift, Lady Byng was upset. She was a fan of Frank Nighbor. A lot of people were. Fans followed him the way they would Gordie Howe and Maurice Richard in the years ahead. No one wanted to see a guy like that getting his arm broken. As it happened, Nighbor was also her neighbor.

The Senators won the Stanley Cup the next year, 1922–23, and then lost to the Canadiens in the 1923–24 playoffs. In 1924–25, when the ownership changed hands, they failed to make the play-offs for the first time in seven years. That spring, Frank Nighbor received an invitation to drop by the governor general's residence, Rideau Hall, to see Lady Byng.

He came in and she walked him into the drawing room, where there was a tall, silver cup on a marble stand. She said, "Frank, do you think the NHL would allow Lord Byng and me to donate this cup as an annual award to the player who shows great ability, gentlemanly conduct and sportsmanlike behavior?" Frank told her they'd probably be happy to. She nodded and then asked him to pick it up. "Well then, I present this trophy to you, Frank Nighbor, as the most sportsmanlike player for 1925."

That probably marked a change in the game. Fighting was just part of the play back then. It was a part of my era too, but thanks to skill players in the 1920s like Frank Nighbor and Frank Boucher, who were part of the first generation of hockey players who didn't want to fight, a code started to develop. If you don't go looking for trouble, no one should expect you to fight.

I played with and against so many of them—Peter Driscoll, Dave Semenko, Marty McSorley, Dave Hunter. All the Hunter brothers were gamers. These were honest tough guys. People have the wrong idea about them. They think they're crazy or that they like violence. That's very rarely the case. They weren't cheap-shot guys. They weren't trying to run guys after whistles.

Don Cherry always argues that if players are allowed to fight, they'll police themselves. He says tough guys fight tough guys in order to calm the waters. And he's right. What people don't realize is that 90 percent of the time when two tough guys fight, they are all fired up like boxers, but they aren't angry. They fight for a reason— to protect a teammate or to change the momentum of a game. They actually prevent violence. If there is a beef, it's better to settle it right there. It's when things go unaddressed (or a score is lopsided) that a game gets out of hand. A lot of times the tough guys are among the smartest guys on the team. They are strategists. They're always some of the most popular guys in the locker room, and often the funniest. Players respect the fact they are risking their necks to protect the team. It's probably no coincidence that fans love them too.

But no one needs to see the Frank Nighbors of the league fighting. Lady Byng thought guys like that should be allowed to play the game, and she was right.

The same goes for Frank Boucher. By 1935, Boucher had won the Byng seven times. Lady Byng asked him to keep the original trophy and she sent to England for a replica. Boucher thanked her but asked her to take him out of the running in the future so other guys would have a chance at winning. I've had the honor of winning the Lady Byng five times and it means a lot to me. It's a privilege to follow great pioneers of the game like Frank Nighbor and Frank Boucher, Syl Apps and Dave Keon.

But I can tell you it's not always easy to keep your cool. The first year the Flyers won the Stanley Cup was in 1973–74. They were called the Broad Street Bullies by then. I was thirteen and I remember my dad saying, "This is not good for you."

I said, "What do you mean it's not good for me?"

He said, "Hockey's going to go in that direction. Now the Flyers have won, other teams will imitate them."

My dad was right. In the NHL, in probably every sport, we're just a big herd of cows. When one team does it every team does it. It's like morning skate. When I was with the Oilers and we were winning we did a morning skate, so everybody started doing a morning skate. Then, in 2015, Joel Quenneville's Blackhawks won the Stanley Cup, and he doesn't do them, so nobody does the morning skate. Everybody wants that edge and you always look to the team that's most successful.

I tried fighting a couple of times, but my fights were just kind of funny. On December 22, 1982, we were playing the North Stars. That night I was presented with the *Sports Illustrated* Sportsman of the Year award. I was pretty excited about it. A guy flew in from New York, and he got on the microphone and gave a speech about what a great role model I was for the game. Basically he said I was getting the award because I didn't fight.

Second shift I was in a fight with Neal Broten. To this day, I have no idea why. It was just one of those things. We were just kind of grabbing each other. It was silly. We were sent to the penalty box and I looked over at him and we both started laughing. I came back to the bench and Dave Semenko said, "That was the worst catfight I've ever seen."

Two years later we were playing Chicago on March 7, 1984. Bob Murray, who now runs the Ducks, was an honest player. He played hard, but he was always fair to me. Back then teams would get a guy to just dog me. And I got frustrated. Bob was just doing his job, but I got mad at him and dropped my gloves at center ice. He grabbed me and flipped me over. I was on the ground staring up at him and he had his fist over my face. He said, "Don't move. I'm not gonna hit you."

I said, "Okay. I'm not moving!" But out of the corner of my eye, I could see four sets of legs come over the boards. Messier, Dave Semenko, Dave Hunter, and Donny Jackson. I yelled, "Hey, nobody touch him, he didn't do anything." And I saw the legs all swing back onto the bench.

When you look at the guys who have won the Lady Byng, one thing they have in common is that they were incredibly unselfish. Dave Keon, Johnny Bucyk, Jean Ratelle, Butch Goring, and Marcel Dionne had to keep their composure in a league that was pretty wild by today's standards. In the 80s my teammate Jari Kurri won it, Mike Bossy won it three times with the Islanders, and Joey Mullen won it twice with the Flames. It goes on and on. From Ron Francis to Paul Kariya, Joe Sakic to Pavel Datsyuk. There was never any question about how hard any of those guys played. They just knew how hard you can play and stay within the rules.

Nobody illustrates the spirit of the Lady Byng better than Stan Mikita, possibly the best center of the 1960s. As a rookie, he played on a line with Ted Lindsay, easily one of the most feared guys in the league. Lindsay advised his linemate to earn respect by playing with a mean streak. So that's what Mikita did, and he ended up being nearly as feared as Lindsay. Until one day he came home from the rink, and his four-year-old daughter asked him why he had been sent to sit by himself after the whistle, when the rest of his line went to sit with all their friends on the bench. When he couldn't offer a good explanation for himself, he vowed to play a cleaner game. He went on to earn the Lady Byng for his efforts.

Today's NHL is policed by TV. Before TV, we would go in the locker room at the end of the period and somebody would say,

"Did you see that guy cross-check our guy over the head?" And the next period someone would straighten it out. Gordie Howe used to say, "Get a number and get him next time." Well, you can't get a number and get him next time anymore because there are now two referees out there, so the officials have a much better sense of what is going on behind the play and there are probably eight TV cameras in the stands. When something happens it's carefully examined by four NHL employees who go through replay after replay from lots of angles in super slow motion. And if the professional cameras don't get it, somebody will have it on a cell phone.

There will always be a place for tough guys who can play the game, like our Oilers enforcers Dave Semenko and Marty McSorley. And fans will always love skill guys who are willing to drop their gloves, like Brendan Shanahan or Wendel Clark. Who can forget Vincent Lecavalier and Jarome Iginla going at it in the 2004 final? Both of those players inspired their benches.

In today's game, you look at a team like Anaheim, which doesn't really need a guy to watch over its stars, because Corey Perry and Ryan Getzlaf don't need anybody protecting them. Edmonton just picked up Milan Lucic for the same reason. It wasn't that long ago that both benches would empty and it would be a free-for-all. But now some of these guys are more like Bobby Orr and Gordie Howe—they can take care of themselves.

I really think in the next maybe ten, fifteen years, you won't see fighting in hockey. You don't see it in European hockey or in college. More and more guys are coming into the league without ever having fought. For most of our game's history, fighting just felt normal. The time is coming when not fighting will feel just as normal. It's slowly being weeded out of the game. I think that would have made Lady Byng very happy.

Eleven

THE FIRST ALL-STAR GAME

E ddie Shore changed the game in a lot of ways. As one of hockey's first true superstars, he actually helped shape the game we know today. But there is one defining moment everyone involved wished had never happened.

Shore was a generational talent on the blue line—he has one more Hart Trophy to his name than Bobby Orr. And everyone remembers how tough he was. In his first year as a Bruin, Shore got into a fight with Billy Coutu in practice and lost a part of his ear. When the trainer refused to sew it back on, Eddie found a doctor who would. He refused to have it frozen and instead used a little mirror to watch the doctor reattach it. It sounds like a made-up story, but I believe it because I saw things like that with my own eyes. Just ahead of a game in L.A., Marty McSorley yanked his own broken tooth out with a pair of pliers. Our captain in Edmonton, Lee Fogolin, did the same thing with a coat hanger. Shore was as tough as they come.

In 1933, the Leafs were playing the Bruins at Boston Garden in front of 12,000 fans. It was a rough game, lots of penalties. King

Clancy, Red Horner, and Ace Bailey were sent out to kill a five-on-three. Bailey was a great stick handler for the Leafs. His manager, Conn Smythe, called him "one of the smoothest men in hockey." Bailey played eight seasons for the Leafs. One year he was the leading scorer in the league with 22 goals and 32 points in 44 games. He was looking at many more years among the league's best players.

Bailey won the faceoff and ragged the puck for a full minute. He won a second faceoff, ran a bit more time off the clock, then dumped it into the Bruins' zone. Shore picked it up and started to break up the ice when King Clancy got a piece of him with a hip check and turned the puck over. Shore got up and went after the first blue-and-white sweater he saw. It belonged to Ace Bailey.

He took a run at Bailey and caught him hard from the side. Bailey was airborne, then came down hard on the right side of his head. He was out cold.

Bailey's teammate Red Horner, a future Hall of Famer who happened to be the league leader in penalty minutes, punched Shore in the mouth and sent him to the ice. Both teams came over the boards, ready to go, but when they saw Shore was unconscious and his head was bleeding, and Bailey was blue and convulsing, they cooled down pretty quickly.

The Leafs carried Bailey into the locker room and the Bruins carried Shore off to theirs. Conn Smythe was trying to make his way to Bailey through some of the fans who'd left their seats and come down into the tunnel for a closer look. One fan named Leonard Kenworthy was pointing at Bailey and yelling that he was faking. Smythe lost it. He punched the guy in the nose and broke his glasses. He was arrested right then and there.

King Clancy cleared the rest of the fans away with his stick. Shore got stitched up and headed over to the Leafs' dressing room to see Bailey. He told him he was sorry. Bailey replied, "It's all part of the game, Eddie." That was the last thing Bailey would remember for the next ten days.

He was rushed to the Audubon Hospital in Boston, where surgeons drilled a hole in his skull to relieve the pressure on his swollen brain. They gave him less than a fifty-fifty chance to live and a priest was called in to give him last rites. There is a story that Frank Selke had to have Bailey's father intercepted when he arrived from Toronto with a gun to kill Shore.

Bailey pulled through, but he wasn't the same. It took a year for him to get his full functions back and he had a hospital bill that ran over $1,000. At thirty, hockey was over for him and he was out of a job.

To raise money for Bailey and his family, the NHL board of governors arranged for the first benefit All-Star game to be played between the Leafs and the rest of the league's star players on Valentine's Day 1934. The money helped Bailey tremendously.

They did the same thing three years later after Howie Morenz died. Morenz left behind three kids—Howie Jr. who was eight, Donald who was six, and Marlene who was three. His widow Mary was just twenty-six years old and faced a tough challenge to raise three kids on her own. The league arranged a game between a team full of Canadiens and Maroons and an All-Star team at the Forum on November 2, 1937.

But the money went only so far. Mary had to find a job so she moved back in with her parents and put her three kids in an orphanage. She spent hours on the trolley to see them every Sunday and never missed a visit.

Eddie Shore was suspended indefinitely but was eventually given sixteen games for that hit. Conn Smythe settled a lawsuit with Kenworthy, the fan he had slugged, for $200 plus $100 for his own lawyer. He said it was the best $300 he ever spent.

At the All-Star game, Shore and Bailey shook hands at center ice. Bailey was wearing a topcoat, fedora, and dark glasses, but you could see a six-inch scar from the top of his ear straight up into his hairline. It covered the silver plate the doctors had to put in his head. The Leafs retired Bailey's jersey number 6 that night. It was the first time a number was retired in the NHL.

Hockey's past has a way of finding its way into hockey's future. Marlene Morenz, Howie Morenz's baby daughter, would grow up to marry Boom Boom Geoffrion, one of the greatest right-wingers in an era that included Maurice Richard and Gordie Howe. (Though he played the point on the power play, along with Doug Harvey. In part that was because of his legendary shot, and in part because Richard was on the right wing, playing with Jean Bélieveau and Dickie Moore. Back then, penalized players served the full two minutes. That line could score a couple goals or more with the man advantage. Finally the league had to take mercy on opposing teams, and let the penalized player out of the box after a goal.)

I played against their son, Danny Geoffrion, when I was with the Oilers and he was with the Jets. Danny's son, Blake Geoffrion, played at the University of Wisconsin and was the 2010 Hobey Baker winner, the top college player in the country.

Blake was drafted in the second round by the Nashville Predators and traded to the Canadiens in 2011–12. In November 2012, he was playing with the AHL farm team, the Hamilton Bulldogs, at the Bell Centre in Montreal. In the first period, his fourth shift going down on the left-wing side, he was checked hard by the Syracuse Crunch defenseman JP Côté. As Blake went down, Côté's skate caught him above his left ear, causing a depressed skull fracture that required a four-hour emergency surgery.

The doctors removed all the broken bone and replaced the shattered part with a two-and-a-half-inch plate held in his head with five screws. At twenty-five years old, Blake's hockey-playing days were done. But he has great hockey sense and he's a great kid. Today he scouts for the Columbus Blue Jackets.

Afterward, Côté got hold of Blake and said, "I'm really sorry for what happened." And Blake said, "It was a good, clean hit, JP. No hard feelings." There wasn't anything more that needed to be said.

Twelve

FIRE IN HIS EYES

I t's hard to believe, but in the 1930s, hockey didn't draw much of a crowd in Montreal. Some nights at the Forum there might have been only a couple thousand fans. Then, in 1942, Maurice Richard came along.

Ken Reardon, who would come back to play defense for the Canadiens after his time in uniform, was playing on an army team in an exhibition game against the Habs when he first encountered Richard. "I see this guy skating at me with wild, bloody hair the way he had it then, eyes just outside the nut house. 'I'll take this guy,' I said to myself. Well, he went around me like a hoop around a barrel."

Everybody always talked about the look in Richard's eyes when he had the puck and was coming in on the net. Glenn Hall, who played against him in Detroit and then Chicago, said that his eyes were "all lit up flashing and gleaming like a pinball machine. It was terrifying."

The Rocket got his nickname in his second season with the Canadiens. Left-winger Ray Getliffe watched him pick up an Elmer

Lach pass at the blue line and head for the net. He said, "That kid just went in there like a rocket!'" Dink Carroll, a longtime sports reporter for the *Montreal Gazette*, heard him say it and reported it in the paper. The rest is history.

Dick Irvin was the coach of the Canadiens. Richard played the first part of the 1942–43 season with Tony Demers and Elmer Lach on what was called the "Broken Bones Line" or the "Ambulance Line" because the three of them were so injury-prone. But Irvin juggled his lines a little and when Joe Benoit enlisted after that season, he put Richard in his spot alongside Toe Blake and Elmer Lach. They would go on to become one of the most famous lines in NHL history—the Punch Line. They won the Stanley Cup that year.

In his third year with Canadiens, Richard became the first NHL player to score 50 goals in 50 games. That was 1944–45. The season before, he was the first to score 12 goals in an NHL playoff year. The Forum was now filling up with fans.

Richard was always the first guy on at practice and the last guy off. He'd stay to skate and shoot. He worked to develop speed, accuracy, and the hardest shot in the league. He had a bomb off the rush and would also set up in the slot for the one-timer like Mike Bossy and Bobby Hull. Goalies like Glenn Hall didn't wear masks back then. It wouldn't have been easy to stand in front of that cannon.

The Rocket wasn't a huge man at 5'10" and 170 to 180 pounds, but the strongest NHLers aren't usually monsters like NFL line-backers. There aren't many guys who can move Sidney Crosby off the puck, there weren't many players who were eager to tangle with Wendel Clark, and there was almost no one as fast or as strong as Pavel Bure. They were all about Richard's size. He had incredibly strong arms and legs and a huge chest.

These names also give a pretty good sense of what it would be like to try to stop Richard. He didn't look for fights, but he would drive so hard to the net that guys would have to bend the rules just to slow him down. And he would retaliate. If he wanted to get to the net, he was going to get to the net. There's a famous story about big defenseman Earl Seibert, who was with Detroit at the time. This is the same player who broke Howie Morenz's leg. Detroit and Montreal were playing at the Olympia when Seibert jumped on the Rocket's back to stop him. But Richard just kept on coming. He put the puck in the net and then he shook his shoulders like a big bear and Seibert went flying.

When Seibert got back to the bench, Jack Adams gave him grief for not taking his man. But Seibert, who was a two-hundred-pound player, told Adams that any guy who could carry him in from the blue line to the net and score deserved the goal.

The Wings and the Canadiens played each other twelve to fourteen times a season, and although Gordie Howe and the Rocket respected each other, they didn't like each other. In Gordie's third NHL season, on January 29, 1949, in their only recorded fight, King Clancy was the referee. He let them go at it. Gordie landed a couple of punches and Richard ended up on the ice. Clancy tied Gordie up, so his linemate Sid Abel came up to the Rocket, stood over him and made some remarks. Richard got up and broke Abel's nose.

The two teams hated each other so much that the police had to stand by at the Westmount station in Montreal when both teams had to catch the same train.

In the 1952–53 season, the Wings finished number one, fifteen points ahead of the Canadiens. In the last game of the season, they were up against Montreal. Gordie had accumulated forty-nine goals and was going for number fifty. At that point the Rocket was the only NHL player ever to have scored fifty in a season. Gordie had a couple of good chances in that final game, but Canadiens left-winger Bert Olmstead was all over him all game. Gordie didn't score.

Gerry McNeil was in goal for the Canadiens and when they got back to the dressing room he said, "Well, Rock, he's got to start at one again." I know a little what they must have felt about Richard's record. Glen Sather used to push us as individuals to pursue individual awards. You could be totally unselfish and still strive to be the best. I think that's because he had played with Orr in Boston and so many greats in Montreal. He knew that players who wanted to be the best made their teams better. So in training camp he would say, "This year I want to win the Stanley Cup. And I want to win the scoring race, and I want to win the Norris," and so on. In his view, individual honors are team awards, so I can see why the Canadiens wanted to protect Richard. His record was theirs too.

On December 29, 1954 in Toronto, in the last minute of the first period, the Rocket scored his 401st goal and the crowd gave him a standing ovation. He was fifteen points ahead of Gordie in overall scoring that season. And then in the third period with five minutes left, twenty-three-year-old Bob Bailey, who was just up from the Leafs' farm team, the Pittsburgh Hornets, and trying to make a name for himself, went after the Rocket. During the fight, Bailey tried to gouge Richard's eyes. The linesmen separated them, but the Rocket was furious. He somehow got a stick and went after Bailey, but one of the linesmen, George Hayes, tried to stop him. The crowd was booing. The referee, Red Storey, gave Maurice five for fighting and two ten-minute misconducts.

A few months later, on March 13, things got even uglier. Richard and former teammate Hal Laycoe got into a stick-swinging incident that quickly spiraled out of control. The linesmen jumped in to break it up and one of them, Cliff Thompson, held the Rocket down. Richard later said that this action opened him up to a few punches from Laycoe.

In a move he may have regretted later, Doug Harvey pulled Thompson off Richard, who then grabbed another stick. Hal Laycoe covered up as the Rocket came after him. Bruin player Fleming Mackell said it was at this point the fight wasn't fun anymore. The crowd went silent. The *Montreal Gazette* reported that Thompson tried to intervene again and the Rocket "nailed him against the boards."

First of all you've got to be courageous to be a linesman because the game is so fast and players are so strong. You may not have to be quite as fast, but you've got to be at least as strong. Today, if you hit an official, that will cost you twenty games. Back then it was up to the league president, Clarence Campbell. He suspended Richard for the last three games of the regular season as well as the playoffs. That would be like taking Peyton Manning or Tom Brady out of the Super Bowl. Habs fans were furious.

The Canadiens and Detroit Red Wings were tied for first place when they played at the Montreal Forum four nights later. Clarence Campbell was in the rink, and fans threw tomatoes, eggs, and programs at him. When someone threw a tear-gas canister into the crowd the fire chief ordered Canadiens manager Frank Selke to clear the building. And so Selke had to forfeit the game. As fifteen thousand people left the building, the bars and taverns were emptying at the same time, and some people started to riot. They picked up bottles and huge chunks of ice and started breaking windows.

They overturned newsstands and kiosks and cars and looted shops along St. Catherine Street.

The Canadiens lost the Stanley Cup to Detroit in the seventh game and missing the final three games of the regular season took away the Rocket's chance of winning the Art Ross Trophy as the league's leading scorer. As it turned out, he never won the league scoring race his entire career. Canadiens fans never forgave Clarence Campbell.

On New Year's Eve 1959, Jack Adams told the papers that the Rocket, who along with Doug Harvey formed the backbone of the Canadiens, couldn't go on forever. Richard was thirty-eight and recovering from an injury. Adams said, "When the time comes he doesn't get twenty goals, he'll hang up his skates." It turned out Richard had been thinking the same thing.

Richard had gained a few pounds and that slowed him down. He also started to worry about ending up badly hurt like Howie Morenz. Richard hadn't played a full season since severing his own Achilles tendon with his skate in November of 1957. (By 1964, the NHL had a rule that every skater had to wear a plastic "safety heel" that CCM developed because of that injury.)

Canadiens GM Frank Selke tried to convince Richard that he would have at least five good years left if he got himself into shape. But at thirty-nine, the Rocket was ready to retire. He made the announcement at a press conference at the Queen Elizabeth Hotel on September 15, 1960. He said that the fans had started to boo him and that was something he never wanted to happen. He'd won eight Stanley Cups for Montreal.

I am sure it was the toughest decision he ever made. It was for me.

I thought I would retire an Oiler. When that didn't happen, I thought maybe I would finish my career in Los Angeles. But my ice time was dropping. I understood. I was in my mid-thirties and coach Larry Robinson had some young players he wanted to groom for the future. But I wasn't ready to retire by any means.

I loved St. Louis and thought that might be my last stop. It's Janet's hometown, and I loved playing there. We had fantastic defense with two future Hall of Famers in Al MacInnis and Chris Pronger, and Grant Fuhr was in net. I loved playing with Shayne Corson and Brett Hull. Brett was the only player who ever played with, against, and for me. We brought him into Phoenix when I was coaching there. The trouble was that I was a little older when I played in St. Louis, so when my contract with them was up I started looking for the right place to end my career.

When I was a kid, there were really only two teams in my eyes—the Leafs and the Red Wings. The Leafs because they were down the road from Brantford and the Red Wings because of Gordie Howe. Playing in Toronto would give me the opportunity to move back closer to my family and to finish on one of Canada's greatest teams.

At the start of the 1996–97 season the Leafs had a lot of pieces in place. They had a lineup with some good young guys like Mats Sundin, Sergei Berezin, and Fredrik Modin and some great veterans like Dougie Gilmour, Wendel Clark, and Larry Murphy. In a way they were like the 1967 Leafs. I thought Toronto had the potential to go deep into the playoffs, as they had in '93 and '94. And if I could help the team at the same time, it would be fulfilling a boyhood dream.

My agent, Mike Barnett, had known Toronto's GM Cliff Fletcher for a long time. Cliff consulted with their owner, Steve

Stavro, who owned a grocery chain called Knob Hill Farms. But the timing was off. Steve was under some financial pressure and so Toronto was out.

I was also interested in playing for the Canucks but didn't approach them until Toronto was off the table. At that point Mike and I flew on our own dime to Vancouver as a show of good faith. I loved the team, loved the city, and really respected Pat Quinn, who was now GM. They had a deep, talented lineup. Marty Gelinas had won a Cup with the Oilers in 1990, Pavel Bure had led the league in goals in 1993–94, and Alexander Mogilny was an absolute wizard with the puck. They had defense covered with Dave Babych and Bret Hedican, and they had goaltending in Kirk McLean and Corey Hirsch. Needless to say, Trevor Linden was a well-respected young captain, who had led his team to the final in 1994.

Mike and Canucks VP Stan McCammon were negotiating final terms and it got late. I went to bed pretty happy at the thought of playing for Vancouver. At about one a.m., Stan said, "This is the best we can do, this is where we're at."

Mike said, "Well, it's pretty close. We'll have an answer in the morning after breakfast." But Stan wanted an answer that night. Mike assured him the offer looked positive but told him it was unreasonable to wake everyone up when he could get a decision first thing in the morning.

Stan said, "If you don't give me an answer now, the offer's off the table."

Mike came to my room and woke me up. I told him, "I like it, but I'm not going to call Janet in the middle of the night and I'm not going to make the decision without talking to her. So if they honestly are giving me an ultimatum after we've come up here at our own expense and told them we like the offer and given our word we are not going to shop it, then it's up to them if they take it off the table, but I hope that they don't."

Mike called Stan back and said, "Look, we are not attempting to do any better in negotiations. We are not taking the offer anywhere else. It's simply that Wayne's not going to bring his wife into the final decision and choice of cities and schools and their lives and all that in the middle of the night. He'll call as soon as he gets up so you won't need to wait long. We'll be back here very early."

Stan said, "Well, I wish you would have told me otherwise." And the next morning they told us that the offer was off the table. Maybe because they were convinced we were trying to leverage their offer, they followed up by sending out a fax to all the other teams in the NHL saying that they were ceasing further negotiations to acquire my services.

One of the teams that received the fax from the Canucks that morning was the New York Rangers. Mike and I were at the Seattle airport heading back to Los Angeles when he got a phone call from Dave Checketts and Neil Smith saying, "We just received this fax that Vancouver's out. Will you talk to us?"

We talked to them in the Seattle airport for forty-five minutes and picked it up again when we got back to Los Angeles. New York, with Mark Messier, Brian Leetch, Luc Robitaille, and Adam Graves, was a good fit. It was a really good fit. On July 21, 1996, I signed with the Rangers.

It was great being back with so many guys I had played with before. But the thing that really made it feel like I had come full circle was having Keith Acton and Craig MacTavish as assistant coaches. At one point I had a small injury that kept me out for about ten days, so I was out skating with the coaches to stay in shape. I used to play with these guys, and now they were telling me how many laps to do—fourteen one way and fourteen the other. I laughed. I don't think I ever did twenty-eight laps in Edmonton.

John Muckler was there too, still making me do sprints by myself up and down the ice. Players were getting bigger and stronger and faster, and throughout my whole career I was always one of the smaller guys. Now I was one of the older guys too. So I was still working hard. I have always had tremendous respect for every coach I've had.

Hockey players have a lot of respect for each other and it's such a physical game. My last year was kind of funny. Players on the other team would be coming down the boards and I'd hear, "Heads up!" or "Wayne, get out of the way!" They were warning me. I remember thinking, "Okay, this is not good."

In March 1999 I decided it was time to retire. The only other person who knew was Janet. I didn't want to do a city-to-city tour with a thousand questions. I just wanted to bow out.

We were scheduled to play a home game on Sunday, April 18, in New York. I decided to announce my retirement the day before. New York had been so good to me and I didn't want the news leaked out, but it kind of did anyway. Thursday, April 15, 1999, was the day of my last game in Canada, in Ottawa, against the Senators at the Corel Centre. And I think it was a dead giveaway when my dad and wife and family were at the game.

Jim Dolan, the owner of the Rangers, was a great guy, really nice. Saturday morning the day before my final game he said, "Will you meet me for coffee?"

There was a little deli called Gardenia's near my place in Manhattan. We met there at nine a.m. In those days before the cap, the Rangers could get anybody they wanted. Jim said, "Wayne, you're still the top scorer on the team. We're going to build a stronger team here and I want you playing for the Cup in a couple years."

He handed me a check for a million dollars and said, "I'll give you this million dollars and you can keep it either way. Just think about it for seven days. And if in seven days you still want to retire, you can keep the million."

I handed him back the check and said, "In good conscience, I can't take it. I know in my heart I'm done."

He asked me why, and I told him, "The older you get as a professional athlete the more time and commitment you have to put in no matter how good you are. I just don't have the energy physically or mentally to train for three to four hours a day, six days a week to get ready for the next training camp."

Off-season training was essential. For one thing, it helped prevent you from getting seriously hurt. People say, "Oh, Gretzky never got hit," which is kind of ridiculous. Guys sticking and whacking and basically tackling you to slow you down is part of the game. You had to train very hard, for hours and hours each day— cardio, Tae Bo, light weights, three-on-three basketball, tennis to stay quick and agile. Training in the off-season is the reason Jagr is still playing and how Gordie Howe made it to fifty-two and Messier and Chelios were able to go for so long.

I told Jim, "Hockey isn't the reason I am retiring. I could go to practice every day, play every game, travel, compete. That part of it is still great. It's not about playing hockey, that part of it I can handle. In fact, I feel like I could play another ten years, but I know I don't have ten years of *training* left."

My parents were staying with us at our apartment in New York. My dad had driven me to the first NHL game I ever went to at Maple Leaf Gardens when I was seven years old.

I asked my dad to drive with me to my last game to complete the circle. It's quiet in New York on Sundays, easy to get around. It was only fifteen minutes to Madison Square Garden. So I was looking forward to our special father-son time.

When I got home after the game Janet said, "How was the drive?"

I said, "You know, it was really hard."

She said, "What do you mean?"

I said, "He spent the entire ride trying to talk me into playing one more year!"

That final game at Madison Square Garden, I played with fifty sticks. One for each of my teammates, and the rest for different people and charities and organizations like the Hockey Hall of Fame that had requested them. Leechy made the whole night really special with a speech he made in the locker room after the game. I can't remember it word for word, but he talked about how much fun we had playing together. He let me know that being my teammate was special and he thanked me for everything I did for the game overall. He made us laugh when he said that I was just a part of their team, the guy sitting next to you, until every once in a while he'd look over and think, "Holy cow, that's Wayne Gretzky!" He wasn't one for long talks, but what he said will always mean a lot to me.

I enjoyed Leechy's company so much. That was what I was going to miss most. Every single day for three years I'd sit in the locker room beside him, drinking a cup of coffee, talking about what had happened the night before, or about our families, or about another team or player. We used to giggle and laugh all the time, but hey, life goes on.

I think, for the Rocket, when he got on the ice, trouble seemed to disappear. It was his happy place. It's how I felt, and I think it was the same thing for Gordie and lots of the guys. When you are on the ice, nothing else seems to matter except going out and doing what you love to do. If I had three points, I wanted four. I always played full-throttle no matter what the score was.

If you're playing well, it doesn't matter how old you are. In professional sports, you play from buzzer to buzzer and you don't stop. You never let up. That never changed. I know that family and kids and all that—that's the most important thing in life. But doing what you love to do is something that energizes a guy, something that gives a man's life purpose. The Rocket, Gordie, a few others, and I have had the privilege of retiring on our own terms. And I think for guys like us, it's always better to leave the game before the fire goes out.

Thirteen

THE FORGOTTEN
MIRACLE

H ockey teams love being underdogs. I can't speak with much authority about other sports, but in hockey, feeling like the odds are against you creates a kind of confidence. When no one expects you to win, you're loose. And a loose hockey team is dangerous.

In 1981, the Oilers faced the heavily favored Montreal Canadiens in the first round of the playoffs. They were the Wales Conference and Adams Division champions and had finished twenty-nine points ahead of us in the standings. No one gave us a chance. And for good reason. They were the better team, hands down.

The first round was best of five back then, and the first two games were in Montreal. We won the first game 6–3. We had no business winning Game Two, but Andy Moog stood on his head and stopped forty shots. We won that one 3–1. When we got back to Edmonton, we were a different team. Still loose, but now we knew what we were capable of. We swept the series with a 6–2 win.

I sometimes think the American victory at Squaw Valley was a little like that.

The eighth Winter Games, held in 1960 at a pretty little ski resort in Squaw Valley, close to Los Angeles, marked the beginning of the Olympics' modern era. Scoring was computerized, and for the first time at the Games, a snow-scraping, ice-flooding machine called a Zamboni was used. It was the first time the Games were televised. CBS was the host broadcaster, with Walter Cronkite at the anchor desk. Walt Disney had designed cartoon-like statues of athletes representing the various sports, and Hollywood stars mixed with the athletes and the public.

The 1960 U.S. Olympic hockey team was made up of the very best college players from across the country—players like Bill and Bob Cleary, John Mayasich, Paul Johnson, Jack McCartan in net, and two brothers with one of the most famous names in American hockey: Bill and Roger Christian. But the American media, which didn't pay much attention to hockey in those days, didn't see them as contenders. No one gave them much of a chance.

The team's new head coach was Jack Riley from West Point. Riley named Jack Kirrane, a tough, stay-at-home defenseman, as his captain. Kirrane brought a veteran presence. He was a thirty-one-year-old firefighter and had played all the way back in the 1948 Olympics.

The opening ceremonies lasted only an hour, compared with at least four hours today. Vice President Richard Nixon welcomed 740 athletes from thirty countries. Nine of those nations had brought a hockey team. The Americans were predicted to place no higher than fifth, behind Canada, the Soviet Union, Sweden, and Czechoslovakia.

To everyone's surprise, the Americans went undefeated in their first four games. But they had yet to play Canada. The sportswriters gave them no chance, predicting a blowout that Canada might win by seven goals. The Canadians had been playing NHL teams as a warm-up to the Olympics (and some of them would go on to great careers in the NHL).

In those days, there was no distinct Team Canada. The team that had won the previous year's Allan Cup—awarded to the top senior league in the country—simply pulled on the maple leaf sweater and headed to the Olympics. The winners in 1959 were the Whitby Dunlops. They declined and were replaced by the Kitchener-Waterloo Dutchmen, coached by Bobby Bauer. Bauer, of course, was a future Hall of Famer. He'd played right wing on the Boston Bruins' Kraut Line with Woody Dumart and Milt Schmidt. The Dutchmen, with Bauer behind the bench, had also represented Canada at the 1956 Olympics, so they were clearly a pretty special team.

Defenseman Harry Sinden would serve as the Bruins' coach or general manager over twenty-eight seasons and would win a Stanley Cup when Bobby Orr scored his famous overtime goal in 1970. He was also behind the bench for Team Canada in 1972. Bobby Rousseau would go on to score 245 NHL goals and win four Cups, and backup goalie Cesare Maniago would join the Leafs the next year and then go on to play nine seasons for the Minnesota North Stars. Defenseman Darryl Sly would see three seasons of NHL action, and so would forward Cliff Pennington. So the Canadians were solid.

The Americans, meanwhile, had played college teams across the country—and lost to half of them.

The Americans knew that their only chance against Canada was to get ahead early. So they attacked hard in the first period. Bob Cleary batted in a rebound while Harry Sinden knocked him down in front of the net. In the second period, Paul Johnson intercepted a pass and raced down the ice on a clear breakaway. When he got to the blue line he let go a perfect slap shot that beat

Canada's goalie, future Boston Bruin Don Head, over his shoulder into the top corner.

From that point, the Canadians got desperate. They took thirty-one shots on McCartan in the last two periods, and pulled within one about halfway through the third. Sinden remembers that they had scoring chance after scoring chance but were getting nowhere. Afterward a newspaper reporter wrote that Jack McCartan had been "operating with radar." The Americans hung on for a 2–1 win and rushed off the bench to grab McCartan, throwing gloves and sticks in the air as though they'd just won the Stanley Cup.

Suddenly, the dream of a home-ice gold medal seemed possible for the Americans. But they still had to get by the Soviets. They'd never beaten them. Before the tournament one reporter had called the U.S. team a "ragtag crew of insurance salesmen and carpenters," but after the win over the Canadians, American fans suddenly discovered hockey. Ten thousand people were packed into a stadium built for eighty-five hundred. The American trainer even had to kick California governor Pat Brown off the bench.

As the clock ticked down to the end of the second period with the score tied at two, American winger Roger Christian got a penalty for slashing. In those days you had to serve the full two minutes regardless of whether your opponent scored on the power play, and you weren't allowed to ice the puck. But the Americans killed it off without allowing a single shot on goal.

In the third period, the U.S. started to take the play to the Russians. The Christian brothers, Roger and Bill, put the U.S. up 3–2. The Russians retaliated by pressing hard, peppering McCartan, but he kept everything out, even a shot on a clear breakaway. The Russians had never trailed so late in a game. It was also the first time they'd ever pulled their goalie—Nikolai Puchkov didn't even know to go to the bench for an extra attacker. He simply skated over to the side of the rink and sat on the boards. And suddenly it was over. The American team was on its way to making history.

They'd beaten Czechoslovakia three times in the past couple of weeks and now they were set to take them on with a gold medal on the line. The game started at eight a.m. There were only a thousand fans in the stands. The ref dropped the puck. The Czechs skated it into the American zone, took a shot, and scored. Not the way you want to open a gold-medal game.

But the Americans came back in a seesaw battle through the period. The score was tied 3–3 after the first. The Czechs notched the only goal in the second to lead 4–3 and went into the break just twenty minutes away from the win.

In the second-period intermission, a strange thing happened. The captain of the Russian team, Nikolai Sologubov, came into the U.S. dressing room. This was just never done. He couldn't speak English, but he kept putting his hand over his mouth. American captain Jack Kirrane figured out what he was saying. He was telling them to take some oxygen to combat the sixty-two-hundred-foot altitude at Squaw Valley. As a firefighter, it made sense to Kirrane. He said, "Okay, Solly, bring it in." Sologubov rolled a tank into the room and a few of the players tried it.

The Russian wasn't acting out of the goodness of his heart. If the Czechs won, the Soviets would be out of the medals. The way it was set up, if Czechoslovakia lost the game against the U.S., they would finish fourth with a 2–3 medal-round record, which meant the Soviets would win bronze with a 2–2–1 record. But if the Czechs won, the Canadians would win gold, the Americans silver, and the Czechs bronze.

Whether it was the oxygen or something else, the U.S. was a different team in the third period. They threw everything they had at the Czechs. Roger Christian moved in and tied the score. They kept shooting from the point and deflecting in the shots. Then Bill Cleary skated through the entire Czech team and deked the goalie. They scored six in the third and won 9–4. Christian played the game of his life, scoring four goals.

Even though this was the first U.S. gold medal in hockey, there weren't any celebrations. Only captain Jack Kirrane was handed a medal—the rest of the team found them on their bunks in their rooms. Hockey wasn't an American sport yet. Outside a few hockey communities like Minnesota and Michigan, there wasn't much interest. The team won the gold on Sunday and most of the guys simply went back to work on Monday.

One interesting sidenote to the tournament is the battle of future equipment moguls. The famous Bauer company was run by Bobby Bauer's father-in-law. And on the American team, Bill and Roger Christian went on to found the Christian stick company. In fact, Roger's nephew Dave used a Christian stick in Lake Placid. But more on that later.

Much more importantly, the American victory in Squaw Valley started to make hockey an American game. In 1981, when the Oilers hit the ice for Game Three in Edmonton, we got a ten-minute standing ovation. Before 1979, people in Edmonton were either Leafs fans or Canadiens fans. When we came back from Montreal, everyone in Edmonton was an Oilers fan. I think American fans started to feel something like that in 1960. Hockey was *their* game too. And that made the game better.

Fourteen

THE GREATEST
OF THEM ALL

I n the 1960s you were either a Leafs fan, a Canadiens fan, a Red Wings fan, a Bruins fan, a Rangers fan, or a Black Hawks fan. My grandmother was a huge Maple Leafs fan. My next-door neighbor, Sil Rizzetto, was a huge Montreal Canadiens fan. He had the first color TV in the neighborhood, and so I used to spend a lot of time over there watching *Hockey Night in Canada*. Sil's favorite player was Béliveau. Once you identify your guy or your team, you don't really change. I was a fan of Gordie Howe, and that never changed.

The greatest Christmas gift I ever got was when I was five. It was a Gordie Howe sweater. I can remember opening it and putting it on like it was yesterday. Every kid loves Christmas, right? But I never really wanted anything for Christmas except that jersey.

It was wool and it really itched. My neck would be all red, but it didn't matter. I wore it every time I went onto the ice in the backyard. At that time Gordie wrote a hockey column in the newspaper, and my dad would read it out loud—things like how Sid Abel had taught him "Anytime you see that net, drill it." And there was a song the radio stations played during hockey season called "Gordie Howe Is the Greatest of Them All," by Bob Davies. When I laced up my skates or walked to school or my dad drove us somewhere and I looked out the window, I'd be hearing that song in my head: "Gordie Howe is the greatest of them all. The greatest of them all. Yes, the greatest of them all. You can have your choice of all the rest. If you're a Howe fan, you've got the very best." Sometimes even today, I'll be doing something and it will run through my mind.

Everybody pictures the classic hockey player as a bull-necked Saskatchewan farm boy, with arms like Popeye, who learned the game playing on frozen ponds. Well, that was Gordie Howe. He grew up during the Depression without many luxuries. But according to Gordie, that's what got him into hockey. A neighbor was selling odds and ends to make ends meet, and that's how the first pair of skates found their way into the Howe household. From that point on, Gordie was a hockey player.

The first NHL team to scout him was the New York Rangers, where his younger brother Vic would later play. Gordie attended the Rangers' training camp in Winnipeg when he was fifteen. Coach Frank Boucher (the same Frank Boucher that Conn Smythe signed to the Rangers as a player) and GM Lester Patrick wanted to sign him there and then, but Gordie was homesick. Some of the vets at camp had given him a hard time and he couldn't wait to get back to Saskatoon. When the Red Wings came calling the next year, however, he was a year older and a year tougher, so he decided to give it another go. He ended up at their training camp in Windsor, Ontario. This time it was Jack Adams who wanted him to sign, and he did.

It took him a while to work his way through the minors. He

was riding the bench in Omaha until one day he hopped over the boards to defend his roommate, who was getting thumped in a fight. His coach was impressed, and Gordie took a regular shift after that—and ended up dropping the gloves more than a few times. He was only eighteen years old, but he was as strong as an ox from working for his father's construction company. He could carry a ninety-pound bag of concrete under each arm.

By the following year, 1946–47, he was in the NHL. But the greatest player in history had a slow start to his career—only seven goals and fifteen assists in his first season. It shows how difficult it can be to judge a hockey player when he's eighteen. Even Gordie Howe had to learn how to succeed in the league. But by 1949–50 he was putting the puck in the net, and the next year he won the Art Ross Trophy for most points in a season. He won it again the next year, along with the Hart Trophy for league MVP. Then he won them both again the following year. And so on. The most dominant player of his era, and possibly any era, had arrived.

Ted Lindsay said that before each season Gordie used to worry that he wasn't going to make the team, and so he was tough on the other right-wingers in training camp. Gordie would say, "The only way that guy is getting my job is over my dead body." In a 2014 TSN interview I did with Gordie, he told me that he thought the Original Six had more depth in the talent pool than today's teams have. He said that back then there were easily eight players with NHL talent who could take your place if given the chance, and that even if you were hurt you'd play through the pain, because if you were out of the lineup you might not get back in. And that's what made the games so competitive and intense.

Not that I believe for a second that there were eight guys who could take his place. I don't think there has ever been even one. Gordie was a complete player. He was ambidextrous—he could put either hand on top of his stick, and so through the course of a game he'd switch to protect the puck or to step around someone—but he had a great backhand shot too. Especially when he was cutting in off the wing, he had so much momentum behind him that he could let a shot go with a lot of power on that backhand.

At the beginning of Gordie's career, sticks had totally straight blades so he always shaved around the toe to round it. Today sticks are custom-made, but back then you just got what you got. Blades came very square, and so Gordie would take a rasp to the toe. His philosophy was that the more blade you put on the ice, the easier it is to handle the puck at your feet. If your blade wasn't rounded, the point would dig into the ice and stop you from getting enough power on your shot.

The other thing he liked was a short stick. It seemed to help both him and his son Mark stickhandle. I think that's because they skated in a more upright style and it pulled the puck in. Gordie's advice was to hold your stick with your top hand just as you'd hold a hammer when you're driving a nail. It will give you the most leverage and you won't get your wrist broken.

Gordie was so strong that he'd often break more than a hundred sticks a season. He could bend a solid wooden stick the way Patrick Kane bends a modern composite. But he didn't have to reach down the shaft to get off a hard shot. His wrists were so strong that he could keep his hands together at the top of the stick and still rip it. Goalies would have no idea that he was even thinking about shooting.

That strength allowed him to play along the boards, holding guys off with one hand and carrying the puck with the other. And it allowed him to set up in the slot and defy anyone to move him. He could skate through the middle with guys draped all over him. And if he wanted the puck, he was going to push you off it.

But the legend of Howe's strength doesn't do him justice. You don't rewrite the record book just by being big. His real genius was that he didn't need to bulldoze through the other team. He moved smoothly and methodically, following effortless patterns around the ice. He never seemed to have to hurry, but the puck always found him. And he could always find the open man. Part of that is just the respect the rest of the league had for him. Guys knew that if they tried to beat him one-on-one, they were probably going to lose. That allowed him to dictate the pace. Sometimes that's a trade-off you have to make against a player that dominant.

At the start of the 1950–51 season, Gordie's fifth in the NHL, he was the only player in the league wearing a helmet (made out of leather) because of an injury he'd suffered the previous season. The first game of the semifinals, on March 28, 1950, was a battle. The Leafs were going for their fourth straight Cup. Halfway through the third period the Wings were behind 4–0. Gordie took a run at Leafs captain Ted Kennedy, and Kennedy stepped out of the way. Gordie went headfirst into the boards, with his teammate Jack Stewart right behind him. Stewart was known as one of the heaviest hitters in the league, and he'd had his sights on Kennedy as well. Gordie hit the boards so hard that the crowd went quiet. Then blood started to pool around his head. He'd fractured his nose and his cheekbone, his eyeball was scratched, and he suffered a serious concussion.

They operated on Gordie after midnight. A neurosurgeon named Dr. Frederic Schreiber drilled a hole in his skull to relieve the pressure. Gordie later said that it was awful listening to the drill and feeling the force of it penetrating his skull.

While Gordie recovered, the Wings went on to beat the Leafs and the Rangers to win the Cup. It was the start of a run of four Cups in six seasons: 1950, 1952, 1954, and 1955.

The incident left Gordie with a facial tic that made him blink. When I was with the Indianapolis Racers in 1978 and Gordie was with the New England Whalers, I once looked over at him during a game. We had been friendly for a while, as his son Murray and I played together in Toronto when I was fifteen, and Gordie would come to watch the games as often as he could. So I thought I saw him winking at me, kind of wishing me good luck. I mentioned this to one of my teammates, who told me, "Nah, he just blinks a lot. In fact, some of his teammates call him Blinky."

Stories about Gordie Howe tend to fall into one of two categories. In the first category are the examples of his generosity and graciousness. He would help strangers, he was adored by children, and he was unfailingly polite. The only enemies Gordie ever had were the nineteen guys sitting on the opposing bench. But those nineteen guys had to be on their best behavior.

That leads us to the second category—the stories about how intimidating he could be. One of his mottos was "Do unto others before they do unto you," but he could be counted on to do unto others *after* as well. In fact, he was known for his long memory. If you ever crossed Gordie Howe, your punishment was coming—it was just a question of when. Before he was known as Mr. Hockey, he was Mr. Elbows. He left a trail of broken noses, missing teeth, and stitches through the league.

And then there is the Gordie Howe Hat Trick—a goal, an assist, and a fight. Players love them, and if a guy has two of the three, his teammates will try to set him up for the third. If you look at the players who have racked up a few "Gordie Howe Hat Tricks," you can see why it's something to be proud of. Guys like Brendan Shanahan, Cam Neely, and Jarome Iginla are in the double digits. But the funny thing is, Gordie had only a couple. And it wasn't because he didn't score that much. It was because he actually didn't fight all that often after his reputation was established. No one wanted to fight him. Only a true heavyweight would tangle with Gordie, and it was a risky move even for a guy like that.

There was one fight in Gordie's career that probably served as a warning. It started because of Eddie Shack, who always played with a full head of steam. This was a guy who traveled in a straight line, and if you got in his way he'd go through you, not around you. (His linemate with the Leafs, Bert Olmstead, loved Eddie despite their rocky start. Eddie was skating wildly and accidentally hit Bert hard. Bert got up, grabbed Eddie by the jersey, and said, "What color is this, Eddie?" Eddie said, "Blue." Bert said, "Right. So whenever you see a blue uniform, steer clear of it.")

Back in 1959, nine years after Gordie's brain operation, Eddie Shack was a rookie with the Rangers. On February 1, the Rangers were up 4–1 in a game against the Wings. Eddie was being a pest, so Gordie sliced his ear for a couple of stitches with his stick.

But Shack didn't get the message. Later in the game he was mixing it up with Gordie's teammate Red Kelly. When Gordie made a move to sort things out, Rangers' heavyweight Lou Fontinato grabbed Gordie and probably wished he hadn't. Gordie's later account was, "Lou was coming like a madman. It took me a while to get the gloves off, and then things were busy." Fontinato's version was that Gordie had "rearranged his nose." But Fontinato was as tough as nails. He needed surgery to straighten out his nose, but he finished the game before heading to the hospital.

Gordie did eventually work things out with Eddie Shack, who by that time was with the Leafs. In January 1961, Detroit was at Maple Leaf Gardens when Eddie and Gordie collided. Gordie went down and was knocked out cold when his head hit the ice. He got up feeling dizzy and with a bad headache, so they took him to the hospital for X-rays. He had a concussion and needed ten stitches. Gordie didn't blame Shack, but Jack Adams was furious.

In a game soon after, the score was 1–1. It was well known that Eddie was taking classes to read and write, so Jack yelled at him from the bench, calling him "an illiterate so-and-so." Eddie rushed the puck down the ice, put it in the net, and then skated past the bench and said, "Hey, Jack, that's spelled s-c-o-r-e."

In 1967, when Eddie was with the Bruins, he knocked Gordie out again. He came in on him elbows up and sent him off balance. Gordie hit his head hard on the ice once again.

In those days the NHL would hold a summer golf tournament and bring in someone from every Original Six team. Eddie was sitting with Gordie. Gordie said, "Shackie? You don't hit me and I don't hit you. Put 'er there." Gordie held his hand out.

Shack said, "Gordie, it's a deal," and they shook on it.

At the start of the next season during a Boston–Detroit game, Coach Harry Sinden called Shack over to the bench. He said, "Eddie, Gordie Howe is the meanest, most competitive man out there. What are you doing skating around him with your head down?"

Shack replied, "Aw, don't worry about it. We got a deal."

I t stands to reason that a guy as tough and as selfless as Gordie Howe would be the ultimate teammate. And who would know that better than his sons, Mark and Marty? In 1973, they were drafted into the WHA as underage juniors, just as I would be later. Gordie thought about it for a while, then offered his services to his sons' new team, the Houston Aeros. He had retired from the NHL two years earlier, and his sweater was hanging from the rafters in Detroit. He was forty-five years old, and his arthritis was bothering him. But he had a lot more hockey left in him.

It took him a while to get back into shape, but on opening night, Mark and Marty Howe were playing with their father. The WHA was a tough league, but God help anyone who took liberties with a player with "Howe" on the back of his sweater. And Gordie wasn't just riding shotgun. He scored over thirty goals almost every year he was in the league. Tom Webster, our coach in L.A. from 1989 to 1992—we made it to the playoffs all three seasons he was there—had played with Gordie in both the NHL and the WHA, so he knew him well. Webby tells a story that captures in a nutshell why players thought so much of Gordie.

Webby joined the Wings in 1970–71. It was Gordie's last year in the NHL. In order to help make room for Webby, the coach, Ned Harkness, decided to put Gordie back on blue line to play defense. That way, Webby would have a chance to play with Alex Delvecchio and Frank Mahovlich. That's a bit like asking Mario Lemieux to play defense. Not that he couldn't do it—but this is one of the biggest stars the league has ever seen.

Gordie Howe had played on the Production Line with Ted Lindsay and Sid Abel since 1947–48—four years before Delvecchio and ten years before Mahovlich even joined the league—and he'd led the league in scoring from 1950–51 to 1953–54. The only guy who came close to his numbers was the Rocket in 1953–54, and he was fourteen points behind. Now the coach comes and asks him to move back—and of course he does it, because he's the ultimate team guy.

And then two seasons later Gordie came out of retirement and joined the WHA. He moved over from the Houston Aeros to the New England Whalers in 1977–78 and joined up again with Tom Webster who played on his right wing. Gordie was at center ice and his son Mark was on left wing. What a great line.

Gordie came up to Webby and said, "Listen, I don't have the touch like you do right now, so you just make your way out into the slot. I'll go into the corners and I'll find the puck for ya." At forty-nine years of age, Gordie would go into the corners instead of making the young guys do it. But that's the way Gordie Howe was.

All Gordie wanted to do was play hockey. He didn't seem to worry about the money. He felt he could put his trust in Jack Adams and in return Adams would treat him fairly. Gordie had only one request as a player during salary negotiations with Adams: he didn't want anyone to be paid more than he was. It was a fair request, considering that he was often the best player in the game.

But a conversation with Bob Baun broke the trust Gordie had in the front office. Baun had been drafted by Oakland in the 1967 expansion draft, and then was traded to Detroit in 1968. (Baun was famous for a goal he scored for the Leafs in the sixth game of the 1964 Stanley Cup finals against Detroit. Halfway through the third period with the score tied 3–3, he broke his ankle blocking a Gordie Howe shot while killing a penalty. Baun went to the dressing room, had his ankle shot up with freezing and taped, and came back out.

He scored in overtime and the Leafs went on to win the Cup in Game Seven.) In 1969 Gordie and Baun and some other vets decided to take the rookies to lunch. Back then players didn't discuss their salaries. But Baun had served as interim president of the new players' association. So it was not just idle conversation when the talk turned to contracts and money. Baun disclosed his contract. He was making more than Gordie Howe.

Gordie was very, very hurt. It was a tremendous blow to his ego or his pride or whatever you want to call it. He felt betrayed because of all the sacrifices he'd made based on the loyalty he had for the Red Wings. Gordie was so upset that he went down and talked to owner Bruce Norris. Gordie was given the $100,000-a-year raise he requested, but the incident destroyed his trust in management.

That's when Gordie's wife, Colleen, stepped in. Her attitude was, "I won't let this happen again. I'm going to take care of my husband and I'm going to take care of my boys." She became their manager and the first female player agent in the NHL. I give her a tremendous amount of credit for that.

When Gordie Howe retired from the NHL a second time in 1980, the league and the game lost a player the likes of which we will never see again. He was a legend even when he was still playing. One glimpse of his greatness is reflected in the career of another true legend of the game—Bobby Orr. Bobby's first NHL All-Star game was in 1968. Gordie played in that game. In fact, he got into a rare All-Star game fight with Mike Walton, then of the Maple Leafs. It's hard to believe, but Gordie's first All-Star game was in 1948, the year Bobby was born (and Gordie dropped the gloves in that game too). Most astonishing of all is that Gordie's final All-Star game was in 1980, two years after Orr had retired.

That game was at Joe Louis Arena, and even though Gordie was returning as a member of the Hartford Whalers, the crowd gave their hero a standing ovation that went on for minutes. I was there. It was my first All-Star game and his twenty-third. The players were introduced one by one. As each guy skated out to his blue line, the announcer called out his name and the team he was representing. Gordie was the last to step on the ice. The crowd spontaneously rose to its feet as his name was called, and he was introduced as representing not this or that team but all of hockey. The applause went on for several minutes. The adoration of that crowd—and the humility on Gordie's face—is something I will never forget.

No matter how you look at it, his numbers are staggering. He scored 801 goals, in a defensively oriented league, with a straight blade, back when the season was only about seventy games long. And that doesn't count the 174 goals and 508 points he scored in the WHA. He was among the top five scorers for twenty consecutive seasons. I may have broken some of his records, but I never came close to that. And no one ever will. And there's another record no one will ever come close to: Gordie scored fifteen goals in the NHL—as a fifty-one-year-old. Anyone who can do that at forty is a legend. No one is ever going to do it at fifty again.

Like the true sportsman Gordie was, he went on the road with us in 1994 when I was with the Kings and close to breaking his record of 801 goals. It got kind of crazy, and after about two weeks we were beginning to wonder how long we could ask Gordie Howe to follow us around. I was certainly feeling pressure. I idolized Gordie and felt as if I was letting him down.

What was really crazy was that in each game I was using nine sticks, three sets of gloves, and three or four different helmets. In a record-setting situation, everybody wants something when the big goal is scored. The Hall of Fame wanted something, the NHL wanted something, the team wanted something, and on it goes.

We were at home on March 23, 1994, when Vancouver came in. The Canucks played a big game and were a good skating club, so it was always tough to go up against them. But at 14:47 of the second period on our power play, the right guys were on the ice—Marty McSorley, Luc Robitaille, and Jari Kurri.

Luc made a drop pass to me just inside the blue line and I gave it to Marty, who returned it cross-ice. I picked it out of the air past the middle of the right circle and put it in past Kirk McLean. Of all the goals I scored in my career, that goal means the most because of the connection to Gordie Howe, the greatest of them all.

Fifteen

WILLIE O'REE

W illie O'Ree is one of those great characters in hockey. Born in 1935, he was the first black player in the NHL and paved the way for guys like Tony McKegney, Grant Fuhr, Anson Carter, Jarome Iginla, and P.K. Subban.

Although his parents were born in Canada and he grew up in Fredericton, his great-grandparents had been slaves who came through the Underground Railroad to Nova Scotia and from there to New Brunswick. But O'Ree's childhood story isn't just about race. He was a lot like any other Canadian kid who fell in love with hockey. When he was only three years old his dad gave him his first pair of skates. They were basically blocks of wood with double blades on the bottom and straps that went over your shoes. With the two blades on each foot, they worked like training wheels. O'Ree would lean on a chair and push himself back and forth across the backyard rink.

When O'Ree was a kid, there were only two black families in Fredericton, so all his friends were white. Still, he later said that he could have been purple for all the difference it made. He wouldn't learn about racial discrimination, in hockey or in life, until later.

As he saw it, in those early days, black meant puck and white meant ice.

As O'Ree grew older he became aware that there were things he couldn't do and places he couldn't go. When he was a teenager, it was pretty much impossible to have a girlfriend. There were no black girls his age at school. It was an unwritten rule, but very much understood by everyone, that white girls were off-limits for a black man. O'Ree would have secret crushes on girls, but that's as far as it went.

He also couldn't go into the barbershop. There were no signs, but it was understood that it was a white barbershop. O'Ree was good friends with the barber's son, Joe McQuade, so he asked him what would happen if he went in for a haircut. Joe said he didn't know. So one afternoon, O'Ree walked in and sat down and Mr. McQuade cut his hair. Joe's father was criticized for it, but he always took care of O'Ree. O'Ree made up his mind then and there that he wasn't going to let prejudice stand in his way.

He played every sport—baseball, basketball, tennis, volleyball, soccer—but mostly he loved hockey. He'd listen to Foster Hewitt's play-by-play on *Hockey Night in Canada* on the radio every Saturday night. His favorite players were Rocket Richard and Gordie Howe. (When O'Ree finally made the NHL, he once found himself in the corner with Gordie and got a faceful of the famous Howe elbow. As Gordie skated away with the puck he called back to O'Ree, "Keep your head up, rookie.")

In his first year in high school, O'Ree was good enough to make the Fredericton Junior Capitals. A year later, he moved up to the Senior Capitals. When he turned nineteen he moved on to major junior with the Quebec Frontenacs, where he made sixty dollars a week. That was great money for a kid in those days and it was enough to help his family buy their first house for $3,000. His family had always been renters, so that was a big day.

O'Ree's coach in Quebec was Phil Watson, who'd played thirteen years in the NHL with the Rangers and Canadiens. Phil told O'Ree that he had the skills to play in the NHL but that people might not accept him because he was black. The next year O'Ree went to play for the Kitchener-Waterloo Canucks in Ontario, coached by Hall of Famer "Black Jack" Stewart—the teammate Gordie Howe had got tangled up with the night of his dangerous head injury.

Then something happened that threatened O'Ree's NHL dream. A shot from the point deflected off Willie's stick and struck him in the right eye, breaking his nose and his cheek.

After the operation on his eye, the surgeon, Dr. Henry Soon, came into the recovery room. "Mr. O'Ree," he said, "the impact of the puck completely shattered the retina in your right eye. You're going to be blind in that eye, and you'll never play hockey again." Ten days later the twenty-year-old was back on his skates. He kept the news about being blind in one eye to himself. Instead, as a left-handed left-winger, he learned to compensate by turning his head all the way around to the right to pick the puck up. At first he was overskating the puck and missing the net, and then he told himself, "Forget about what you can't see and just concentrate on what you can see." So his game started to improve. He scored a few goals, and then the season ended. That's when Punch Imlach, who was with the Quebec Aces, asked him to come to training camp. Imlach signed O'Ree for $3,500 plus a $500 signing bonus and another bonus if he scored twenty goals.

In 1949, O'Ree's baseball team in Fredericton won a league championship and was rewarded with a trip to New York that included a Dodgers game at Ebbets Field to meet the great Jackie Robinson, who'd broken baseball's color barrier with the Dodgers two years earlier. The kids lined up after the game and Jackie shook their hands. He was about to move on when O'Ree told him that he was a hockey player. Jackie stopped and said, "I didn't realize there were any black kids playing hockey." And O'Ree said, "Yeah, there's a few."

Herb Carnegie—a center who played senior hockey in the 1940s and 50s—had come close. Conn Smythe would say of him, "Somebody get me a paintbrush. If I could paint him white, he'd make the team." Carnegie played in the Quebec Senior League with Jean Béliveau, who saw him as "a super hockey player [with] a beautiful style, a beautiful skater, a great playmaker. In those days, the younger ones learned from the older ones. I learned from Herbie." Carnegie was also part of the first all-black line in the Quebec Provincial League, known as the Black Aces—he played center while his brother Ossie and Manny McIntyre were wingers. Named most valuable player in 1946, 1947, and 1948, he tried out for the New York Rangers in 1948, but there were some racial problems there too. Although he was among the best players at camp, he was only offered a contract to play in the minors. Carnegie decided to stay in Quebec, where the money was better.

O'Ree, too, spent time in an American training camp when the Milwaukee Braves of baseball's National League brought him down to Georgia. It was his first time in the Deep South and he was shocked. He had to stay in a blacks-only hotel, and for the first time in his life he was told to sit at the back of the bus. But at the end of the tryout, he too headed back to Canada to play hockey. After all, O'Ree liked playing with the Aces. (For a short time in 1958–59, O'Ree played on an all-black line with Stan Maxwell and twenty-year-old John Utendale, who had earlier played with Mark Messier's father, Doug, on the junior Edmonton Oil Kings.)

O'Ree's teammates and their hometown fans in Quebec treated him well, but when the Aces went on the road, fans in other rinks would call him names. There was no glass between the stands and penalty box, and sometimes they'd spit and throw drinks on him. Opposition players went after him too—there was a lot of name-calling, stick work, elbows, and hits from behind—but O'Ree gave as good as he got. He had to let them know he wasn't an easy mark or they'd run all over him.

I n August 1957, Lynn Patrick, the Bruins' GM, invited O'Ree to the Bruins' training camp. O'Ree framed the letter and still has it today. On January 18, 1958, he was called up to replace Leo Labine, who had the flu. It was a Saturday night, so the game was broadcast on *Hockey Night in Canada*. O'Ree played on a line with Don McKenney and Jerry Toppazzini against his heroes Jean Béliveau, Doug Harvey, and Jacques Plante. The Bruins beat the Canadiens 3–0 that night.

O'Ree had no idea of the game's significance until he opened the newspaper the next morning to search for his name in the box scores, and to his surprise he found a couple of lines in the third paragraph saying that he was the "first Negro ever to play in the N.H.L., at left wing for the Bruins."

Once O'Ree was in the league, the name-calling escalated—not so much in Canada, where he was known from his junior days, but in Detroit, Chicago, and New York. If O'Ree told the refs, they'd brush him off.

Eric Nesterenko, a winger with the Black Hawks who finished his career with over a thousand penalty minutes, once skated up to

O'Ree and made racial comments during the warm-up. He knew then that he would have to fight Nesterenko that night.

Seven minutes in, Nesterenko butt-ended him in the mouth. He broke O'Ree's nose, split his lip, and knocked out his two front teeth. Then he stood over him, calling him the N-word several times. But that wasn't what set O'Ree off. As Nesterenko stood there and laughed at him, daring him to do something about it, O'Ree thought, "You have to do something now or he'll be chasing you the rest of the year." So O'Ree clubbed him over the head with his stick. Nesterenko needed fifteen stitches.

O'Ree was traded to Montreal a year after they won five Stanley Cups in a row. Montreal was so deep that he was sent to the minors in Hull-Ottawa, and then traded to the WHL's Los Angeles Blades, where he was moved to right wing. That meant the passes and the checks came at him from the left where he could see them, so his totals jumped to twenty-eight goals and twenty-six assists in 1961–62, and he won the goal-scoring title in 1964–65.

In Los Angeles, 1962, O'Ree was at an NAACP luncheon in Jackie Robinson's honor. Robinson was standing over in the corner when O'Ree's coach brought O'Ree and a couple of other players over to meet him. He said, "Mr. Robinson, I'd like to introduce you to a couple of players. This is Willie O'Ree, newly acquired from Canada to join our team." And Robinson looked O'Ree in the eye and said, "Willie O'Ree. You're the young fellow I met in Brooklyn." It just goes to show, you don't forget a guy like Willie O'Ree.

Sixteen

STAND FIRM

No one is exactly sure where the game of hockey started. Some people think it is a Canadian adaptation of the traditional Irish sport of hurling. Others claim it was an invention of students at McGill University in Montreal. But there is a solid claim that a sport not unlike hockey was played by Native North Americans before Europeans ever arrived. Certainly, some of the first hockey sticks were made by the Mi'kmaq First Nation in Nova Scotia. In fact, the "Mic Mac" stick was the most popular stick in the game in the first decades of the twentieth century (and was used by Lord Stanley's sons).

Even though the First Nations were part of the evolution of the game from the very beginning, it wasn't until 1954 that Fred Sasakamoose, a short, speedy center with great skills, became the very first Native Canadian player with treaty status to make the NHL. Born on Christmas Day 1933, Sasakamoose grew up on the Ahtahkakoop reserve in Sandy Lake, Saskatchewan, and began playing hockey at a residential school in Duck Lake. His Aboriginal name, pronounced tah-saw, means "stand firm," and that is the man he became.

When Sasakamoose was very young, his grandfather, who was deaf and mute, would put him in a sleigh and take him to the slough near their cabin to play hockey. He would scrape off a bit of the ice and help Sasakamoose pull on three or four pairs of socks and a pair of moccasins, and then he'd slide a little pair of box skates over the boy's feet. Next, his grandfather would hand him a little hockey stick that he'd whittled from a willow branch.

Sasakamoose's grandfather would stand him up and let him go, and then turn his own attention to chopping a hole in the ice to fish. Sasakamoose would rush around pushing a chunk of frozen horse manure all over with his stick. When he fell down, his grandfather would pull himself up off his seat on an upside-down five-gallon pail, pick Sasakamoose up, and make him try again.

Later in the day, when it got too cold, his grandfather would pack up and take Sasakamoose home. He would hold the boy on his knee in front of the stove, warming him up by rubbing his back while he peeled off the frozen layers of his outer clothing.

All six members of Sasakamoose's family lived in a tiny, mud-daubed log house. His mother used to braid Fred's and his brother Frank's hair every day. There was no such thing as welfare in those days. If you didn't work, you starved. The closest hospital was eighty miles away in Prince Albert. The family used traditional medicine—roots, leaves, grass, whatever was taught—and that's how they survived. They lived off the land and they were happy.

In 1940, when Sasakamoose was six years old, an RCMP officer, a government agent, and a Catholic priest came for him and his brother. They pulled into the yard in a three-ton truck already filled with crying children. His grandfather tried to pull Sasakamoose close to protect him. Sasakamoose could see the tears dropping down his cheeks. But the government agent shoved the old man back. It was the last time Sasakamoose ever saw his grandfather. He died that winter.

It took about five hours to get to Duck Lake Residential School. The first thing the priests did when the boys arrived was cut off their braids. Then they poured coal oil, which is like kerosene, over their heads. Next, they threw the boys into a large steam bath, about thirty or forty kids at a time. Sasakamoose remembers how he sweated in that steam bath and how the coal oil burned his eyes. His parents were only 120 miles away, but they were not allowed to see their boys for two years. Terrible things happened to him at Duck Lake.

In the spring of 1943, when Sasakamoose was nine years old, he and a friend named Charlie ran away. They made it to the banks of the Saskatchewan River, about ten miles from the school. The river was a couple of hundred yards wide—a long way across. But Sasakamoose was too ashamed to go back and face the teasing from the other kids, so he and Charlie waded in. They'd made it about five or six feet when they got caught in the current. Later, Sasakamoose would say that river didn't want them to drown, so it swept them back to the shoreline.

The priests eventually found them and brought them back. But first they took their shoes. They made the boys walk all the way back in bare feet on gravel.

Fred was eleven years old when Father Georges Roussel came to Duck Lake from Quebec. Father Roussel was an athlete and a sportsman. He played basketball, baseball, and soccer. In the winter, he ran a hockey team. When Fred had milked enough cows, made enough beds, and cleaned enough toilets, he earned a pair of secondhand skates and was able to join the Duck Lake team.

Father Roussel would turn on the radio on Saturday nights at six o'clock so he and the boys could listen to *Hockey Night in Canada*. Foster Hewitt was so good at play-by-play that the boys didn't need to watch TV to "see" the games. Hewitt took them by the hand and gave them front-row seats.

When Sasakamoose was fourteen, Father Roussel came to him and said, "Freddie, you're going to hate my guts, but I'm going to make you skate for four hours every day in the cold. I'm going to make a champion out of you." But Sasakamoose didn't hate it. He loved the four-hour outside practices. It didn't matter how cold it was—it didn't matter that his hands and feet were stiff and numb—because when he was in his skates with a stick in his hand, he was back home on the slough with his grandfather.

Father Roussel noticed that Sasakamoose seemed much stronger on his right than his left. So he nailed tobacco cans on top of the boards and had Sasakamoose shoot left and then right for hours and hours until he was accurate on both sides. That old priest was determined. He made Sasakamoose into a left-handed shooter just like Gordie Howe.

In 1949–50, the Duck Lake team led by Sasakamoose won the Saskatchewan midget championship, and although he didn't know it, Sasakamoose had been scouted.

He was sixteen and finally free to go home for good. He had been away for almost ten years. All he could think about was having his mom and dad hug him and kiss him and care for him. He had been without the love of another human being for too long.

That summer, Sasakamoose, Frank, and their parents were piling grain for a local farmer. Each of them made fifty cents an acre. Sasakamoose was in the middle of a field when he saw a car pull up and two people get out. As they got closer, Sasakamoose recognized Father Roussel. The other person was a big white man, wearing a long coat. Sasakamoose hid behind a stack of grain. No way was he going back to Duck Lake.

A little while later, he heard his mother calling. His parents had been talking to the priest. Sasakamoose couldn't ignore her, so he put his head down and went over with tears in his eyes. She said, "They want you to play hockey." George Vogan, the man with Father Roussel, put out his hand and said, "Come with me to Moose Jaw." Sasakamoose's father put his arm around his son and whispered in Cree, "Go now, but come back in two weeks."

In early September, Sasakamoose moved in with Vogan and his family. There was a lot to get used to—a bathroom inside and running water. Back home when he wanted to clean up, he went to the lake.

Sasakamoose thrilled the Vogans with his fast hands. He would take four quarters and throw them up high in the air, catching them one at a time on each knuckle of his left hand. He also liked to open the birdcage so the family's budgie could fly around the room. Sasakamoose would stand very still, watching it go, and then reach out and snatch the bird right out of the air.

Sasakamoose went to the training camp of the Moose Jaw Canucks, and on the morning of the second week, he headed to the highway and started the five-hundred-mile walk home. He picked dried Saskatoon berries and chokecherries from bushes that grew along the ditch and drank water from nearby creeks when he got thirsty. Late that afternoon, having walked for eight hours, he sat down to rest. A car pulled up—it was Vogan. He said, "Where are you going?" Sasakamoose replied, "George, it's been two weeks. I'm going home to my reservation, where I belong."

Vogan got out of the car and put his arms around him. Vogan was half crying when he said, "Freddie, you're going to make it. You're going to make that team." He took the boy to a diner in Chamberlain, a small town nearby, and talked to him for a long time.

It was dark out when they got back in the car and headed home for Moose Jaw. It was the first time a white man had made Sasakamoose feel loved.

When he was twenty, Sasakamoose was named MVP in the Western Canadian Junior Hockey League. After his last game in junior, the team was sitting in the dressing room when Vogan walked in carrying an envelope. He opened it and read it to the room. It was from the Black Hawks, who were calling up Sasakamoose to play against the Leafs in Toronto. On February 27, 1954, he became the first full-blooded Native Canadian to play in the NHL. He played the rest of that season for Chicago.

They called him Chief. And whenever Sasakamoose stepped onto the ice, the organist would play the song "Indian Love Call." In the years to follow, the same thing would happen to pretty much every First Nations player. But as a pioneer for his race, Sasakamoose heard a lot worse in opposition rinks.

George Armstrong, a player with some First Nations ancestry (his mom was part Ojibway), had established himself as an NHL regular in the early 1950s. Like Sasakamoose and a lot of guys with First Nations heritage, he too was known as Chief. But it was meant with true respect—Armstrong was the captain of the Toronto Maple Leafs in the glory days of the 1960s. He played his whole career for the Leafs and was captain for twelve seasons, the longest term of any captain in Leafs history.

George Armstrong was a legend to Leafs fans. In the last game of the 1967 Stanley Cup finals, when the Leafs won their fourth Cup of the decade, it was Armstrong who scored the very last goal of the Original Six era. (The Leafs haven't won a Cup since.) From

1950 to 1971, he played twenty-one seasons for the Leafs, a total of 1,187 games. That's a franchise record. Armstrong is now one of only two First Nations players in the Hockey Hall of Fame. The other is Bryan Trottier.

S ince the days of Sasakamoose and Armstrong, there have been many great First Nations players, including Dale McCourt, Reggie Leach, Chris Simon, Theo Fleury, T.J. Oshie, and Jordin Tootoo (who is Inuit). Carey Price, one of the best goalies in the world, is Métis. His mother, Lynda, is a former chief of Ulkatcho First Nation.

Price's father, Jerry, is also a goalie. He was drafted by the Flyers in 1978. Jerry played four seasons as a pro but never made the NHL. When Carey was young, the family moved to the remote town of Anahim Lake, in northern B.C. Carey didn't live on the reserve, but most of the kids he went to school with (and a large percentage of the people at Anahim Lake) were First Nations.

Every day after school, Carey would skate on the creek that ran through the family's backyard or head to Anahim Lake to play shinny with his friends. He'd be out there until it was too dark to see the puck anymore. Jerry wanted to make sure that his son had an opportunity to play organized hockey. So when Carey was ten years old, he made the commitment to sign him up for peewee hockey in Williams Lake, two hundred miles away. That meant making an eight-hour round trip three times a week by car.

First practice was at six a.m. on Tuesdays, the next at six p.m. on Thursdays. Games were on the weekends. Jerry and Carey would drive to Williams Lake Monday night, practice Tuesday morning, and head back to Anahim Lake for school that day. Carey would go to school on Wednesday and half of Thursday, then head back to Williams Lake for evening practice. He'd return home late Thursday night, go to school on Friday, and then head back that night for the games on Saturday and Sunday. Jerry never saw it as a sacrifice or anything like that. It was just something they both enjoyed. To this day, neither of them would trade a minute of those drives. Carey would do his homework, or they'd listen to CBC Radio. Sometimes they'd catch a WHL junior game on the radio. In remote settings, you can often get AM stations that are normally out of reach.

Jerry got his pilot's license around the time Carey was born. He bought a little Piper Cherokee, and he and Carey flew to practice when they could. Carey couldn't land the plane or take off, but from the time he was eight years old, Jerry let him handle the controls. He says Carey could fly the Piper just as well as he could ride his bike. Unfortunately, they didn't get to fly to practice much because of bad weather and limited daylight. The runway at Anahim Lake wasn't lighted.

Carey is an expert hunter and fisherman, but not just for sport. Like his ancestors, he learned to harvest food from the land. His connections to his Ulkatcho First Nations roots run deep. When he was nine years old, he had a dream one night that Patrick Roy walked by him fully dressed in his equipment. Carey's neck was tingling and he had trouble catching his breath as he stared up at Roy in complete awe. When Carey woke up, he couldn't shake the dream. Being so close to his idol—even in a dream—was too powerful. He could still smell the wet leather on Roy's Koho pads as he moved along. Over the years, in quiet moments, Carey would sometimes let himself relive the thrill he felt that night in his dream.

Carey became a top goaltender in the WHL and was drafted fifth overall by Montreal. He became the Canadiens' starting goaltender during his rookie season, 2007–08. In November of the next season, the Canadiens retired Patrick Roy's number 33.

Carey was twenty-one years old when he found himself standing next to Roy at the Bell Centre in Montreal. He stole a glance at his hero. Roy still had the same bright blue eyes he saw in his dream. As Carey watched Roy's number rising to the rafters, his heart was racing and his eyes were stinging. And then he noticed that the banner was as red as the Indian paintbrush wildflowers that grew in spring alongside the highway back home.

Now Price is a hero to kids around the world, the way Roy was to him. In 2015, he won the Hart Trophy, the Ted Lindsay Award as MVP elected by the players, the William M. Jennings Trophy for allowing the fewest goals, and the Vezina. No one had ever won all four of them in the same season before.

Fred Sasakamoose's NHL career could have been longer, but he fell in love with a girl back home and so he returned to Sandy Lake. But he will always be remembered for doing something no Native Canadian had done before, paving the way for other great players like Carey Price.

Seventeen

THE SECOND SIX

ockey is a game of tradition. That's one of the things I
love about it, and I know that a lot of fans and players
feel the same way. For me, while growing up, hockey
meant the same six teams that had made up the NHL for years. The
same cities, the same colors, the same names. Hockey didn't change
much, and I don't think many people thought it needed to change.

But the NHL is also a business. There is nothing wrong with
that. If it weren't a business, there would be no league. The fact
that the players are professional means they can focus on being
the best they can be. The travel, the bright lights, the crowds—so
much of what we love about the game is possible only because it's
a business.

It's interesting that for so long tradition and business went
together in the hockey world. Hockey is pretty unique in the way it
avoids being too flashy. You think of Bobby Orr scoring a highlight-
reel goal, then barely smiling as he heads back to the neutral zone
for the faceoff. For a long time, the whole league was the same way.
Just drop the puck, and let's play hockey.

Hockey games were first broadcast over telegraph. During the Stanley Cup playoffs, newspapers would often send a hometown reporter across the country by train; between periods, the reporter would fire off bulletins to the paper, and then someone there would use a bullhorn to keep the hometown crowd up to date. On Valentine's Day 1923, CFCA radio (owned by the *Toronto Star*) broadcast the first live NHL play-by-play ever as the Toronto St. Pats defeated the Ottawa Senators 6–4 at Mutual Street Arena. Two days later, Foster Hewitt, a sports reporter at the *Toronto Star* (his father, W.A. Hewitt, was its sports editor), was the second person to call hockey play-by-play on the radio.

Hockey Night in Canada (known then as the *General Motors Hockey Broadcast*) debuted in November 1931 with Foster Hewitt barking out the play-by-play of a Toronto Maple Leafs game for about a hundred thousand rapt fans. *HNIC* broadcast thirty games that season.

By the next spring Conn Smythe had hired Hewitt as the director of radio, and more and more stations were picking up the games. At that time Canada's population numbered only about fifteen million, and a third were listening to the show every Saturday night. In 1935–36, the Mutual Broadcasting System picked up a few Chicago Black Hawks games in the States, but they never caught on. Fans in border towns and cities were able to listen to the games on CBC.

Hockey sounds great on the radio, as generations of fans know. If you know the game and you know the players, a guy like Foster Hewitt could re-create a game in your imagination. But the thing is, you had to have already seen a lot of hockey, or played it, for a radio broadcast to make any sense at all. Otherwise, a hockey broadcast is like a foreign language. In other words, radio is a great way to broadcast to people who already love the game, but it is never going to reach new fans.

Television is a different story. Hockey is all about speed and power and free-flowing athleticism. You have to see it to believe it. A lot of people are hooked by their first game. But there has to be a first game for that to happen. In 1949, Clarence Campbell vowed that hockey would never be televised. He figured the cameras would pick up the violence, but that the small, grainy screens would not be able to communicate the grace and speed. He also worried that if fans could watch the games at home, they would have no reason to go to the rink.

He was overruled, of course. The first publicly televised hockey game in Canada was on October 11, 1952, as the Montreal Canadiens defeated Detroit 2–1 on *La Soirée du hockey*, the French-language version of *Hockey Night in Canada*. René Lecavalier called the play-by-play for French Canada. Conn Smythe saw a closed-circuit broadcast of a Memorial Cup game that year and hated it. "If that's what hockey looks like on television," he said, "then the people of Toronto won't be seeing it."

But it was his own son, Stafford Smythe, part owner of the Leafs, who started pushing the league to harness the power of television. He knew he couldn't bring every sports fan in North America into Maple Leaf Gardens, but he could try to convince his fellow owners to take the game to those fans. He started pushing the other NHL team owners to expand the league into the biggest television-viewing audiences they could find. It took him five years to get them to agree.

In March 1965, NHL president Clarence Campbell announced plans to expand to twelve teams. In February 1966 the franchises were awarded to Philadelphia, Los Angeles, Minneapolis–Saint

Paul, Pittsburgh, St. Louis, and San Francisco–Oakland. CBS had the television broadcast contract in the U.S. and the network wanted all American cities. Each team had to come up with $2 million and guarantee a building with at least 12,500 seats. The game was changed forever.

Eighteen

BLACK, WHITE, AND SILVER

The world seemed very big to us back in 1967. Boston, Detroit, New York, Chicago. I knew where those were. But Los Angeles? Oakland? I really had no idea.

People were very excited about it. I was excited, of course. There was nothing about hockey I didn't love. I knew by the way my parents and neighbors would talk about it that everyone was eager to see the puck drop in the new NHL. When we saw the colors of the new teams, I admit we were a little surprised. Yellow and purple? It didn't look like hockey to me. But everyone I knew was excited, and everyone watched.

The league was split into two divisions, with expansion teams in the West and Original Six teams in the East. The thinking was that they didn't want a league with all six originals at the top and all six new teams at the bottom. Four teams in each division would qualify for the playoffs. The winner of the Clarence Campbell Bowl in the West would compete with the Prince of Wales Trophy winner in the East for the best-of-seven Stanley Cup finals.

St. Louis was by far the best expansion team out of the gate, appearing in three straight finals. But they didn't win a single game—they were swept twice by the Canadiens and once by Bobby Orr's Bruins. In fact, the Blues have not been back to the finals since. For a while, a lot of fans started to think that while these teams were in the NHL, they weren't very good. But four of the teams have won the Cup since then, and some of them have gone on to become the class of the league. But there were a lot of ups and downs before that could happen.

The *Washington Post* has called Jack Kent Cooke the best owner in the history of sports. He was a Canadian who moved to California in 1960. Although he'd never even seen a professional basketball game, he bought the L.A. Lakers five years later for $5,175,000—the most anyone had ever paid for an NBA franchise. He won his first NBA title in 1972, and then five more in the 1980s with Kareem Abdul-Jabbar and Magic Johnson. He also owned a share of the NFL's Washington Redskins. But Cooke's real love was hockey.

When he acquired the Los Angeles Kings he immediately started making plans to build a fifteen-thousand-seat showplace on thirty acres in Hollywood Park for hockey fans. He called it the Fabulous Forum and chose royal purple and gold as the team's colors. After all, he predicted that Los Angeles would one day become the most important hockey city in the world. When he was awarded the franchise, Cooke called it the happiest day of his life.

Yet hockey wasn't selling in L.A. And although Cooke was an intelligent guy, it takes real dedication to and passion for a sport to make it fly. In 1979, Cooke decided to sell to Jerry Buss. Buss was both a businessman and a visionary. He bought the Forum for $33.5 million, the Lakers for $16 million, the Kings for $8 million, and a thirteen-thousand-acre ranch in Kern County for $10 million—$67.5 million in total. At the time, it was the biggest sports transaction ever. Buss would take the Lakers to ten NBA championships, but hockey still wasn't selling.

Enter Bruce McNall, an ambitious young guy who dealt in ancient coins. He'd taken a very small business that nobody cared about, opened an establishment on Rodeo Drive, and started bidding on coins at auctions around the world. Bruce always paid high, which drove up the price and made his coins more and more valuable. He'd also gotten involved with the Dallas Mavericks when the NBA expanded in 1980. Dallas was football country—no one cared about basketball there in those days—but Bruce was really good at sales and marketing, and so with his help they turned things around.

Bruce was a huge hockey fan. (He hesitated to buy season tickets to the Kings because you could pick up tickets for almost nothing on game nights outside the Forum back then.) Kings players like Rogie Vachon, Whitey Widing, Gene Carr, and Mike Murphy were his heroes. Meanwhile, although Jerry Buss loved the Kings and would have given anything to win with them, whatever magic he had with the Lakers he never really had with them. One of the problems was that he doubled up on his people in the organization—the PR people, the ticket people, and the sponsorship people were all the same. And if you're in that business and you work on commissions, you're going to focus on the team that brings you the most personal success. Now, as it happened, Buss was into coins and so had known Bruce for many years. Bruce would kind of teasingly say to him, "I want to buy the Kings!" and Buss would laugh it off.

But at one point Buss was a little pressed for money. That sounds crazy for someone who owned the Lakers, but he had a high overhead. Bruce would lend him small amounts, $25,000 or $50,000, until those amounts had built up to a couple of million dollars. So Buss approached Bruce and said, "If you want to use the debt for partial ownership in the Kings, okay, we can do that."

Bruce said, "Great, but I'd like to have the option to be able to buy the balance." Buss, to his credit, felt that Bruce's enthusiasm for the game would make a difference. So in 1986, Bruce bought about 25 percent of the team, and by 1988 he'd acquired 100 percent ownership.

That's when Bruce said, "Look, we have to get away from being the Lakers and become our own team." Instead of departments sharing offices, he hired his own staff and literally put up doors and walls to mark out a clear distinction between the two groups. Next, he changed the team colors. Bruce felt that purple and gold made people think Lakers. Also, who the heck wears purple and gold? Bernie Nicholls, one of the Kings' top scorers, told him that they looked like bananas on ice. Bruce said, "Okay, what do you want?"

The team responded with "Well, white at home, obviously. Black on the road is cool because it makes us look bigger."

Bruce said, "Okay, what about the third color?"

"Well, you're in the coin business, and coins are silver."

The team unveiled the new colors in 1988, at the same time I was traded from Edmonton. At the press conference back in L.A., Bruce went up on stage to announce the new team colors and introduce their "model," and then I came out wearing the new sweater.

O nce I'd been traded to the Kings, my number-one concern was winning the Cup. Bruce and I talked a lot about how we could accomplish that. By 1992–93 we had a very good team and a very good coach in Barry Melrose. We played an eighty-four-game regular season—except that I missed the first thirty-nine because of a back injury that went back to March 22, 1990, in a game against the Islanders. I was checked by Alan Kerr and went flying headfirst into Kenny Baumgartner's chest. It wasn't a dirty or a bad hit. I just got hit from behind, and thankfully Kenny caught me and kind of cradled me. If he'd been coming at me full force, I would have been hurt really badly. I was lucky because I'd roomed with Kenny a year before, when he was with the Kings. All guys are good friends when they're teammates, but when you're roommates you become even closer.

I was out for three of ten playoff games that season. And then eighteen months later, on September 14, 1991, I was checked from behind by Gary Suter in a Canada Cup game and sustained another injury. Again, not a dirty hit. It was my own fault. The Americans were on a power play and I was first to the puck at the side of the net. I think Gary thought I was going to take the puck behind, but instead I turned into him. I didn't see him and I don't think he anticipated it. When you play against a guy, you know his tendencies. He probably thought I knew he was there. It all sort of settled down until I got reinjured in a game later that year. I must have seen four doctors. They all had different ideas as to what was wrong—from a cracked rib to a strained ligament.

About eight of us were at dinner in Hawaii at the end of the season when suddenly that injury flared up. Bad. I couldn't sit or stand, so I lay down on the floor of the restaurant.

Come June, I started training to get ready for the next season. Things were better. I felt really comfortable. But after the first day of training camp I couldn't walk. This time they sent me to the Kerlan-Jobe Orthopaedic Clinic—those are the guys who invented the Tommy John surgical graft procedure where they replace a ligament in the elbow with a tendon from somewhere else in your body. A lot of major league pitchers have had it.

I met with Dr. Robert Watkins at the clinic, and the first thing he said was "Has anybody checked your back?" I said, "'No, it's my ribs." He ordered an MRI, and when I met him mid-December to go over the results, he said, "The good news is that it's not cancer." I thought, "Cancer? Geez. He thought it might be *cancer?*"

It was a herniated thoracic disc. They started me on an IV for inflammation in my upper back and lower neck while Dr. Watkins spent the next four days talking to doctors around the country. Three recommended surgery and three recommended physical therapy. The only other professional athlete who'd been treated for the same injury was a downhill skier. She had the surgery and had to retire, so we went with 120 days of rehabilitation instead. I asked Dr. Watkins, "Am I allowed to golf?"

He shook his head and said, "You'll be playing hockey before I let you golf."

I started skating lightly and was feeling really good—eager to get back in the lineup. On Christmas Eve I practiced by myself, and then on Christmas Day I skated for two hours. That was one of the best presents ever.

The team was having a great year. We were in first place in the division. And then, on my first game back, January 6, 1993, we were beaten 6–3 by Tampa Bay. I remember coming off the ice and Marty McSorley, who never held back, looking at me funny and saying, "Good job."

I made the team worse for about fifteen games. We were forty-five games into the season and near the top of the division. I wasn't playing well—and you reward players for how they're playing now, not for their past history. I didn't want to take time from the other guys who were contributing. And yet I had to catch up because my timing was off, and even though I was in shape, I wasn't in *playing* shape. It was kind of a catch-22 situation. So I asked Barry Melrose, "Okay, how are we gonna make this work? How are we going to make this comfortable for the team and still let me get in enough time so that I can be ready for the playoffs?" But the turning point for me was on February 22, during a road trip to Tampa Bay. I had a really good game that night—I could feel the momentum and the timing of my game come together. I became a different player for the rest of the season.

Now, the flip side of the long layoff is that in the last ten games of that year and heading into the playoff run, I was the freshest I'd ever been in my career. There were years when I'd played 130 games when you factor in preseason, regular season, playoffs and the Canada Cup. After that many games you're ground down.

That year we played Calgary first round, followed by Vancouver, Toronto, and then Montreal. We played all four Canadian cities, and because we'd finished third in our division, we started on the road in every one.

In the first playoff game in Calgary, five minutes into the first period, I was in a faceoff with Joel Otto, who was a really good player. He was tough, really tough. Kind of like Mark Messier tough. If you did something stupid he was going to get even with you, but he was honest and pretty fair. I won the faceoff, but when I turned away from him he cross-checked me right in the side. Joel was a big man, 6'4", 220 pounds, and those sticks were solid wood. He broke my rib. I went to the locker room as soon as it happened.

As I lay on the trainer's table, I was thinking, "Oh my God, what do I do now?" The doctor came in. In the regular season you use the home team's doctor, but in the playoffs you don't want the other team to know who's injured and so you use your own. Joel had gotten me pretty good, though. I was in a lot of pain and worried about the rest of the playoffs.

The doctor said, "You know what we're going to do, Wayne? We'll just put a flak jacket on you." In those days a flak jacket was like a quarter inch of rubber. Hardly better than nothing. And so for every single game during the rest of the playoffs, at 7:25 after warm-up and right before we'd go on the ice, I'd put this vest on. The doctor would come in and take me to the trainer's room, where he'd use a long needle to inject freezing into my upper thigh.

I used to tease the doc: "Don't hit the wrong spot or I'll be walking around on one leg." I played the entire eight weeks of playoffs with a broken rib and never felt it once in a game. His reasoning was, "It's not going to get worse." But for about an hour after the game as the freezing came out, it was pretty painful.

We started the series in Calgary and we won it in Game Six. We started the next series in Vancouver and won a big game in double overtime in Game Five and then Game Six at home. We were on our way to Toronto for the semis.

One of the reasons we love sports is that anything can happen. But how Marty McSorley and Wendel Clark played in that series was a privilege to watch. Dougie Gilmour and I might have been the skill players, but Wendel and Marty were the heart and soul.

Wendel Clark was a phenom. He wasn't born with the natural talent some guys have. But he was one of the most dominant players in the league. His wrist shot was a laser, his open-ice hits were like being run over by a truck, and he was absolutely impossible to intimidate. It seemed as if he scored two goals every single game. He was the one guy on the Leafs we couldn't control. We did manage to slow Doug Gilmour down a little, though we were never going to stop him. But Wendel was just out of this world. Barry Melrose tried everybody against him, including Robbie Blake and Marty McSorley, yet Wendel still found a way to score. What was interesting is that Barry and Wendel Clark are cousins. Barry's mother's mother, Norrie Clarke McLean, and Wendel's father's father, Bud, are brother and sister. So Barry and Wendel grew up together.

There was a saying at that time: "You can't stop Wendel Clark. You can only hope to contain him." At the end of the night, if Wendel had scored only one goal, we thought we did a great job. It was such a tough, physical series, with Marty on our side and Wendel on theirs. Those two guys played above their talent level. Neither one would give an inch.

On May 17, 1993, in the third period of Game One, we were a little flat. The travel had been really tough. This was our third series and we'd yet to open at home, so we needed to get that bad blood and emotion back. Marty, who saw that as part of his job, was looking for an opportunity to fire us up. And then Gilmour came across the middle with his head down. Marty stood up inside the blue line and just drilled him. Dougie is a tough guy and I can guarantee that's the hardest he was hit all year. It was an important move. It sent a message to Toronto that we were going to challenge them. And it told Gilmour that he wasn't going to have free ice. He'd have to pay a price. It really brought us into that series.

And then Wendel came in and did what everyone in the rink knew Wendel would do. He challenged Marty. That's when I saw one of the greatest fights I've ever seen in my career. It was an incredibly emotional clash. Neither Marty nor Wendel hung back.

Each of them was swinging from his heels and making contact. It was a classic toe-to-toe scrap that you just don't see anymore in today's game. Both guys had black eyes the next day.

That fight really set the tone for the series and inspired our team. Wendel was one of the toughest guys in the league—absolutely the toughest guy in Toronto—and for Marty to take him on like that propelled us into the Stanley Cup finals.

There was still a ton of incredibly intense hockey to be played in that series. It was hugely emotional and physical, and the momentum tipped back and forth. And sometimes mistakes happen. When I accidentally clipped Dougie Gilmour on the chin in Game Six overtime, was it a penalty? Probably. It was a tie game when Glenn Anderson, who was now with the Leafs, tried to run Rob Blake through the boards from behind. He got a charging penalty. At the faceoff, the puck seemed to stall and I took a shot that deflected off Jamie Macoun's shin pad and bounced back to the faceoff circle. I came over behind Gilmour and we both went for the puck. He bent over, grabbed his chin, and the play stopped.

The rule back then was that you were in charge of your stick. Even if a guy skated into it, you got a five-minute penalty. I know what the league was trying to do, and yet it was a stupid rule. Some rules come in and work and some don't. But in those days the rules were arbitrary. An owner would say, "This is what we've got to put in the game," and snap, new rule. A GM might say "Hey, I don't like the guys standing in the crease!" and they'd change the rule the next day. That's how the league operated. Now they have a rules committee, a management committee, and a players committee that all have to decide together.

When Kerry Fraser asked him what happened, Dougie said it was my follow-through that clipped him. On a normal

Howie Morenz was the game's first superstar. Sportswriters voted him the best player of the first half of the twentieth century. When you think of the stars of the second half of the century, you realize just how good Morenz was. He is right up there with the guys in this photo: Jean Béliveau, Bobby Hull, Gordie Howe, and Phil Esposito. (Beside me on the left is my friend Mike Barnett.) But I imagine him playing the game like Paul Kariya. Not a big guy, but smooth and smart, and tough enough to pick himself up after a big hit.

Some defensemen are just playing a different game from everyone else. Bobby Orr was the only defenseman ever to win a scoring title. Like Orr, Paul Coffey could start behind his own net and go end to end. We were teammates in 1985–86 when he broke Bobby's scoring record. All you had to do was watch Paul skate with the puck for ten seconds to know that he was a special player. Eddie Shore was like that. The phrase "power play" was invented to describe the way the Bruins could dominate when Shore was on the attack.

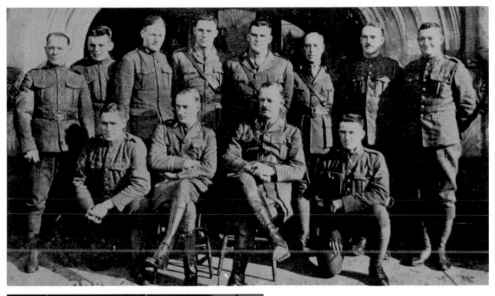

As important as our game is, our countries are more important, and that has always been reflected on the ice. In the First World War, an entire team of servicemen played a season in the NHL as the Northern Fusiliers before shipping out for the battlefields of Europe. In the Second World War, the league's top-scoring line enlisted all at once. The Kraut Line, as they were called (because they were all from a town of German heritage), was carried off the ice as heroes at Boston Garden when they left for service. I personally experienced a small taste of that patriotism at the 1991 All-Star Game, which was played during the first days of Operation Desert Storm. The cheers that shook the Chicago Stadium during "The Star Spangled Banner" were unforgettable. (Here I am trying to get a saucer pass over the stick of one of the greatest defensemen I ever played against, Ray Bourque.)

There is a reason the annual trophy for the NHL's best goaltender is named after Georges Vezina. During his career, he was a brick wall in net for the Canadiens, and recorded the first shutout in NHL history. I have played with some truly great goalies over the years, but I have to say that Grant Fuhr was the greatest. When the game was on the line, the whole team knew that Grant could shut the door. He won the Vezina in 1988.

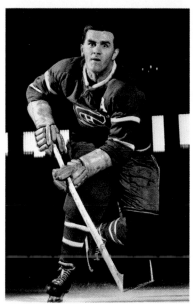

Maurice "Rocket" Richard played the game with a ferocity anyone could see. He had pure speed, and he was strong enough to bulldoze his way to the net when he had to. There was just no way to stop him. But one thing we all have in common is that we slow down. I always respected Richard for hanging up his skates while he still had a little of that fire left, as hard as it must have been. I wanted to do the same.

I am very proud to have won the Lady Byng Trophy. The list of guys who have won it over the years would make a pretty impressive hockey team, from Frank Nighbor (Lady Byng invented the trophy for him, so he was clearly a deserving winner) through Stan Mikita and Bobby Hull (seen here with Gordie Howe, who was nobody's idea of a Lady Byng candidate), and Pavel Datsyuk. These guys had the kind of toughness that shows up not in penalty minutes, but in victories.

I know what it is like to lose to the United States in international competition. But back in 1960, the Americans were perennial underdogs. That year, they shocked the hockey world with a gold-medal victory at Squaw Valley (above). Then they did it again at Lake Placid in 1980. That's when the sport really took off in the United States. In fact, it was the kids who were inspired by the "Miracle on Ice" that defeated Team Canada in the World Cup in 1996.

Hockey has always been a game of ice and sticks and pucks. But it was the owners who shaped it into the game we have today. It was Tex Rickard who saw the potential for a rough Canadian game to bring in crowds at Madison Square Garden and Boston Garden. Lester Patrick and his brother Frank came up with innovations as fundamental to hockey as artificial ice, numbers on sweaters, changing on the fly, and the blue line. Jack Kent Cooke did as much as anyone to expand the NHL in 1967 (that's the Los Angeles Forum under construction in the background). There can be no doubt what the Oilers meant to owner Peter Pocklington. That's him to my right at the press conference announcing my trade to Los Angeles.

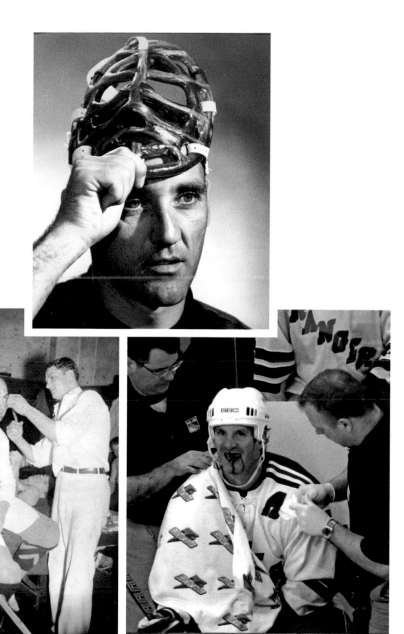

Stitches and hockey have always gone together. That's just the way it is when you're playing a fast game with sticks and pucks. In 1959, Jacques Plante took a puck to the face from the Rangers' Andy Bathgate. He went to the dressing room, got patched up, and returned wearing a mask. He played only one more game without one for the rest of his career. Howie Morenz, seen here getting stitched up thirty years before Plante changed the game, didn't even wear a helmet. But a helmet didn't help Brendan Shanahan, seen here getting some medical attention. A bit of discomfort is just part of the game.

When I look at these Boston Bruins in their practice sweaters from the 1935–36 season, it seems as though they could step out of the photo and play today. And they would certainly have been good enough. If you could hold onto a roster spot on an Original Six team, you were a very, very good hockey player. Dick Irvin certainly was. He came in second in league scoring after returning from the First World War, then went on to coach both the Leafs and the Habs to Stanley Cups. That's Punch Imlach at the bottom, celebrating the Leafs' Stanley Cup victory over the Black Hawks in 1962. They would win the last Cup of the Original Six era in 1967.

No matter how you define greatness, Gordie Howe was the greatest player ever. There will never be another player to finish in the top five in the NHL scoring race for 20 consecutive seasons—I didn't come close. There will never be another hockey dad who rides shotgun for his sons—or plays at the highest level of international competition with them. But as great as he was on the ice, no one was warmer, funnier, or more generous off the ice either. No one who knew him will forget that the greatest ever was also possibly the humblest.

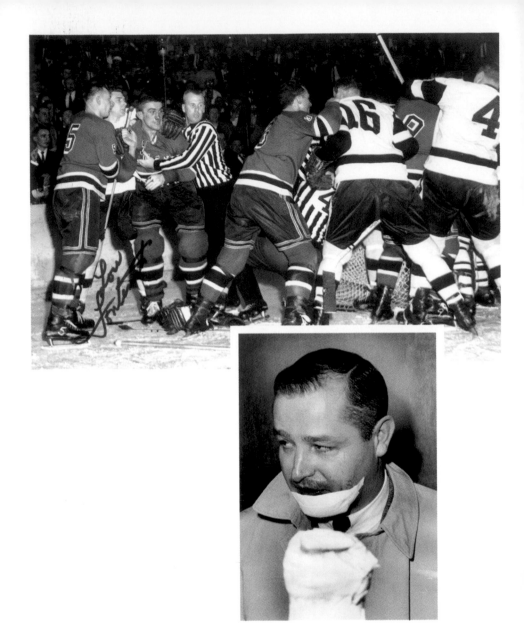

Hockey is about speed and vision and finesse. It also requires you fight through adversity. Lou Fontinato (on the left, being held by the linesman) was one of the toughest players of the 1950s. He led the league in penalty minutes three times, and his bout with Gordie Howe was legendary. Glenn Hall played over 900 games in net in the NHL without a mask, and lost only one tooth. He did take a few stitches though. On the opposite page is Ted Lindsay, one of the tougher guys in NHL history, after taking a hit (he scored four goals afterward). At the bottom, that's me getting separated from the puck by Marcel Dionne.

How great was Jean Béliveau? The Montreal Canadiens bought an entire league just to secure his rights. Howe and Béliveau were very different players, but they were both big men who played the game with a kind of gracefulness that made it look easy. I met him at a tournament when I was a kid, and I spent the whole game worrying that I would let him down.

The history of the game is full of great lines, from the "Bread Line," who played for the Rangers in the '20s and '30s, through to Vancouver's "Brothers Line" of Henrik and Daniel Sedin, along with Anson Carter. But sometimes you end up on a line with your childhood idol, as I did with Gordie Howe in 1979. Famously, Jaromir Jagr came to Pittsburgh just so he could play with Mario Lemieux. Possibly the most lethal line in the history of the game was the Soviets' "KLM Line" of Vladimir Krutov, Igor Larionov, and Sergei Makarov. There was almost nothing those three couldn't do.

Hockey is a game of tradition, and usually that is something we can be proud of. But we also need to celebrate the pioneers, like Willie O'Ree, the NHL's first black player (seen here being interviewed while making history) and Fred Sasakamoose, the groundbreaking First Nations player. When you think of the guys who followed in their footsteps, like Grant Fuhr and Jarome Iginla, or Reggie Leach and Carey Price, you realize what a debt we all owe the players who paved the way.

follow-through there's no high-sticking infraction, and Fraser told him that that meant no call.

Dougie and I are good friends today, and so when people ask me about it, I always say, "You know what? In those playoffs, Dougie got a little cut on his chin. Well, a guy broke my rib and nobody talks about that. So no, I don't feel so bad about it." The real difference in that series wasn't a high stick in Game Six. It's not fair to either team to say that the series came down to one call—or one missed call—by the referee. Both teams should be proud of the way they played, and focusing on one non-call only takes away from the accomplishments and sacrifices of the guys who were going over the boards shift after shift. Both teams left absolutely everything on the ice for seven games, and in the end we were so closely matched that the difference was one goal in Game Seven.

We'd become the first team ever to play all four rounds against Canadian teams. We'd played nineteen games in the first three rounds. The final Toronto game was on a Saturday night. We had an early Monday afternoon flight to Montreal and then a light skate. Game One of the fourth round was scheduled for Tuesday. That game was as good or better than any game we played the entire playoffs. The Canadiens were a little flat-footed from their time off. We won 4–1.

We were on a high, but we were also starting to erode physically and mentally. We weren't as good a team as the Montreal Canadiens. But what we had was maybe better: tremendous chemistry, desire, and heart. Still, we knew they were going be a good team, and they were.

You always want to be up 2–0 on the road if you can. It gives you a tremendous confidence advantage. (We experienced it in '88 against Calgary in the quarterfinals. On paper, Calgary was a better team than the Oilers that season.) And so it was really important to keep the lead in Game Two in Montreal. Even though the Canadiens were playing much better than they had in Game One, we were tied 1–1 after two periods.

In the locker room going into the third, we told everyone, "We know we're a little tired right now, so we gotta simplify things. We gotta keep our shifts short and keep the puck in deep and don't do anything fancy or silly."

Every home team supplied the visiting team with an extra pair of hands to help out the trainers with equipment and sticks. After all, you can travel with only so many people. Edmonton did it, we did it in L.A., and Montreal did it. The Canadiens had a fellow named Doc who came in, and there were times when he was in our locker room by himself. It's not as though he did anything wrong, but all you had to do was eyeball Marty's or Luc's sticks and you could see that they had big curves. A curve helps with puck control. It hugs the puck, making it tougher to lose. The NHL has restrictions not only on a stick's weight, height, width, and length, but also on its maximum curve. And so we've got a Montreal Canadiens employee in our dressing room working with our sticks that are clearly illegal.

Before we went out, I said to the guys, "Look, we're tired, let's be smart here. Luc, you and Marty, they're gonna come after you guys. There's no question about it in my mind. So make sure you take out a legal stick."

Luc nodded okay and Marty looked at me and said, "My stick's good."

I said, "Okay, we're good to go."

We were in the third period, now leading 2–1, with 1:45 left when Guy Carbonneau and Kirk Muller, captain and assistant captain of the Canadiens, came over to ref Kerry Fraser and said, "Jacques wants Marty McSorley's stick measured."

Kerry said, "What is it specifically that you want measured?"

Carbonneau said, "The curve."

Kerry said, "Okay." He went over to Marty and requested his stick, which Marty gave over. Reluctantly.

I skated up to Marty and said, "Is your stick okay?"

"Yeah, it should be fine."

I was hanging at the edge of the referee's crease as Kerry pulled out the plastic gauge. He had his back to the players, and Ray Scapinello, the linesman, was holding the stick. Kerry measured it twice—it was a big call—and then turned to me and said, "Here, have a look at this." He showed me the slide measure: it didn't touch from the heel to the toe. There was a wide-open gap. Fraser called a penalty. Montreal coach Jacques Demers pulled Patrick Roy to make it six on four. They scored on us barely thirty seconds in.

No one was more devastated by it than Marty. Even though he sometimes puts on a brave front, I know him better than anyone, and I know he was crushed.

That night in the locker room there was a tremendous mood swing. We went from being up a goal with a minute and a half left, playing great and looking to take a two-game lead back to Los Angeles, to heading into sudden-death overtime. Montreal had only two shots in the last eight minutes, and then a power play, and then suddenly a tie. And then, suddenly, a loss. Montreal scored in the first minute of overtime to tie the series. We were pretty disheartened to let the opportunity to go home up 2–0 slip away.

I think in his heart Marty wanted to get five or six minutes in with his stick because he knew they wouldn't check early in the period. But he was playing so much and the emotions were so high that I think he got caught up in the game and just forgot to change it. I have some friends on the other team, and when you retire you talk. They told me that the plan was to check either Luc's or Marty's stick—whichever guy was on the ice in the last two minutes. Had it been Luc, there would have been no problem. Luc's stick was fine.

The crazier part of it was that we ended up losing three games in a row in overtime. Patrick Roy played so well in the series. He won the Conn Smythe that year.

Let's not take away from what Roy did by blaming Marty. Sometimes all you can do is sit back and say, "We played hard and we played good."

Montreal deserved to win the Stanley Cup, but we had a group of guys who'd played beyond their level—a lot like the '86 Montreal team. They maybe weren't the best team in the NHL that year, but they beat Calgary in the final. Our effort and our team commitment were definitely special, and that's what made the run so great.

In the end, we wouldn't have gotten through the playoffs to the Stanley Cup finals had Marty McSorley not played at the level he did. Marty was the kind of player who could lift a team, and he did that for us many times that spring. As far as I'm concerned, if it wasn't for Marty and how he played against Toronto in that series, we wouldn't have been playing Montreal anyway, and there would have been no curved stick story.

Nineteen

THE ST. LOUIS BLUES

T he St. Louis Blues were in so many Stanley Cup finals in the late 60s and early 70s that they almost didn't seem like an expansion team. Even their colors looked like classics from the beginning. Over the years they have had some great teams, and it's easy to reel off the names of the Hall of Famers who played there. Hull, Pronger, MacInnis, Shanahan, Fuhr, and many more. Those guys all came well after expansion. But one of the things that made the Blues so successful right from the beginning is that even in their first years, they had guys destined for the Hall of Fame.

First off, the general manager was hockey royalty. Lynn Patrick was the son of Lester Patrick, one of the brothers who had done so much to improve the game of hockey in the first place. That first year, Patrick had only enough money in the budget for one employee, and he hired the right guy—someone who would go on to earn a reputation as one of the shrewdest minds in the game— assistant GM Cliff Fletcher. Fletcher went on to win a Stanley Cup in Calgary as the GM and built the gritty Leafs team the Kings met on the way to the final in 1993. Not a bad front office.

But the expansion teams faced an uphill battle. In later rounds of expansion, the league understood that teams needed to be viable from the very beginning if the market was going to warm up to them. But they hadn't figured that out in 1967, and didn't yet think of the new teams as partners in the success of the league. Not surprisingly, the Original Six owners kept all the best players for themselves.

At the June 1967 expansion draft, the original teams were allowed to protect eleven skaters and a goalie. The expansion teams selected goalies in the first two rounds and then skaters in the following rounds. The Black Hawks protected Denis DeJordy, who had just shared the Vezina with his teammate Glenn Hall. Terry Sawchuk had just won the Cup with Toronto that season, but Toronto coach Punch Imlach protected Johnny Bower instead. (The Leafs would not do well in the years after expansion, in part because Imlach protected too many of his veteran players. He protected George Armstrong even after he had announced his intention to retire. Montreal, on the other hand, traded some veterans they felt they could spare to expansion clubs in exchange for draft picks. It set them up for the future, and it worked. They won eight Stanley Cups in the next twelve seasons. That strategy works even better today under a salary cap.)

Patrick knew he'd be happy with either Terry Sawchuk or Glenn Hall, but he had third pick. Jack Kent Cooke took Sawchuk for the Kings. Philadelphia had next pick, but Glenn Hall was asking for $50,000. Too much for Philly's GM Bud Poile. He told Hall, "*I* don't make that much." And Glenn said, "Yeah, well, you're not a goalie." So Poile picked Bernie Parent from Boston.

Patrick's team budget when he was in Boston for the 1964–65 season had been $250,000, and he always came in under budget. The

Blues had $475,000 to pay players, but expansion salaries were much higher. Hall had started out twelve years earlier in Detroit being paid what all the other rookies were making: $6,000 a year. In his last year with Chicago he made $25,000. Moving to an expansion team was his chance to get paid what he was worth, so he was still asking for $50,000 when he talked to Patrick. The Blues offered $45,000, and they split the difference. Patrick knew that Hall deserved it—and that if he didn't get the raise he'd stay home. It's a testament to the depth of those Original Six teams that St. Louis could pick third in an expansion draft and still get a Vezina winner and future Hall of Famer (as were the two guys picked ahead of Hall).

Hall was the first butterfly goalie. This was thirty years before Patrick Roy, who's often credited with that innovation. When Glenn butterflied, he taught himself to keep his inside blades on the ice so that he could get up in one motion. He said the butterfly was a natural way to play because a goalie could get up so much quicker than he could stacking the pads.

The game was changing. Starting in the late 60s, defensemen were becoming better skaters, making it much more difficult for forwards to speed through or around them. So teams started working the puck back to the point to spread out the defense. Now, instead of snipers picking corners, goalies were facing bombs from the blue line and deflected pucks. That is just incredibly dangerous for a goalie who's not wearing a mask. Hall always thought it was amazing that no one got killed in goal back then. Bobby Hull was shooting harder than most guys in the league right now, and no one in their right mind would stand in front of even a midget player today without a mask, let alone an NHL defenseman.

Hall complained only about the shots that caught him in the mouth. That happened to him three times, and all of them needed at least twenty-five stitches. He was playing in Detroit when a puck hit him right below his bottom lip. In those days they didn't use freezing when they stitched you up. As the doctor was sewing, Glenn kept saying, "Ohh, that's enough, that's enough." The doctor said, "No, just a few more." But Glenn stopped him, and so he had to go back a few months later to have a big lump of scar tissue removed.

The next puck was in Chicago. Gordie Howe deflected an Alex Delvecchio shot from the point and Glenn took it in the mouth. He went back to the dressing room for thirty stitches. No freezing again, but he let the doctor finish this time.

The third in the mouth happened during the second-last game Glenn played with Chicago. It was the biggest cut yet, requiring thirty-six stitches, and the only time he lost a tooth. He played 1,021 games in the NHL, most of them without a mask, and he lost only that one tooth.

For Glenn's second year with St. Louis, he signed for $50,000, which made him the third-highest-paid player in the NHL behind Bobby Hull and Gordie Howe. He played with the team from 1967–68 to 1970–71, and they made it to the playoffs all four years and to the finals in the first three. You know that famous picture of Bobby Orr at the Stanley Cup finals in 1970, as he's flying through the air after scoring the shot that won the Bruins their first Stanley Cup since 1941? The goalie in the net is Glenn Hall. He still jokes that no one ever talks about all the times he shut the door on Bobby.

The guy behind the bench also ended up in the Hall of Fame, with 1,244 regular-season wins, another 223 victories in the playoffs, and nine Stanley Cups—all records.

Lynn Patrick's son Craig had played junior in Montreal for

Scotty Bowman in the 60s. So he asked him what he thought of his former coach. Craig liked the fact that Bowman taught solid defense and that he was an innovator. He had the players keep notebooks on every game they played and rate themselves. And then he'd rate each player and compare. Bowman taught accountability, and Craig thought that would translate to the NHL. He was right.

Bowman lived with the Patricks that first year, so his boss could see that he was all business. He was also methodical. He worked hard on preparation and would labor all through the night on matchups. He wanted to see how certain coaches would put people out against certain guys so that he could match his lines and defense against the opponent's. No one could beat Bowman as a bench coach.

Bowman also continued a tradition started by Lester Patrick and other coaches like Dick Irvin. Before the morning skate, Lester would have the players study the rules for half an hour. He made it mandatory that you had a rule book on you at all times. And in those morning meetings he'd call out a rule and then call on a player—and that player had better know it. Lester felt that if you're going to go to the referee you've got to know what you're talking about, because then he'll listen to you. But if you aren't sure, he'll blow you off.

That's why you'd see players from certain teams, like Lester Patrick's old New York Rangers and Lynn Patrick's Blues, grow into management and coaching. That culture has been passed down through their players, like Emile Francis. Even today, look at the St. Louis team's management legacy: Jim Nill, Paul MacLean, Mark Reeds (who recently passed away). They all played in St. Louis.

For Scotty Bowman, on the other hand, it wasn't so much about rules. He wanted his players to think like he did as much as possible because a lot of players don't worry about who they're playing next. So Bowman would put a board up in the room to show his team what the opposition was doing with the power play, with the penalty kill, with breakouts and positioning.

Now and again he'd also do a pop quiz. He'd call a team meeting and single out different players. "Who do we play next week?" or "What's our goals-against?" or "What's our objective for the rest of the season? We've got twenty games left. How many goals can each guy get?" Scotty would have his players verbalize things just to keep them on their toes. He learned that from broadcaster Dick Irvin Jr., who'd told him that his dad would do it.

Bowman wasn't personable or warm, but he was good at getting the players motivated. During the 1968–69 season the Blues had a two-day break, but they hadn't been playing well. So for those two days, Bowman scheduled nine a.m. and four p.m. practices. Most of the guys lived in the suburbs. That meant they had to drive back and forth to the rink with the rest of the commuter traffic. Before their next game, Bowman asked them, "How'd you enjoy the drive over the past few days?" And they all grumbled about it. He said, "All that traffic coming in in the morning—it wasn't fun, was it?" "Nope." "And the traffic going home wasn't fun either, was it?" "Nope." Scotty said, "Yeah, well, welcome to the world of the people who sit in the stands and pay your salary." It got their attention. The team went on a winning streak, taking five in a row.

In 1968, goaltender Jacques Plante had been working for the Molson's brewery. He'd announced his retirement in 1965, so he sat out three years until the Blues obtained his rights from the Rangers and Bowman convinced him to come to St. Louis. Jacques and Glenn Hall, both in their mid- to late thirties, shared a Vezina Trophy that season. They split the season and were a terrific team, thirteen shutouts between them and twenty-two games of one-goal losses.

Like most goalies, Jacques was eccentric. He was the cheapest guy in the whole world. He wouldn't buy a newspaper. He'd wait until someone was finished and then he'd grab it. When he was younger, he started knitting his own hockey socks and toques to keep his ears warm in those freezing cold outdoor games in Shawinigan Falls, Quebec. When he got into the NHL, he kept on knitting to calm his nerves.

In the 1940s, the Canadiens had one of the great goaltenders of all time, Bill Durnan, a six-time Vezina winner. Montreal GM Tommy Gorman described him as being "as big as a horse and as nimble as a cat." But in 1950, three games into the Stanley Cup semifinal against the Rangers and a year into Jacques Plante's contract with Canadiens affiliate the Montreal Royals, Durnan quit. When he told his coach, Dick Irvin, that he had to leave or he was going to crack up, he was crying.

Goaltender Gerry McNeil was called up from the minors and Plante became McNeil's backup. Plante got his chance when McNeil struggled in the 1953 playoffs against Chicago. They were down three games to two and so coach Tommy Ivan took a gamble, throwing Plante, a rookie, in there. Plante won his first NHL playoff game with a shutout and then won Game Seven too. He played the first two games of the final against Boston, and then McNeil took over. The Canadiens went on to win the series, and in 1953 Plante had his name engraved on the Stanley Cup for the first time. He was in net for the Canadiens five Cups in a row, from 1955–56 to 1959–60. And his name was spelled four different ways.

Bowman would dress only one of his big goalies, Glenn Hall or Jacques Plante. Whichever guy wasn't playing would sit in the stands and rest and relax. But if either Hall or Plante got hurt or was having a bad game, the team would stall and stall and stall while the other would come down from the stands and get dressed. So the NHL changed the rules. Now only dressed goalies can play, unless they're both injured, and then you can dress a third.

The final piece of the puzzle was the character of the team. The Blues had character in spades. The Plager brothers, Barclay, Bill, and Bob, were the original Hanson brothers from *Slap Shot*, very tough and very colorful. You didn't want to turn your back on any of them because you never knew what would happen. And it didn't matter who you were. When owner Sid Salomon fell asleep on a flight home, Bob cut his tie—just as the players did to each other. Not to be outdone, Salomon cut the leg off Bob's suit pants during the game. Bob, being who he was, wore the suit anyway.

A team like that needs a leader, and Patrick and Fletcher found another future Hall of Famer to wear the *C*. Al Arbour played on the Blues from 1967–68 through to 1970–71 as a veteran player. He was one of the very, very few players who wore glasses. In those days you didn't see many helmets and very few goalies wore face masks. He was thirty-four years old when he arrived and the captain during the Blues' three-year run to the finals. He wasn't a great offensive player, but he was a warrior, in the best sense of the word. In the days of the six-team league, Arbour was always on the bubble. He started with Detroit in 1953–54, but he didn't play much on that Cup-winning team. Then he went to Chicago, where he won a Cup in '61. He won another in '62 with the Leafs. But he also spent time in the minors and never broke through as a top regular. So he knew about winning, and he knew what a player had to do to make it.

When he was nearing the end of his playing career with St. Louis, he was playing part-time. Scotty Bowman used him as an assistant coach. (Today everyone has assistant coaches, but in those days you had only a head coach.) When Arbour coached, the guys weren't going to fool him because he'd seen everything, and if a guy wasn't playing a lot, Arbour could relate because he'd been there. A lot of great coaches were players who got by as players not on natural talent but on hard work and willpower. And Arbour was certainly a great coach. He was behind the bench of one of the great dynasties in NHL history, the 1979–83 New York Islanders.

On January 6, 1972, St. Louis was in Philadelphia. The Flyers were leading 2–0. Arbour, now the Blues' head coach, and referee John Ashley were standing at the top of the ramp leading to the tunnel at the end of the second period arguing over a two-minute penalty call. Philadelphia fans started throwing garbage, and one guy dumped a beer on Arbour. Barclay Plager jumped the railing and went after the fan.

That led to a brawl, with fans starting to come onto the ice. The Philadelphia police got involved, and there was some back and forth. Al and defenseman John Arbour (no relation to Al) were hit over the head with nightsticks—John needed thirty stitches. A couple of fans and two officers were injured. The police went into the St. Louis locker room and tried to arrest the whole team but settled for Al, wingers Phil Roberto and Floyd Thomson, and John Arbour. The game was delayed while the four were taken to the police station. Each of them posted a $500 bond, and forty-five minutes later, Al was behind the bench without a shirt and tie on. St. Louis won the game 3–2.

Hockey was getting rougher, and expansion was a big reason for it. There were six more teams to fill a roster of twenty players and two goalies. That meant 132 new slots for players. The league basically increased the demand for talent on the ice by 100 percent in one year. Not every team could keep up with the league's best, so that brought on more clutching, grabbing, stick work, and fighting to slow things down. When you look back at the bear hugs and the hooking, it's incredible that players got away with that.

But we should not lose sight of the fact that there was some truly beautiful hockey played in those days too. You could clutch and grab all you liked, you weren't going to stop the Bruins when Phil Esposito and Bobby Orr were battling each other for the scoring title. Or the Habs when Béliveau, Cournoyer, and Lemaire were on their game. It was far from just goonery out there, and the fact that the Blues could compete with teams like that from day one just shows that if you get the right people in an organization, it's going to succeed.

Twenty

THE MINNESOTA
NORTH STARS

M ike Modano's last NHL contract made him an employee of the Dallas Stars for one day in 2011. He used that day to retire. When he did, the last active player from the 1980s was gone from the league, and the last connection to one of the most exciting of the 1967 expansion teams was gone. Modano was also the last of the Minnesota North Stars.

When Mike was drafted, everyone expected him to mature into a pretty special player, and that is a lot of pressure, especially for an American kid drafted first overall into a market that knows hockey. Mike was only the second American ever taken first overall. The fact that the first was Brian Lawton, who was also taken by the North Stars, only made the challenge more daunting. Lawton scored his first goal only nineteen seconds into his first shift but never did manage to silence the critics who thought Minnesota should have taken Steve Yzerman, Cam Neely, or Pat LaFontaine, who were all available in that same draft year. That couldn't have been easy for Lawton, and it only made Mike's career harder.

But.Mike exceeded every expectation. He was very similar to someone like Connor McDavid. He was a big boy, but he could skate as well as anyone I've ever seen out there. He could absolutely fly, and he had incredible vision. The thing about Mike was that he could do everything at full speed. He could shoot from mid-stride, thread a pass in full flight, and get three head fakes in after a goalie had already bit on the first one. Sometimes a defenseman wouldn't even react as Mike blew by. He literally would have no idea which way to go.

No American player has ever scored more goals or total points. He led the Dallas Stars to the 1999 Stanley Cup, and he is now in the Hall of Fame. He was just a special player.

The thing is, if you live in Minnesota, you probably wish a player like that had retired playing for the city that drafted him.

When it was announced that Minnesota was getting a team, a lot of people thought it was a sure thing to succeed. Detroit has become known as Hockeytown, but Minnesota is definitely the State of Hockey. You could fill an NHL rink with the fans who come out to high school hockey tournaments there, and NCAA hockey is huge. They love hockey, and they know hockey. We all thought of Minnesota as a lot like Canada.

And over the years, there were a lot of great teams there. They had some phenomenal players, and a lot of success. They made it to the Stanley Cup final twice over the course of their twenty-six years, and drafted some players who more than made their mark on the game. Bobby Smith, Craig Hartsburg, Brian Bellows, Derian Hatcher.

One of their most exciting players was a guy who started with the team in their first season, Bill Goldsworthy. He played junior in the Bruins' system with Derek Sanderson and Bernie Parent, but never established himself as a regular in Boston even when they were a last-place team. When he got his chance in Minnesota, he became the team's offensive star, scoring more than a point a game in the team's first post-season and coming within one game of making it to the Stanley Cup final. He turned out to be good enough to be named to that legendary 1972 Summit Series team. The fans in Minnesota loved him.

One thing I remember about Bill was his enthusiastic way of celebrating a goal—it was known in the media as the "Goldie Shuffle." Players were a little more conservative in the way they celebrated back then, and even now guys get called out for celebrating too enthusiastically. But I don't blame them. It's so hard to score in today's NHL. It's hard to score twenty goals now, never mind forty or fifty. When a guy scores a goal, I love to see that excitement and jubilation.

I got to know Goldie a little when I went to Edmonton. He didn't play much that year, due to injuries. And one thing that all hockey players have in common is that we all get old. There was a group of older guys on that team—Ace Bailey, Paul Shmyr, Dave Dryden, Bill Flett. They were all great to me. Because Goldie was a little banged up, I got to know him more away from the ice than at the rink, and he was a great guy. He called me Kid. That kind of thing means a lot to a rookie.

The North Stars' coach was a fiery character. You never knew what Wren Blair was going to do. People in Minnesota weren't familiar with professional hockey, and Blair felt he had to coach the fans as much as the players. If the team was bungling a power play, he'd stand on the bench or the boards, turn toward the crowd, and wave his hands and yell at the fans to boo his players.

Blair was famous for signing Bobby Orr. In 1959–60 Wren was managing the Kingston Frontenacs of the Eastern Professional

Hockey League (EPHL), a Bruins-affiliated team. Harold "Baldy" Cotton, who was scouting for the Bruins (and had been involved with the NHL since playing left wing with the Pittsburgh Pirates in 1925), saw Bobby playing with his bantam team in Parry Sound. At that time Boston was building up its farm system and starting to get its hands on some young players. Cotton went to Lynn Patrick and said, "You gotta see this kid." So a group of them, including Blair, drove up to Gananoque, Ontario, to watch Bobby Orr, who had just turned thirteen, take over the ice for a full sixty minutes. Scotty Bowman, who was scouting for the Canadiens, was there that night too. He thought Bobby was so small that it was hard to figure out how good he'd be, but he also saw that Bobby had the puck the whole night.

Scotty sent a report to Ken Reardon, a former Montreal defenseman who went on to scout, manage minor-league affiliates, and become team vice-president. He told Ken, "You know, Bobby could really move and he'll be ready to play junior in a year." But Bobby wasn't even in high school, so Reardon replied, "We're not moving guys in public school." (In fairness to Reardon, it is absolutely unheardof for a kid in grade eight to play junior hockey. But Bobby did it.)

Blair was the point man assigned to get Bobby. In the days before the draft, NHL teams developed young players through affiliated amateur teams. That meant that they could own a kid's rights from the time he was fourteen. At that age, a player would be invited to sign what was called a C card. Most kids couldn't wait to sign those cards because it guaranteed that at least one of the six teams was going to take a really good look at you. But Bobby's parents were in no rush to sign anything—they wanted him to have as many options as possible. So Blair had his work cut out for him to bring them around.

He got the Bruins to sponsor Bobby's Parry Sound team for $1,000 a year. Eventually he built up enough trust with the family that, in 1962, Bobby's parents signed his C card. Bobby was thrilled. In return, the Orr family got their house stuccoed, his dad got a car, and Bobby got $1,000 cash. He would be playing for the Oshawa Generals, a team Blair had all but built himself. He had also been GM of the world champion Whitby Dunlops. So he knew what he was doing when he helped build the North Stars.

In 1963, the NHL began to phase out team sponsorship, and held its first amateur draft of sixteen-year-olds. By 1969 the draft was universal and there were no more protected junior players. So by the time I was Bobby's age, the C cards were gone. But you had to be twenty to be drafted to play pro. At sixteen, I was an underage junior in Sault Ste. Marie.

I really got along with my coach, Muzz MacPherson, who was a great guy. When Muzz left he was replaced by Paul Theriault. Paul was very big on positional hockey, which is a very good way to develop players. In fact, when he was coaching for Oshawa and Marty McSorley was with the Belleville Bulls in 1981–82, Marty was playing in an All-Star game and Paul was his coach. He was really good to Marty and taught him a ton. Marty just loved him.

But without sounding egotistical, I didn't need to start with the basics. I'd been studying hockey all my life. When I was seven years old and watching *Hockey Night in Canada* with my dad, he handed me a piece of foolscap and a pen. He told me to follow the puck on the paper without looking down. It developed my peripheral vision, which in turn helped me develop a more creative approach. I knew where guys were, so I could go where the puck was going to be. That's why Paul Theriault's style of coaching didn't really work for me. I started thinking about going pro, but the NHL didn't draft underage juniors.

My agent, Gus Badali, called the WHA and got me an offer for $80,000 from John Bassett with the Birmingham Bulls. John was building a team full of great young guys like Rick Vaive, Michel Goulet, Craig Hartsburg, and Rob Ramage—a collection of future NHL captains, Team Canada players, and Hall of Famers. Paul Henderson was their veteran. I would have loved to play with those guys, but Gus thought the offer was too low. And then he got me an offer from Hartford to play with Gordie Howe for $200,000. That would have been a dream come true, but they pulled it back. The WHA owners were all hoping their teams would fold into the NHL, and since I was underage, they thought I might be out of it. I believe everything happens for a reason.

Bassett recommended me to his friend Nelson Skalbania, a wealthy real estate developer from Vancouver who was starting to invest in sports teams. Nelson owned two WHA teams. In 1976 he bought the Edmonton Oilers but then sold them to Peter Pocklington the next year. Then he bought the Indianapolis Racers on speculation that the WHA would merge with the NHL. He wanted to pump up the value of the league, and had decided that his best bet was to buy a good underage junior. That way, the NHL would have to come to the WHA, either to take the teams in or to keep plugging them with money to get the underage kids.

Nelson called my mom and dad in June 1978, and along with Gus, we flew out to Vancouver on Nelson's private plane. I was seventeen, too young for the NHL, but I really wanted to play professional hockey. As soon as we got there Nelson asked me to go for a run with him. I think it was his way of testing my endurance.

Starting all the way back when I was a kid, six, seven, eight, nine, ten, eleven, I didn't just play hockey. I used to look forward to the summertime because I loved lacrosse and track and field too. I was a huge track and field guy. Even at ten I was running long distance, eight hundred meters, fifteen hundred meters, cross-country. I trained hard every day and I loved it.

We used to drive out to my grandmother's farm every Sunday, and the first thing I'd do is put my running shoes on and take off along the country roads. I'd run for miles and miles. I wasn't doing it to become a hockey player, but it built up my endurance and oxygen intake, or VO_2. So did playing box lacrosse (that is, indoor lacrosse). We'd play four games on a Saturday and then three games the next day. I played almost each entire game, four fifteen-minute quarters. That's like seven hours of lacrosse each weekend.

Years later, when I was with the Oilers, Jari Kurri always had the highest VO_2, next to Paul Coffey, and Messier was always ridiculously fit. It was just a part of their makeup and a result of their hard work and training. But the difference was my heart recovery time. They took twice as long to recover. I could go, say, one minute and be completely recovered in ten seconds, ready to go back on the ice at a high level, whereas Jari and Paul might take twenty seconds. That was my strength.

Back in '84 when I got eight points against Minnesota, after the second period Glen Sather came in and said, "When you wanna go on the ice, just go. The door's open." It was the only time in my career that something like that ever happened. Glen always played me a ton, but that was only time a coach said, "Just go." So in the third period of that game I gave myself a four-minute shift.

Athletes today are incredibly conditioned. When I see defensemen playing thirty-minute games it's unbelievable. I can remember

Paul Coffey and Kevin Lowe playing twenty-seven minutes. That's nine minutes a period. You've got to be in immaculate shape to do that. Duncan Keith plays twenty-five to thirty minutes every single game. That's amazing to me.

I was a centerman who played twenty-one minutes a game. Again, a lot of minutes. Seven minutes a period. That's a lot of hockey. If I played seven, Mark Messier was playing seven, and the third and fourth guys might be splitting six. But I see some of these centermen today who can play eight and a half minutes in a period. That may not sound like a big difference, but every additional minute on the ice is one less minute of recovery. It catches up to you quickly. The shape these guys are in is remarkable.

Back in 1978, all those years of playing a lot of hockey and skating and running and lacrosse had built up my endurance to a high, high level. So when Nelson and I went for that six-mile run and I came back fresh, I think it impressed him.

That month we signed a personal services contract that I hand-wrote as he dictated it to me on his private plane. It was for four years, $550,000 total, with a signing bonus of $250,000. If the merger happened and the NHL refused underage players, I could keep any money I'd already received. It was a good deal, and I was thrilled with the offer.

Something most people don't know is that even though I signed that contract with Nelson and went on to play with the Oilers in the WHA, when the league folded into the NHL I came close to going back into the draft. That's because at first the NHL owners couldn't agree on a deal to take in the WHA teams.

So they called in Lou Nanne, the longtime Minnesota North

Stars GM, to meet with the owners on Chicago Black Hawks owner Bill Wirtz's yacht in Florida and hammer out a deal. Nanne was a legend. He was a Canadian-born American who hung in with North Stars for a long time. If it weren't for him, the team would have moved to Dallas a lot sooner.

Lou structured the proposal so that each WHA team could keep two players and two goalies, but that the rest of the players would be dispersed throughout the league. And underage players, like me, who'd signed with the WHA but weren't yet NHL-draft eligible, would have to go back into the draft when we came of age. That meant Edmonton wouldn't be able to protect me.

Then Frank Griffiths, who owned the Vancouver Canucks, stepped up and said that unless I was allowed to stay in Edmonton, he wouldn't vote for the deal. Sometimes NHL owners get a bad rap, but I think that showed the generosity and the consideration of a man like Griffiths.

When Minnesota started out, it wasn't a great defensive team. But by 1978–79, when Lou Nanne took over as GM from Blair, he hired Glen Sonmor, a former tough guy, as coach. Nanne thought he was the best coach the North Stars ever had. Sonmor put his heart and soul into the game.

In 1978 Lou drafted Bobby Smith, Steve Payne, Curt Giles, and Steve Christoff. This was a strong core group of players. And then, when the Cleveland Barons folded and joined the Minnesota North Stars that same year, they got some more key guys, including Gilles Meloche in goal.

Minnesota was already strong up the center, and then in 1979 they drafted Neal Broten, who, along with Christoff, was part of the 1980 Miracle on Ice win. Neal played seventeen years and 1,235 games in the NHL and scored more than a thousand points including playoffs.

The Stars drafted Craig Hartsburg with their first pick (sixth overall) in 1979. Hartsburg was terrific. I played with him in the Soo in 1977–78. (He'd play with Minnesota for the next ten years. And if Craig hadn't had such bad luck with injuries to his knees, groin, back, and hip, he might have been another Bobby Orr.) Although they didn't draft Dino Ciccarelli, they were smart enough to sign him as a free agent when he went undrafted in 1979.

In 1980, Sonmor made history when the North Stars faced off against a Flyers team coached by Pat Quinn. As a young player, Quinn had faced a choice between playing minor-league hockey and accepting a scholarship. He had asked a high school phys-ed teacher in his hometown of Hamilton for some advice. The teacher was Glen Sonmor. He told Quinn to take the scholarship.

Quinn went on to have solid career as a bruising defenseman (and ended up captaining the expansion Atlanta Flames), then quickly became one of the best coaches in the league, winning the Jack Adams Trophy for coach of the year in 1980. Part of what he did to earn that honor was coach the Flyers to the longest unbeaten streak in North American sports history—thirty-five games. That streak ended in Minnesota in front of the largest crowd the North Stars had ever drawn. The North Stars smoked the Flyers 7–1 to keep a twelve-game home unbeaten streak of their own going. The teams met again in the semifinals. This time Quinn's Flyers had their revenge, and took the series 4–1.

By 1981 they made another solid run for the Cup. In the history of the club, Minnesota had never beaten Boston at the Garden. But on February 26, 1981, Glen Sonmor took Lou Nanne aside and said,

"Lou, I think we gotta make a statement here and show them what we're made of." When Nanne agreed, Sonmor told the team, "We're going to fight every one of them every time they look at us."

By the end of the game, Minnesota had five guys left on the bench and Boston had six. They set the NHL record in penalty minutes. It seemed to set the table for the playoffs. Minnesota beat Boston and then they beat Buffalo. The North Stars then came across Calgary, who had a very good team, and they put the Flames out, which set them up in the finals against the defending-champion New York Islanders. They lost the first two games on Long Island, but started out playing well in Game Three. The Islanders' Butch Goring recorded a hat trick, including two goals right after Minnesota power plays, and it turned the tide. The Islanders took the game 7–5 and won the series in five games. But no one was going to beat New York that year. The Isles lost just three games in the four series they played.

Norm Green already had a history of moving hockey teams when he bought the North Stars from George and Norman Gund in the early 1990s. He had bought the Atlanta Flames in 1979 and moved them to Calgary, and he was still a part owner when they won the Cup in 1989. But still, it was a shock when he decided to move the North Stars to Dallas in 1993, not even two years after the team had made a Cinderella run to the final, where they had the misfortune of running into Mario Lemieux.

Green had his reasons, of course. The Met Center, the North Stars' rink, was notoriously cold and aging—though players loved it because the ice there was the best in the league. Green claimed to be losing money, and local government was doing little to help make staying look more viable. Green wanted to move the team to Los Angeles, but the NHL already had plans to partner with Disney in Anaheim. Green's next option was Dallas.

At the North Stars' last game, fans were carrying signs blaming Norm Green and making their feelings about him pretty clear. Others were tearing up the seats, either to take them as souvenirs or throw them. Today there is an Ikea where the Met Center used to be, but the North Stars' legacy has not been erased. Hall of Famer J.P. Parise was on the North Stars' roster in their first season. His son Zach was born there and has gone on to stardom in the league—now playing for the Minnesota Wild, who joined the league in 2000–01 as part of the three-year process of expansion that included Nashville in 1998–99, Atlanta (now Winnipeg) in 1999–2000, and Columbus and Minnesota in 2000–01. It's ironic that, while the Minnesota Sports and Facilities Commission wouldn't spend $15 million to keep the team, it took $285 million to bring the NHL back.

But Minnesota fans have not forgotten their first team, and the Stars haven't forgotten their roots either. In 1991, they created a patch to commemorate their twenty-fifth anniversary. It featured Bill Goldsworthy in the original green sweater facing off against Mike Modano in what became Dallas black.

Twenty-One

THE OAKLAND SEALS

D on Cherry has a lot of great Bobby Orr stories. But there
is one he calls the greatest. Bobby was killing a penalty
in Oakland one night, ragging the puck for over a minute, circling back behind his own net as no one else could do.
There was no way the Golden Seals were going to touch the puck.

But then Bobby saw an opening, and he was gone, up the right
wing and in on goalie Gary Smith (who I would later play with).
He tried to go top corner on his backhand, but Smith got a piece
of it. He didn't catch it cleanly though, and the puck squirted up.
By this time, Bobby's momentum was carrying him around the net.
But he saw the rebound sort of hanging there, just under the crossbar, so he tapped it out of midair as he skated by. According to
Cherry, it was the only time in hockey history that both teams have
given a standing ovation.

There is a reason there aren't more standing ovations like that.
Hockey players are taught to never give up. You may be behind in
the game, but anything can happen out there. I am not blaming
those Seals players. I'm sure I would have been impressed too.

But if you're standing up to cheer the other team, that's not a good sign. You're probably not going to win a lot of hockey games.

Unfortunately, the Seals (or the Golden Seals, as they were called by the time Bobby scored that goal) didn't win a lot of hockey games. They seemed to have problems from the very beginning, and even though they had some solid players on the roster, they never did manage to establish the game in the Bay Area.

The 1967 expansion was always about television. And the league's deal with CBS called for two teams in California. Their number-one target was, unsurprisingly, Los Angeles. San Francisco was the next obvious choice. That expansion team went to Barry Van Gerbig, godson of the famous crooner and movie star Bing Crosby. A year earlier Barry had partnered with Crosby, his brother Mickey, and fifty other investors to buy the WHL's San Francisco Seals, who were supposed to play out of a brand-new rink to be built when the NHL rejected the Cow Palace as a venue (though the San Jose Sharks would play there decades later). But the rink was never built, and it was decided that the Seals' home ice would be across the bay in the Oakland–Alameda County Coliseum. The Seals relocated before they ever played.

The Seals also had trouble selling tickets—there were games where the players themselves might have thirty tickets they couldn't give away. Bing Crosby and his famous friends tried to help them out. *Peanuts* creator Charles Schulz even made a couple of program covers for them. In fact, Schulz went so far as to give Snoopy a number 9 hockey sweater in his comic strip in honor of his friend and favorite Seals player, Bill Hicke. (Schulz and Hicke would later open a hockey school together in Santa Rosa, California.)

Still, Barry Van Gerbig and the investors were losing money. They wanted to sell the team to Vancouver, but the league wouldn't let them. Jerry Seltzer, who owned the original Roller Derby League, put in a great offer, but the NHL owners didn't like his association with roller derby, not to mention his long hair and flashy clothes. Then Charles O. Finley, the owner of Major League Baseball's Oakland A's, met with Bruce Norris and Bill Wirtz in 1970 and convinced them to sell to him instead.

But the organization had its share of respected hockey people, particularly coach Bert Olmstead. Bert had played on the number-one line with Elmer Lach and Maurice Richard in Montreal, and was known as a mucker. When he played with Jean Béliveau and Boom Boom Geoffrion, he told Béliveau to stay out of the corners—he'd dig out the puck instead and send it to the last place he'd seen him standing. Olmstead always seemed to find Béliveau's stick, and when he didn't, he'd chew him out on the bench for moving. Olmstead played in a Stanley Cup final an amazing eleven out of his fourteen seasons in the league. He pushed his players hard. Eddie Dorohoy, a tough little center, once said, "If Bert Olmstead was Santa Claus, there wouldn't be any Christmas."

Bill Torrey was hired as general manager, and would go on to help the Seals gain a playoff berth in their second season, 1968–69, and again in 1969–70. But he didn't see eye to eye with new Seals owner Charlie Finley.

Finley had all kinds of ideas that didn't work for hockey. One of those ideas was white skates. After training camp, the trainer came into the locker room and announced to the team, "We've got a great surprise for you guys." In their stalls were white skates. Now, there were quite a few old-school players on the Seals, senior guys like Harry Howell, Earl Ingarfield, Bill Hicke, and Gerry Ehman. Howell shook his head and said, "I am not going to wear white skates! Those are *figure* skates."

Bill Torrey had warned Finley. He'd said, "Charlie, hockey players don't wear white skates." Finley had replied, "Well, they might if they work for me."

When the team later played an exhibition game up in Sudbury, Ontario, Finley showed up with no advance notice. Halfway through the first period, Torrey, who was up in the press box, got a note: Mr. Finley was downstairs waiting to see him.

Torrey went down and said, "Charlie, I didn't know you were coming."

Finley said, "Where's the white skates I sent you? Nobody's wearing them."

"No, they're not."

Finley said, "Well, I didn't come all the way from Chicago not to see somebody wearing white skates, so you'd better go and tell them."

At the end of the first period, Torrey found coach Freddie Glover and said, "Go in there and tell the boys that the boss is here and that somebody better come out in white skates."

Glover said, "*You* go in there and tell them."

So Torrey went in. "Gentlemen, the man who signs your checks is outside and he wants one of you to put on those white skates." There was dead silence in the locker room. No volunteers. So Torrey walked around the room and said, "I guess you didn't hear me. I said the man who signs your checks wants someone in here to wear the white skates." He walked out of the room and waited in the hallway. A few minutes later, left-winger Gary Jarrett came out wearing the skates. After the game Torrey found Finley and said, "Well, Charlie, how did you like those white skates?"

Finley said, "I didn't like them. They didn't look good on the white ice." And so he got CCM to make up skates in Seals' colors—kelly green, wedding gown white, and California gold. And actually, other teams then followed suit. Toronto had blue skates made and the Detroit Red Wings came up with red skates with a white toe. The trouble was that when pucks or sticks hit the skates they made black marks, so it became a real nightmare for all the trainers. After about a year, colored skates kind of disappeared.

Another time, Finley decided that he wanted a live seal for a mascot. He instructed Bill Torrey to find one, saying, "I think fans would really like that."

Torrey said, "If that's what you want, let's see what we can do."

Torrey's management team had a hard time locating one. But a couple of weeks before the start of training camp, his PR guy came in and said, "I found a seal at a sea park. Its trainer will bring it over for $500."

Torrey said, "As long as he's alive and flaps. Anything to satisfy Charlie."

On the opening night of the season, right before the anthem singer stepped onto the ice, a guy came out from the Zamboni entrance with his seal waddling behind on a leash. The seal got to center ice, barked and flapped his flippers for a few minutes, and then suddenly decided to lie down on the nice, cool ice. After that it never moved. The PR guy, with the help of the ice crew, dragged it off the ice.

Finley came by the dressing room and remarked, "That looked like a dead seal."

Torrey said, "Charlie, we had no way of testing him."

"Well, how much are we paying the trainer?"

Torrey said, "I think it's $500."

"Give him $250 and tell him to get the hell out of the building."

Torrey was also forced to spend hours and hours designing team uniforms and brochures. Worse still, despite a clause in Torrey's contract that no player could be traded or moved without his agreement, Finley interfered with the running of the club. In 1970, he wanted Torrey to make a player-and-money trade with the Rangers.

Torrey said, "Charlie, I wouldn't be a good general manager if I agreed to that. It'll hurt our team."

Finley told him to make the deal and gave him a forty-eight-hour deadline. Torrey ignored it, and Finley fired him. Torrey sued and won. He left the team and accepted an offer from another expansion team, the New York Islanders. Today, Torrey is special adviser to the general manager and alternate governor of the Florida Panthers.

Charlie Finley was also notorious for not paying his players what they were worth. In 1970–71, his first year with the Seals, Ernie Hicke scored twenty-two goals and had twenty-five assists. Dennis Hextall, his centerman before he was traded to Minnesota, scored twenty-one goals and recorded thirty-one assists. That summer, Finley started negotiating with Hicke. As a rookie, Hicke had made $10,000 his first year. Finley offered him a $1,000 raise. Hicke called Dennis Hextall and found out that he was making thousands more.

So when Finley called back and said, "Ernie, how are you doing? Have you thought about my offer?" Hicke said, "Yeah, Charlie. Yeah, I've thought about your offer. I'm not gonna accept it."

"Why not?"

Hicke said, "Well, Hextall was on our team last year. I scored more goals than he did and he's getting $55,000 and you wanna give me $11,000?"

Finley said, "Well, the only thing you can do, Ernie, is you can go to arbitration in Montreal. I'll be there and so will NHL president Clarence Campbell, and he won't give you another dime. In fact, you'll lose $1,000 because you've got to pay for your flight there, your hotel, and your meals."

Hicke flew to Montreal and went in and for the next hour or so he made his case to Clarence Campbell. Campbell listened and then said, "I don't even really have to wait on this. You're getting what Finley offered you."

Hicke said, "What? Are you kidding me?"

Campbell said, "Nope, that's it. End of conversation, end of meeting, we'll see you at training camp."

The next season, 1971–72, the Seals had a completely a different team—all great young players like goalie Gilles Meloche, Joey Johnston, Carol Vadnais, Gerry Pinder, Paul Shmyr, and Bobby Sheehan. Only four guys on the team were over twenty-five. Garry Young came in as the GM and Vic Stasiuk was the coach. The team played really well. And Finley would sometimes go on road trips with them.

In October 1971, Meloche stopped tons of shots and the team beat Boston 2–0. Finley came into the dressing room and said, "Okay, we're going to New York tomorrow because I'm gonna take you to Gucci. I want to buy each of you a nice pair of Italian shoes."

Later they played the Rangers and beat them 2–1, and again Finley came into the dressing room. "Unbelievable, guys. The limos will be there tomorrow morning. We're going to the Burlington Factory. Everybody gets a trench coat."

You never knew with Finley. For Christmas that same year all the wives were given recycled pendants that were inscribed "Oakland A's, World Champions 1970."

When the WHA started up in 1972, most of Finley's players jumped over, and so the nucleus of that team was gone. The WHA was offering much more money. Dennis Sobchuk, a junior star with the Regina Pats who was drafted eighty-ninth overall by Philadelphia in 1974, made a million dollars when he went to the Cincinnati Stingers in 1975.

The same thing happened to the Oakland Athletics in baseball. Finley lost his top hitter, Reggie Jackson, and future Hall of Fame pitchers Catfish Hunter and Rollie Fingers. Reggie Jackson led the league in home runs and hitting, but Finley didn't care. His attitude was, "Go to New York. I'll get some other players."

In 1973–74 the Seals ended the season 13–55–10. The NHL stepped in and bought the team from Finley. The team was a drain on league finances until they were sold to San Francisco hotel owner Mel Swig, who moved them to Cleveland in 1976–77. They were called the Barons and lasted just two seasons before they were folded into the Minnesota North Stars.

But that is not to say that hockey had no place in the Bay Area. The San Jose Sharks have one of the loudest rinks in the league today. The same can be said for Minneapolis–St. Paul, which lost a team, then got one back. Or Denver. Or Winnipeg for that matter. When a team goes under, people say the problem is the market. But that is not necessarily the case. Often, when we say that one market is better than another, what we mean is that one team is better than another. No one wants to see their home team get embarrassed every night. Eventually, they are going to stop coming. If the Seals had been on a level playing field with more established franchises, they probably wouldn't have left in the 1970s. Maybe the same can be said for the Cleveland Barons and the Kansas City Scouts. If teams have the right support from the league, and if they do the right things to reach out to their communities through charities and youth hockey programs, I don't see why hockey shouldn't thrive anywhere sports are played.

Twenty-Two

THE PITTSBURGH
PENGUINS

M y father was a big believer in education. He *hated* the idea of his kids missing school for any reason. But in early September, he would let me miss one day a week.

That was when the Pittsburgh Penguins would be holding their training camp in my hometown of Brantford, Ontario. For four or five hours a day, I would be in the stands, just amazed at how big the players were, and how fast. What may have made the strongest impression was how incredibly hard they worked. No one was standing around out there. They were going flat out the whole time. The other thing I thought was, "That looks like a lot of fun."

One year when I was in peewee, I scored 400 goals, which was also pretty fun. Somehow, the Penguins heard about it and I was invited into their dressing room the next September. There were about fifteen guys in the room, all sweaty and doing pushups and tossing around medicine balls and things. I was a shy kid, and a little bit intimidated by all these huge guys in matching sweat suits. But then one of the more intimidating guys came over to shake my hand

and take me around the room to introduce his teammates. His name was Glen Sather.

Of course, I would learn a lot from Glen over the years, but the first lesson came the first time we met. It meant so much to me that he would go out of his way to welcome a nervous kid, and I never forgot it. For my whole career, unless I'd had the worst day of my life, I always took time to talk to the kids who just wanted to meet some of their heroes.

When they first looked at expansion, the NHL decided to add not only two West Coast teams but also two from the Midwest and two from the East. Buffalo and Pittsburgh were competing for the latter, but Pittsburgh had the inside track. Pennsylvania senator Jack McGregor, who represented twenty-one investors, called on his friend Art Rooney, the owner of the Pittsburgh Steelers. McGregor offered him a minority ownership in the Penguins and then asked him to make a call to the Norris brothers, who owned the Wings and Black Hawks. Rooney got them to swing the vote Pittsburgh's way.

Once they got the franchise, McGregor hired Jack Riley, a well-respected former minor pro player, to be GM. The owners told Riley to follow a "win now" approach and draft proven players, not rookies. Riley hired ex–Rangers coach Red Sullivan, and over the next couple of years they secured a number of former Rangers.

The most famous of them by far was Andy Bathgate, who had played ten years in New York and had actually tied Bobby Hull in the scoring race in 1961–62. He also won a Cup with the Leafs. The Penguins also picked up ex–Ranger Bryan Hextall (father of goaltender Ron Hextall) in 1969. His father, Bryan Hextall Sr., had been one of the top Rangers in the late 1930s and 40s and is a member of the Hockey Hall of Fame. Bryan Jr. was a hothead and would jump in to protect his teammates. That may be a family trait. I don't think anyone who ever played against Ron thought he was the kind of guy who would shy away from confrontation. If you spent too long near Hextall's crease, you'd have bruises on the back of your legs to show for it.

By 1973–74 Pittsburgh was building by getting skilled players in the draft, but one of their main problems was toughness. Now, they did have some agitators who would stand up for the team, guys like Bugsy Watson, who was one of the toughest guys in the league, pound for pound. (Seven years earlier, when he was with Detroit, he shut Bobby Hull down in the playoffs—not a job for the faint of heart.) And yet, in an era where Philadelphia had the Broad Street Bullies, St. Louis had the Plager brothers and Steve Durbano, and Boston had the Big Bad Bruins, the Penguins were getting pushed around.

So, in the late 1970s and early 80s, Pittsburgh brought in more toughness. During that era, and in my era too, the tough guy had a role. He was part of the makeup of a solid team. You had your offensive guys and your defensive guys and you had a couple of tough guys.

There was a guy named Kim Clackson who played for a number of different teams and ended up in Pittsburgh in 1979–80. He looked like a choirboy, but he was the only guy who ever scared me in hockey. At 5'10" and 195 pounds, he wasn't exactly a beast, but he was mean.

Kim wasn't afraid of anyone. He wouldn't try to fight me, but he would try to run me. To him, it was like scoring goals. I always knew who was on the ice and where they were. I also liked to stand opposite the opposition bench—that way I could count everyone in front of me. And in Kim's case, I wanted to make sure I knew where he was at all times. That's paying him a compliment—guys like that get paid to make you think about them.

Clackson used to eat at a place called Alexander Graham Bell's in Market Square in downtown Pittsburgh. The bar manager there was a guy named Ho Hum, a Vietnamese immigrant. Clackson gave him tickets to watch us, the Oilers, play the Penguins on January 19, 1980. It was Ho Hum's first hockey game and he was sitting two rows behind our bench. In the middle of the second period, we dumped the puck into their corner and I came up to forecheck. Their goaltender, Rob Holland, was covering up the puck and Kim was in front.

Kim accidentally high-sticked me as I came in and clipped me across the forehead. I was a little bit shaken up and stayed on the ice for a moment or two, so the Edmonton trainer came out to see how I was doing. Now, usually a player will escort the trainer over so that he doesn't slip on the ice. That night, a couple of my team-mates left the bench, and one of them was Dave Semenko. It was already a chippy game, and Dave was never very forgiving about guys taking liberties. It wasn't long before he and Clackson dropped their gloves. Dave was throwing bombs and had Clackson on his knees, but Clackson wasn't backing down.

Somehow the linesmen got them apart and into the penalty box, but they weren't done. Both guys had plenty more to say, and finally Dave had enough. The benches had cleared by this point and even the goalies were squared off, and no one was watching the penalty box. Suddenly Dave swings his leg over the boards and goes at Clackson. The funny thing was, standing in the box, a few inches above the ice, those extra few inches made Clackson seem as tall as Dave. They threw a few punches while Clackson was still in the box, then he jumped back out on the ice and they started throwing again. The linesmen separated them—and Clackson got free yet again, and the two renewed hostilities.

Eventually, they were separated a third time and led away to their dressing rooms. But Clackson had other ideas. As soon as the officials' backs were turned, he calmly put his helmet back on and skated back out onto the ice, and challenged any Oiler who was willing. Dave Hunter was game, and away they went.

When Glen Sather saw Clackson on the ice, he picked up a water bottle and threw it at him. Suddenly, someone behind Glen tried to come over the glass. It was Ho Hum. In his hand he had a big open safety pin full of keys and he was holding it like a knife. As Glen was moving back and forth trying to dodge the safety pin, Clackson picked up the water bottle and started spraying Glen, who was wearing one of his hand-tailored wool suits. This went on for a couple of minutes until the police grabbed Ho Hum by one leg, pulled him off the glass, and handcuffed him.

A week later, Kim drove over to Alexander Graham Bell's for lunch. He sat down and Ho Hum came over. When Clackson offered him tickets to the next game, Ho Hum shook his head, "No more hockey for me, thank you."

Hockey got off to a rough start in Pittsburgh. It's tough to win when the odds are stacked against you, and it's tough to *learn* how to win when the tradition isn't there. For a long time, the Penguins seemed destined for the same fate as the Seals. The Igloo was full of empty seats, the team had declared bankruptcy once, and a lot of people expected them to relocate. They lost a lot, and they did not draft well. But every once in a while, a guy comes along who is magnificent enough to completely change a city. When the Penguins got their chance to draft someone like that, they made no mistake.

On his very first shift in the NHL, Mario Lemieux robbed future Hall of Famer Ray Bourque of the puck, skated in on net, and buried it. It was his first shot as a pro. Not a bad start for a franchise that hadn't had a winning season since 1979. He scored 100 points as a rookie, and 141 in his second season, which put him in second in the scoring race. In his fourth season he scored 168 points, and beat me in the scoring race.

There was pretty much nothing Mario couldn't do. He came within a point of scoring 200 points one season. He had an eight-point game in which he scored in every way a player can—even strength, power play, penalty kill, penalty shot, and empty-net. He was so powerful, and so smooth, that he could do whatever he wanted out there. Imagine being so good that an absolute legend like Jaromir Jagr is the second-best player on your team.

The Penguins were barely holding on when the Magnificent Mario arrived. It wasn't long before the Penguins were one of the most intimidating teams in the league. (And now they are easily one of luckiest. It's one thing to be able to draft Mario and Jagr to one team—now they have Sidney Crosby and Evgeni Malkin.) Today, Mario has his name on the Cup as both player and owner— the only person ever to do that. But that kind of dominance seemed a long way away in 1967.

Twenty-Three

THE PHILADELPHIA
FLYERS

Whenever a player is interviewed after winning the Stanley Cup, the first thing he does is thank his parents. There is just no way anyone makes it to the NHL without an unbelievable amount of sacrifice and support. And it's not just parents. It's all the coaches and volunteers who keep minor hockey running. I certainly was very lucky in the way my parents brought me up and helped me along. There is no way I could thank them enough.

My parents gave me every opportunity to succeed, and when I was fourteen that meant leaving home. I wanted to play for a team in Toronto called the Young Nationals. Anyone who has played minor hockey at a serious level has probably come across a Young Nats team at a tournament somewhere in North America. A ton of great players have come through that program, including Paul Coffey, Mike Gartner, Larry Murphy, Eric Lindros, and more recently Tyler Seguin and Jeff Skinner. You can see why my parents thought that playing with the Nats would be a good opportunity for me. They signed over guardianship to a Toronto couple, Bill and Rita Cornish, so that I could live in Toronto. The Cornishes were unbelievable to me. Over the years we became very close.

I showed up for school in September, but a week before the season started, the Ontario Minor Hockey Association suspended me and another kid named Brian Rorabach, on the grounds that we were not entitled to play in Toronto, since he was from Brighton, Ontario, and my home address was down the highway in Brantford. We went to court to challenge the suspension, but we lost. Rorabach appealed to a higher court and won, but I didn't want to miss more of the season in court. I wanted to play hockey.

So I had two choices. I could go home, or I could play for the high school team at Upper Canada College, a private school in Toronto. I didn't really want to do either. Luckily, the coach of the Nats' Junior B team (where Murray Howe played), which is a level higher than minor hockey, invited me to come watch a practice. So of course I went. I was about 5'6" at the time, and weighed about 120 pounds. Those Junior B guys looked huge. But after practice, the coach said, "You know, you could play here." I nervously told him, "Yeah, I think I can." My dad just said, "Oh my God, you're going to get killed."

Playing there changed my life in a lot of ways, and it also changed my game. One of the most exciting players in the NHL back then was Bobby Clarke. He wasn't a big guy, but he played fearlessly, and part of that was because he played smart. Nats coach Gene Popeil gave me some great advice. He told me to watch the way Clarke played, particularly in the corners and behind the net, and especially on the power play.

Back then, if you were wearing a Toronto Marlies jacket you could get a standing-room ticket to a Leafs game for a dollar. So whenever the Flyers were in town I would take the subway down to Maple Leaf Gardens to see Bobby Clarke take the warm-up. And then I would pay careful attention when the Flyers were on the power play. Clarke could control the pace by positioning himself in the seams of the defensive coverage. If guys started chasing him, the seams would only get bigger and someone would be open. And of course, when he was behind the net, no one could touch him.

Whenever someone asks me how I started controlling the offense from behind the net, the only honest answer is that I studied Bobby Clarke doing it. And it worked pretty well for me.

In 1981, I scored fifty goals in thirty-nine games. Five of those came in the thirty-ninth game, against Philadelphia. I talked to a lot of people in the dressing room afterward, and it took quite a while to get ready to leave. When the dust settled a little, one of the trainers told me that Bobby Clarke wanted to say hello.

I just couldn't believe that Clarke had waited all that time to have a word with me—it was incredibly gracious. And I'll never forget what he said. "You know, with Bobby Orr, at least I knew where he was out there. With you, I can't even find you half the time." He was laughing, of course, but it was still a huge compliment coming from someone I admired so much growing up.

Clarke went on to become one of the most respected executives in the league and was appointed to run Team Canada for the 1998 Olympics in Nagano—which means he was probably the most respected hockey mind in Canada. He and I would have coffee every morning for a couple of hours in the Olympic Village with Bob Gainey, another very smart hockey player and executive, who also had his fair share of Stanley Cup rings. We would talk about the old times, and players we knew, and the young guys coming up. When you're talking hockey with guys who love the game, time stands still.

Philadelphia is a sports town. The league was looking for television markets, and thanks to the city's three professional teams in football, baseball, and basketball, Philadelphia was already the fourth largest television market in the country. (The NFL's Philadelphia Eagles had been around since 1933; baseball's Phillies—the oldest sports team with the same name in the same city in the United States—got their start in 1883; and basketball's 76ers had been in the city since 1963.) As a matter of fact, Philadelphia had already had an NHL team before 1967. The Philadelphia Quakers lasted for all of one season in 1930–31. Their record was 4–36–4, which still stands as a record for fewest wins by an NHL team. Not surprisingly, the fans weren't interested.

When Ed Snider, part owner of the Eagles (and my eventual neighbor and friend), heard about the NHL expansion, he was sure he could make it work. The 76ers, who'd picked up Wilt Chamberlain in 1965 and won the NBA Championship in 1967, wanted a new building, which could double as a hockey arena. So Snider partnered up with his brother-in-law, Jerry Schiff; Bill Putnam, a young New York financial adviser; and another Eagles owner, Jerry Wolman. They put in a bid and acquired the franchise.

GM Bud Poile hired Keith Allen to coach. Snider bought the American Hockey League's Quebec Aces for $350,000 to kick-start the team and got some great players—guys like André Lacroix, Jean-Guy Gendron, and Bill Sutherland. Then Allen spent a year scouting the Original Six, and in the expansion draft they got Bernie Parent in goal and then two solid defensemen, Ed Van Impe and Joe Watson. In other words, they did what many smart teams do: they built from back to front.

On opening day they held a parade down Broad Street with the players sitting on top of convertibles as they made their way to the

Spectrum. Ed always said that there were more people *in* the parade than actually watching it. That would change sooner than anyone thought, but they still had some tough luck ahead of them. On March 1 of their first season, a storm tore part of the roof off their brand-new building, and so they had to play their last seven home games on the road. They finished first in the western division, but lost to St. Louis in a seven-game semifinal. In their second season, they were eliminated by the Blues once again, only this time they were swept. Noel Picard (the Blues defenseman immortalized in the famous photo of Bobby Orr flying through the air after scoring his most famous goal) and the Plager brothers were really hard on the Philadelphia players. As Ed watched his team get shoved around, he told Keith Allen that they would never be outmuscled like that again.

The first universal amateur draft year was 1969. Bobby Clarke, who played for Manitoba's Flin Flon Bombers, had been ripping up the Western Canada Hockey League for two years, winning the scoring title both years and being named MVP in 1969. (He had also won the scoring title and the MVP award two years earlier, when the Bombers were playing in a different league.) The WCHL was incredibly tough hockey, and absolutely nothing slowed Clarke down. He was unstoppable.

Or almost. When he was fourteen he was diagnosed with diabetes. He'd learned how to inject himself with insulin, and no one who saw him play ever doubted his energy levels. But the diabetes scared off the GMs.

The draft was held in the Queen Elizabeth Hotel in Montreal. In those days it wasn't the big event that it is now. Today, a team will host the draft in its arena with hundreds of team personnel and thousands of fans in the stands. The entire first round is covered on live national television and all the top picks show up with their families and their agents. Back then, though, the GMs just sat around a table, and had a time limit of three minutes per pick. The scouts would phone up the picks and invite them to training camp in the fall.

Despite dominating junior for three years, Clarke went unclaimed in the first round. (The Flyers took Bob Currier. He never played a game in the NHL.) Although scouts were raving about this kid who had been dominating junior for three years, Clarke's diabetes made him seem too risky. Bobby's coach, Pat Ginnell, had taken him down to the Mayo Clinic in Rochester, Minnesota, figuring that a clean report from the doctors there would turn the NHL GMs around. It didn't.

But Ed Snider had done his homework. He made a call to a doctor in Philadelphia, who told him that as long as Bobby lived a healthy lifestyle there would be no problem. So Snider told Bud Poile to go for it. The Flyers picked Clarke in the second round, seventeenth overall.

As soon as Philadelphia took Bobby, the other teams figured the Flyers must have known something they didn't. Detroit Red Wings head scout Jimmy Skinner came up to Keith Allen and Bud Poile and offered four good players for Bobby. Poile said "No thanks." Later, legendary Montreal GM Sam Pollock called Ed Snider and offered him five players and two top draft picks for Bobby. Ed said "No way." Pollock said he agreed that it was a smart move to keep him. And it was. Clarke turned out to be one of the great steals in draft history. No one in his draft year came close to matching his impact in the league.

But Clarke had a rough start in the NHL. He fainted during one of the workouts at training camp. The coaching staff got nervous. A few practices later, it happened again. Luckily, the team trainer, Frank Lewis, knew something about diabetes. When Bobby admitted that he was skipping breakfast, Lewis put him on a diet of energy-rich foods, including candy bars and orange juice with sugar cubes stirred in. (Personally, I loved the concession food. I'd have a couple of hot dogs an hour or so before the game, and maybe some popcorn and a Coke. I remember guys in the locker room eating pizza. I also remember Guy Lafleur chain-smoking cigarettes between periods at the 1981 Canada Cup. Gordie Howe would sometimes play a game on a chocolate milkshake. We just had no idea about nutrition.)

In the fifth and sixth round that year, the Flyers picked up two big guys from Saskatchewan, Dave Schultz and Don Saleski—and that was the beginning of the Broad Street Bullies. After all, Ed Snider had made it clear: the Flyers would never get manhandled by St. Louis or anybody else ever again.

Fred Shero was hired as the Flyers coach in 1971. Fred was a real pioneer in the game. He'd have the guys practice with a tennis ball to sharpen their stickhandling touch and reflexes. He'd also have them bunny hop up and down the ice to loud music in order to build their legs. Things like that made the guys laugh and brought them closer together. The exercises also made them better.

Shero treated his players like men. He encouraged them to argue with him if they didn't agree with his methods. And if somebody screwed up, he didn't punish the whole team. He would just sit the guy on the bench for a couple of days. The experience was so embarrassing that the player wouldn't do it again.

I n 1972, the Flyers made a seven-player deal with Los Angeles. It included a guy who would become a good friend and mentor to me, Bill Flett. Jack Kent Cooke had nicknamed him Cowboy and that's what everyone called him.

Cowboy Flett was two hundred pounds and over six feet. Very powerful, all arms and chest. His hands were huge and he had a strong grip. He wasn't mean, but he was strong. No way could you move him if he didn't want to be moved. He wore a thick, bushy beard that had to be hot as hell, although he always kept it nice and clean. For two years, 1978–79 and 1979–80, I'd sit beside him on the plane when we played together in Edmonton. I remember he smelled like soap, beer, and horses.

Cowboy was a bit of a tragic figure. His dad was Meyer Flett, quite a hockey player himself for the Turner Valley Oilers in the early 1940s. Meyer was a hard man, an oilfield worker. He played senior hockey with Calgary Flames trainer Bearcat Murray, who tells this story: After a game once, when everyone was having a shower, Flett walked past Bearcat, who nudged his buddy and said, "Look at Meyer!" Flett was bruised black and blue from top to bottom. That's the kind of game he played. Nobody fooled with him, especially not his son.

The Kings traded Bill to Philadelphia when he was twenty-eight, a big, strong winger who hadn't scored very much. Then he was paired with Bobby Clarke and put up seventy-four points. Bill hadn't much cared for liquor until he moved to Los Angeles in his early twenties and became a beer drinker. By the time he joined the Flyers he'd had his oilcloth duster custom-made with about eight big pockets on the inside, and he kept a beer in each one.

Cowboy was Bobby Clarke's roommate on the road. They'd go out and have dinner together, and Bobby would make sure he got in on time at night. In those days you could have a couple beers the night before a game and nobody cared.

Cowboy may have needed guidance off the ice but certainly not on the ice. He really gave it to the goaltenders. If he came down the wing and had a clear shot, not even a scoring opportunity but a clear shot, he'd try to hit the goalie in the head. His theory was that when he came down the next time, the goalie would figure he was going to shoot it high, but instead he'd just slide it along the ice. That's how smart he was. It wasn't that he was the fastest or the toughest, but he took being a hockey player very seriously. He partied and all the rest of it, but he was never off his game. He always came up big.

Philadelphia won the Stanley Cup in 1974, when that meant going through a legendary Bruins team. In Game Two of the finals the Flyers were in Boston, twelve minutes into overtime. Cowboy came up the middle and assisted Bobby Clarke to beat them. It was a great play and it turned things around for the Flyers.

Remember, no expansion team had ever won a Cup. And in the Flyers' previous nineteen regular-season visits to Boston Garden, they hadn't won once. They gave Boston everything they could handle in Game One, but just when it looked as though they had gone ahead late in the third, Bobby Orr singlehandedly saved the goal, then went the other way to score. Nothing was going to be easy for Philadelphia.

It was Clarke who finally broke through in Game Two, and it was Clarke who led the rest of the way as the first expansion team from 1967 hoisted the Cup. (Though it was Bernie Parent, who the Bruins had left unprotected in the expansion draft, who won the Conn Smythe as playoff MVP.) Clarke led again in 1974–75 (and Dave Schultz set a record for penalty minutes), and the Flyers won a second straight Cup. That year they squared off against Buffalo in the first-ever matchup of expansion teams in the final. Game Three of that series is still talked about today as the "Fog Game," as a May heat wave created so much fog at ice level at the auditorium in Buffalo that players couldn't see the puck. Officials had to ask them to skate in circles to dissipate the fog. The Flyers lost that game, and the next, but roared back on home ice in Game Five and closed the series out on the road thanks to another shutout from Bernie Parent.

The Flyers haven't won another Cup since then (though Pat Quinn coached them to the final in 1980, and Eric Lindros brought them close again in 1997). But they have become one of the most respected teams in the league. Since 1967, only the Montreal Canadiens have won a higher percentage of their games than the Flyers. And Bobby Clarke has been a huge part of that history of success. He holds franchise records for most games played, most playoff games played, most points, most playoff points, best plus/minus, and many others. He is also fourth all-time in penalty minutes. He played in eight All-Star games, won the Hart Trophy (most valuable player) three times, as well as the Selke Trophy (top defensive forward), the Ted Lindsay Award (formerly the Lester B. Pearson Award, given to the top regular-season player as voted by other players), and many more.

Just as importantly, when Clarke retired, he stepped right into management, and has done as much to steer the Flyers over their impressive history as anyone. Some players are defined by their teams, but the Flyers have definitely been defined by Bobby Clarke.

I think the reason Ed Snider and I got along so well was that we wanted to beat each other. I had so much fun with him over the years, especially after I retired. He got a real kick out of talking about the Flyers with me because I know so much of their history.

He was good friends with David Foster, the music producer, and I've known David since 1979. He once invited Janet and me to a dinner at Christmastime along with Ed and his wife and some of David's other friends. David loves to get on the piano and sing, and everyone joins in. David always says, "I can make anyone sound good—except Wayne." Anyway, at this dinner we were all singing when David shook his head and said, "I didn't think it was possible, but Ed's worse than Wayne."

Ed Snider died this past spring. It was a sad day for hockey. He made such a great contribution to the Flyers and to the league. I remember a conversation we had where he summed up the three things that had changed the franchise. Number one was that they went into the community and started programs for kids to play youth hockey. Number two was when they lost to St. Louis and then made the team tougher. And then Ed said, "Number three, Wayne, was when we drafted a guy named Bob Clarke."

Twenty-Four

THE WORLD HOCKEY
ASSOCIATION

L ooking back now, the World Hockey Association probably
looks pretty crazy. The franchises that came and went, the
wild hair and the wild fights—it was pretty different from
the game we know today, and the game that came before it.

But I honestly think the WHA was good for hockey. For one thing,
the on-ice product was actually surprisingly good. Any league with
stars like Bobby Hull, Dave Keon, Gordie Howe, and Gerry Cheevers
is a pretty serious league. The WHA players hung in there with the
Russians in 1974, and whenever a WHA team squared off with an
NHL team in an exhibition game, they more than held their own.

Part of that was a result of the WHA's openness to European
players and the style of play they brought with them, and part of it
was the fact that by raiding junior teams they were injecting youth
into their lineups. Think of the impact that some eighteen-year-
olds have in the NHL today. That should give some idea of the
effect that guys like Mike Gartner, Rod Langway, Mark Messier,
and Mark Howe had in the WHA as teenagers. Youth wasn't really
part of the game before then.

The other benefit to the game was that it opened up a lot of new jobs for players and raised their salaries. The fact is, I wouldn't have had a job playing hockey at the age of seventeen if it hadn't been for the new league.

A lot of those teams had great fans. People in Winnipeg, Quebec City, Edmonton, and Hartford knew hockey. Those were great rinks to play in. Even Cincinnati and Indianapolis were close enough to Detroit and Chicago that fans knew the game and appreciated it. Now, until the mid-80s, hockey wasn't widely broadcast on television in the United States, so if you didn't grow up with hockey you probably didn't know what was going on at ice level. Even when the Atlanta Thrashers started up in the 1990s, people used to joke that fans would cheer whenever a team iced the puck. But who can blame them? If you've never seen a hockey game, icing probably looks like a great idea. And it's true that we saw some crazy things in places like Birmingham, where fighting seemed to be a big part of the Bulls' marketing. But on the whole, hockey fans should be glad the WHA was there when it was.

The WHA started up in 1971, with its first games played in October 1972. The twelve-team hockey league was the idea of American promoters Dennis Murphy and Gary Davidson, both from California. They'd seen it done in 1960, when the American Football League was formed to take on the NFL, and were directly involved in the American Basketball Association when it took on the NBA in 1967. Now they wanted to do the same with hockey, but they knew nothing about hockey. They hadn't even seen a game. So they recruited Wild Bill Hunter to help them out.

Hunter was the president of Edmonton's junior team, the Oil Kings. Before that he founded the Western Canada Junior Hockey League, which became the WHL. (Juniors now call it "the Dub," for W.) Because Hunter knew a lot of people in the hockey world, he traveled all over North America looking for investors to buy franchises for $25,000 each. One of his first investors was Ben Hatskin, who'd played football for the Winnipeg Blue Bombers and won two Grey Cups in 1939 and 1941. (In 1967, during the NHL expansion, Hatskin had taken a run at a franchise, but then-president Clarence Campbell told him he'd need a sixteen-thousand-seat rink and a $2 million entry fee. Hatskin thought that was too steep.)

In order to bring in good players (and the fans who would follow), the fledgling WHA needed to begin with stars. And fortunately for them, the NHL itself paved the way. Although average NHL salaries were competitive with those in other pro sports, top hockey stars were paid less than top stars in baseball and basketball. So the WHA owners figured they'd be able to recruit a few great players from the NHL—and they were right. By 1972–73, the WHA's first season, sixty-seven players had jumped from the NHL.

But the WHA still needed a big name. Gordie Howe was retired, and there were really only a handful of active players in hockey everybody knew: players like Phil Esposito, Bobby Orr, Bobby Clarke, and Bobby Hull. The trouble was that most of them were tied up in contracts. Except the Chicago Black Hawks' Bobby Hull. At thirty-three, he was still in really good shape with many good years ahead. And he was a huge hockey star.

Bobby Hull had already scored 604 NHL goals. Only Gordie Howe had scored more. Hull had led the league in goals seven out of ten years in the 1960s. And he had one of the hardest slap shots in the history of hockey, shooting the puck at 120 miles per hour. Who does that? No one. Shea Weber can shoot the puck hard enough to go right through the mesh (which he did at the 2010 Olympics against Germany) and he has never been clocked at anywhere near 120, even at the All-Star game, where he is allowed a running start and a stiffer stick than he uses in real games. Bernie Parent says there were times when Bobby's shot would rebound so hard off the glass or the end boards that his own goalie would have to make the save. He used to amuse teammates by firing pucks over the boards and down the tunnels and trying to break the glass doors of the old Chicago Stadium.

Ben Hatskin offered Bobby $250,000 a year for five years with his new Winnipeg franchise, plus another $100,000 a year to coach or manage for five years after that. Bobby said no thanks. He wanted to stay in Chicago. He really liked Chicago and had played there for fifteen years. But he was having problems negotiating his contract with Bill Wirtz. Attendance was dropping at Black Hawks games. Fans could watch the home games of the White Sox and Cubs, the Bears, and the Bulls on television, but not the Black Hawks. Even though Hawks games had been on TV as early as the 1940s—certainly before *Hockey Night in Canada*—Wirtz refused to televise most of his home games because he thought it would mean fewer ticket sales. (Later, when Chicago did decide to air their home games, their fan base grew. So did their crowds at the arena.) In any case, he was in no mood to open the bank for Hull.

Hatskin continued to call Bobby's agent, Harvey Weinberg. Finally, just to get Ben off his back, Bobby said he thought the $250,000 a year for five years was fine, but that he wanted a million-dollar signing bonus up front. He thought it would never fly because no one had ever been paid that much to play any sport, let alone get it up front.

Hatskin said yes. To acquire a star of Bobby's caliber would give the WHA the instant credibility it needed, so each of the first ten owners kicked in $100,000 and raised the million. It was a huge deal in hockey, one of the biggest ever.

When it came out that Bobby was going over to the WHA, Bill's father, Arthur Wirtz, who was still the chairman of the Hawks, sent over a contract for $1,250,000. But Bobby says he told him to "stick it where the sun don't shine."

The WHA owners cost the NHL owners a lot of money and changed the game forever. For the first time since the Western Hockey League folded in 1926, a rival league had the power to compete with the NHL for elite players.

Legal challenges arose involving the reserve clause in NHL contracts, which restricted a player's movement for the rest of his life. But the courts ruled that once a player's contract was finished (and several NHL players were on single-season contracts in 1972), a player was free to sign with the team that held his rights—in either league.

This was the beginning of multiyear deals to keep a player's rights. Several NHL stars followed Bobby into the WHA, including goalies Gerry Cheevers from Boston and Bernie Parent from Toronto, defensemen Ted Green and J.C. Tremblay, and an exciting young center named Derek Sanderson.

Before the WHA, the players had no voice. The teams called the shots because there was no one else to negotiate with. That's why you always hear the story about Glenn Hall threatening to take a year off to paint his barn instead. (It turned out that there was no barn—that was just Glenn negotiating.) The players had no power at all. It was the WHA that finally gave them some bargaining power.

M eanwhile, the NHL thought that if they ignored the WHA it would go away. Consider the case of Tom Webster.

Webster had played pretty well in Detroit, and then got traded to the California Golden Seals. Then, when Webster's Seals contract was up, Howard Baldwin, part owner of the WHA's New England Whalers, offered him a three-year deal for over $50,000 a year guaranteed. At the time, it was a lot of money—Tom was making only $12,000 a year with the Seals. So he called Finley and said, "The WHA has drafted me and offered me a three-year contract and I'm considering taking it."

Finley said, "Well, son"—if he liked you he called you son— "why don't you fly down and meet me here in Chicago?"

Webster jumped on a plane, flew into Chicago, went to Finley's office, and showed him the contract.

Finley read it over. "Well, son, listen, it's a very good offer. I don't blame you for looking at it, but you know what? I've had experience with this kind of stuff in baseball. Do you remember the Pasquels?"

Webster said he didn't.

What Finley was talking about was a Mexican league. In 1946, Jorge Pasquel brought major leaguers to Mexico. He offered them huge contracts. Some big names like Brooklyn Dodgers catcher Mickey Owen and Giants second baseman George Hausmann packed up and headed to Mexico to earn top dollar. Altogether, twenty-seven major leaguers moved down to Mexico. But after just one year, it all started to come apart when the league couldn't pay some of the players. So they headed home. And of course when they came back, the money was much, much less than what they'd been making before they left.

Finley asked, "How much are you making now?"

"Well, last year you paid me $12,000."

"I think I'll pay you $11,000 to come back and play for me next year."

"Sir, this is a legitimate contract here. I'm not trying to pull any punches, or lie to you, or B.S. you . . ."

"Yeah, I understand that. But I told you, I had this experience. Eleven thousand now, much less if you have to come back."

Webster stood up. "Thank you very much, sir, but I'm going over to the WHA."

After Bobby Hull went to Winnipeg and others began to follow, NHL general managers started calling their star players and offering to raise their salaries. Agents weren't above taking advantage. In August 1975, when Bobby Orr's contract with the Boston Bruins was up at the end of the coming season, his agent, Alan Eagleson, began negotiating with the Bruins. But the Bruins were lowballing, so Eagleson went looking for other opportunities. The president of the WHA's Minnesota Fighting Saints, Wayne Belisle, offered Bobby a multimillion-dollar contract with a $1 million signing bonus. Eagleson turned it down. He was just looking for leverage.

But there were other legends of the game who did make the jump to the new league. Dave Keon played in the WHA, as did Frank Mahovlich, Paul Henderson, and Kent Nilsson. And then there was Gordie Howe, who came out of retirement to play with his sons.

I was at a 2015 Kinsmen dinner in Saskatoon honoring Gordie Howe when Mark told a story about him at that first training camp. He said he remembered Gordie huffing and puffing and turning fifteen shades of purple. The boys thought he was going to have a heart attack. But Mark said that his dad had incredible stamina: a week later they couldn't keep up with him. And the special part, he added, was seeing bodies flying around his dad, even in practice. (Terry O'Malley, who played on three Canadian Olympic hockey teams, was once talking with Danny O'Shea, a checker who played against Gordie in Minnesota. Terry said, "It's amazing he can play at such an age." And Danny replied, "I could play at fifty too if I had fifteen feet on each side of me whenever I got the puck.")

Terry Ruskowski was drafted by the Black Hawks but signed with the Houston Aeros instead because Gordie was there. Just before playoffs they were playing scrimmage, and although Terry knew he shouldn't do it, he put the puck between Gordie's legs and stepped around him. Gordie turned and rapped Terry with his stick right above the eye. Cut him for about four or five stitches. There was blood all over the place, and the trainer had to run out with a towel. Gordie tapped his stick on Terry's pants in a friendly way and said, "Hey, sorry about that, kid." And then in a quiet voice, he added, "Don't ever make me look bad."

Gordie always wanted to be the best. He hated to lose. And he was the ultimate teammate. In Houston he would fight guys, make plays, score goals. Everyone knew that when the game was on the line you could sit back because Gordie would be taking over.

Other young guys, like Morris Lukowich, whose brother Ed is a former world curling champion, were offered similar contracts from both leagues, but like Terry, Morris chose the WHA because of Gordie.

Gordie was interested in helping younger guys, but he demanded respect and good manners. Morris would sit beside him in the dressing room and on the bench just because he loved being near him. When Gordie would get ready to go on for his shift he'd have sweat pouring off him, but instead of using his own sweater, he'd always lean to his right and wipe his forehead on the jersey of the guy next to him. Morris told me that the first time Gordie did it to him, he thought, "Wow! I'm hitting the big time!"

If Gordie was tired between periods, he'd sit back in his stall and sleep through intermission, or he'd open up his fan mail, read it, sign it, and hand one of the younger players the envelope to lick it. Morris says he licked so much glue that he'd be dizzy going out for the next period.

In 1978–79, the final season of the WHA, I was seventeen years old. It was my first season of pro hockey and I was just thrilled to be there. I was having a pretty good year with the Edmonton Oilers. We finished in first place, and I was third in the scoring race and starting to find my way. I hadn't expected to get picked for the three-game All-Star series against the HC Dynamo Moscow, a pro team from Russia, but Edmonton was hosting, so that probably helped get me on the team.

Jacques Demers, who'd go on to coach in the NHL for fourteen years and win a Stanley Cup with the Canadiens in 1993, was the assistant coach of the All-Star team. In those days everything was run so differently. The team wasn't put together by the media or a panel. I think Jacques pretty much handpicked the players himself. So when he called me, I knew it was a great honor.

I went down to the locker room one day ahead of our first game thinking, "If I dress tomorrow, great. If I don't, I'm seventeen, I understand."

The trainer told me, "Jacques Demers wants to see you."

I walked into his office. Gordie Howe and Mark Howe were there too. I'd already developed a friendship with Gordie, but I was still really nervous.

Demers said, "You're gonna center Mark and Gordie."

I was kind of shocked. I thought, "Oh my gosh, I'm playing— and I'm playing with *Gordie Howe*."

We practiced, and the next day we had a light skate. When we got to the arena that night before the game I was really scared.

I was sitting in my stall, and at one point I turned to Gordie to ask him a question, but his eyes were closed. He was having a nap.

"Gordie? Gordie, I'm really nervous about this game."

He opened one eye, looked at me, and said, "So am I."

In the end, we won 4–2 and our line had eight points. But for me the real thrill was just lining up for the faceoff beside Mr. Hockey.

I remember how well guys like Paul Shmyr, Rob Ramage, Morris Lukowich, Robbie Ftorek, and Mike Gartner played on that 1979 All-Star team. And I got to spend four days with Dave Keon, the great Maple Leafs captain.

Keon had been a Junior B player at St. Michael's College in Toronto, where he was coached by Father David Bauer, who founded the Canadian men's national Olympic team. He also happened to be the brother of future Hall of Famer Bobby Bauer, of the Bruins' Kraut Line. At a practice one day, Father Bauer began a backward-skating checking drill. But Keon couldn't do it. He was a river skater—a beautiful skater, but not a checker. Father Bauer wasn't letting him off the hook.

Finally Keon said, "I'm not doing this anymore. I'm done."

They had a real argument, and Father Bauer kicked him off the ice and marched him into the dorm. When they got there, Father Bauer said, "I'll tell you what. Let's wrestle, and if I pin you, you practice my checking drills. If you win, you don't have to."

Keon agreed and they went at it. Father Bauer won, and Dave Keon went on to become one of the great two-way players in the game. (When he played for the Leafs, he was checking Gordie Howe one time and had him in the corner. He wasn't riding Gordie or anything, but he was controlling his space, and then pinned him. Finally Gordie had enough. He turned back to him and said, "Look, kid, remember—the elbows come back fast.")

Everybody always talks about good scorers or good defensive rushers, but good checkers get kind of overlooked. The fundamental behind a great check is that you close the distance between you and the player with the puck. You have an angle, your head is up, you're looking at his chest, and when he stops and changes direction you have to be able to stop and recover and then close the gap again. That's the kind of checking that Father Bauer introduced. That's how elite defenseman can play almost half the game. They're not chasing guys around the ice. They're just maintaining their gap.

So playing with Keon was my link to Father Bauer and the Kraut Line. I was always grateful that Jacques Demers gave me that opportunity.

Several established NHL stars moved over to WHA teams in those first few seasons: Pat Stapleton from Chicago; Marc Tardif, Réjean Houle, and Frank Mahovlich from Montreal; and Paul Henderson from Toronto. The WHA also took on good junior players who were too young to sign with NHL teams. I've already talked about how you had to be twenty to qualify for the NHL draft. So when you were seventeen, eighteen, nineteen and someone offered to pay you to play pro hockey, it was hard to say no. Nelson Skalbania, the owner of the Indianapolis Racers, signed me in June 1978. He signed Mark Messier later the same year.

I got to Indianapolis at the end of August because that's when school started. One of the deals I'd made with my dad when I turned pro at seventeen was that I would go to school until I turned eighteen. So I signed up for night school twice a week. Broad Ripple High. David Letterman went there. I made a lot of friends my age, which was good because the guys on the team were much older. One of them even had a baby.

Fridays before hockey season, our goalie Eddie Mio and winger Peter Driscoll would roll up to the Steak 'n Shake in Peter's new baby-blue Biarritz Cadillac. It was his pride and joy. Drisc and Eddie looked like Starsky and Hutch. Drisc had a black shag and wore long, pointy collars and an Indian red leather jacket. He was a big, rugged guy who could really play. The season before (1977–78) he had fifty-six points, forty-six with Indianapolis and ten with Quebec. But he was also our tough guy in Indianapolis. Peter's nickname was Grenade because he didn't have the softest hands and tended to shoot wide. But you had to be careful about calling him that. He had to be in a certain mood. Eddie was blond with a cool mustache and sideburns. He always wore a light calf-leather jacket and a black T-shirt with bell-bottom jeans. Years later he told me that the jacket was actually made of plastic because he couldn't afford the real deal. Didn't matter, he still looked sharp.

Our GM and coach, Pat Stapleton—or "Whitey," as everyone called him—had told Peter and Eddie, "Hey, there's a kid coming up, Wayne Gretzky. He's going to be billeted right around the corner from you guys, so check in with him once in a while until the season starts."

That's why the two of them would drive up to the Steak 'n Shake on Friday nights, where I'd be hanging out with the kids from school. They'd call out, "Hey, everything okay?" I'd wave at them. "Yeah." And they'd drive off.

I wasn't a hit in Indianapolis. I remember my first mall signing. Three people showed up. Eight games in, Drisc and Eddie and I were on a plane to Canada. We'd been traded. Peter Driscoll was a key player in the trade because it gave Edmonton a power winger they didn't have. Edmonton had Dave Semenko, who could fight anybody. He could play hockey too, but he wasn't a power winger like Peter. The Oilers were also looking for a goalie. They had Dave Dryden, but he was getting older and they wanted another guy to back him, so they went after Eddie Mio. It was a package deal: three players for a final price tag of $400,000.

When we got off the ice after practice in Indianapolis, we were told to grab some basics and get on a plane. So we had maybe two suitcases each. We were on this little Learjet 25, the three of us with our hockey equipment. Those small Lears don't have any undercarriages. They're basically puddle jumpers.

We were squeezed in. Eddie and Peter were sitting on their equipment. We were all in a daze. I was a very nervous flier, but the guys didn't know it, so they told me to sit at the back on a little jump seat. Eddie looked over and saw me shaking pretty bad. He opened the cooler and handed me a sandwich and a beer. He said, "It's okay, kid, I don't think there's any air police going to check your ID."

We weren't even sure where we were going. Maybe Edmonton, maybe Winnipeg. Still, I'd known the trade was coming. A few days earlier, after a game against the Jets, their stick boy had come up to me and said, "Bobby Hull wants to talk to you." So I went to dinner with Bobby. He said, "Would you like to play in Winnipeg for the Jets? They're gonna trade you." He told me that they were going after me and our coach, Pat Stapleton. So there I am, seventeen years old, and Bobby Hull is asking me if I want to play with him. I said, "Wow! Okay, sure."

The day after that was a Monday. We went home, and the Racers' owner, Nelson Skalbania, called and told me that I had two choices: Winnipeg or Edmonton. My agent, Gus Badali, advised me to go to Edmonton. He said that the NHL and WHA were going to merge, and that since Winnipeg's arena could hold only eleven thousand people whereas Edmonton's could hold sixteen thousand, Edmonton had a much better shot at getting into the NHL. Going to Edmonton would be a good business decision, but playing with Bobby Hull would have been great too. In any case, Bobby hadn't given up. He and Nelson were still negotiating while we were on the plane.

We had to stop in Minneapolis to refuel. At that point, the pilot told us that we were heading to Edmonton. Jets GM Rudy Pilous had passed on the deal. He thought I wasn't good enough to play pro hockey.

The very existence of the WHA (and speculation about its longevity) could influence contract negotiations within the NHL. Montreal Canadiens GM Sam Pollock's deal with Guy Lafleur is one example.

Pollock knew in order to get Lafleur he would need the first overall draft pick in 1971. He figured the California Golden Seals (formerly known as the Oakland Seals) would come in last. So he traded Ernie Hicke and his 1970 first-round draft pick to the Seals for François Lacombe and their first-round pick the following year. But the Hicke brothers started to gel and the Seals started winning. That meant the L.A. Kings, not the Seals, were going to come in last place in 1971. Sam had to make the L.A. Kings stronger, so he traded center Ralph Backstrom, a guy who averaged forty to fifty points, to Los Angeles in exchange for Gord Labossiere and Ray Fortin. Just as Pollock had hoped, L.A. started winning and the Seals came in last place. And that's how Pollock managed to get the first overall pick to draft Guy "The Flower" Lafleur.

By the spring of 1973 Lafleur had just finished his second season with the Canadiens. That's when the WHA's Quebec Nordiques (Guy's father-in-law was one of their directors) offered Guy a three-year, $150,000 contract. Now, Sam Pollock had gone through a lot of trouble to get Guy Lafleur, and there was no way he wanted to lose him to the WHA. The trouble was that he couldn't pay $150,000 a year. That was way above the salaries of the other players. On top of which, there were guys picked later than Guy in '71 who were putting up bigger numbers.

Pollock decided to offer Guy a million dollars for a ten-year contract for $100,000 a year, but first he called his coach, Scotty Bowman, and his assistant, Claude Ruel. A ten-year contract was unheard of at the time, and so Pollock wanted to know whether they thought a lesser team would eventually want Guy in a trade. Bowman said he didn't know how good Guy would be because he hadn't played up to his potential, but that he was confident Guy would always be an NHL player, not a superstar. Claude, who'd scouted Guy in the first place, was more attuned to his possibilities. He said, "He will develop."

So Pollock offered Guy the contract. And because Guy wasn't sure whether the WHA would survive, he signed it. Guy Lafleur would go on to win five Stanley Cups with Montreal. Larry Robinson, who'd won all those Cups with Lafleur and had signed as a free agent with the Kings a year after I got there, told us how amazed he'd been by him. Robinson said that as long as you passed the puck in Guy's direction, whether it was off his skates or on either side, he'd somehow find it. They say there is no such thing as a bad pass to a good player, but Lafleur was truly phenomenal. And Guy was explosive, so he could move away from a hit like a fly. Years later I'd have the opportunity and the privilege to play on the Flower's line at the 1981 Canada Cup.

When the WHA added two teams for the 1974–75 season, the NHL responded in a defensive move by adding the Kansas City Scouts (now the New Jersey Devils) and the Washington Capitals. That meant thirty-two teams in total—and since almost all the players were from Canada, the talent level was getting thin. Teams started to look to Europe, mostly Sweden and Finland, as well as to a few defectors from Czechoslovakia. No players behind the Iron Curtain were free to leave at that time.

The Jets brought over two Swedes, Ulf Nilsson and Anders Hedberg, to play on Bobby Hull's line, and together they were pretty special. Really entertaining. They played the game with crisscrossing wingers and creative passing. Their opponents had no clue where to pick them up. That line was one of the greatest lines ever in the history of the game. And it really changed hockey in North America.

Hedberg and Nilsson were two of the bravest players ever. When they came and played in North America, they were better than a lot of players here, so they got hacked and whacked a ton. When Glen Sather became coach of the Oilers near the end of the 1976–77 season, he wanted his team to be patterned after what Bobby Hull had built for the Winnipeg Jets.

I t was a sign that things were getting desperate in the WHA when the Houston Aeros and Winnipeg Jets announced that they were going to merge for the 1978–79 season. The Houston Aeros and the Winnipeg Jets were huge rivals in the WHA. The Jets couldn't stand the Aeros and vice versa. They even fought in the penalty box. Now that rivalry carried over into the locker room. They didn't play as a team. Their coach, Larry Hillman, once a defenseman with the Maple Leafs, was caught in the middle. He got fired and Tom McVie came in for the last nineteen games.

Tom and the club's general manager, John Ferguson, went way back—they'd been friends since they were kids growing up in Vancouver's Eastside. McVie was three years older, and when he was leaving bantam and John was just starting, he gave John his old pair of skates.

McVie was a workaholic and a rough, gruff coach. In the locker room the guys would call him Sergeant Major. He would say, "If I can put eighteen hours in at the rink, you can put in two or three." The practices were so tough that the players would leave the ice with their tongues hanging out. And their pregame warm-ups were just as hard. It was like playing two games in one day. As for Ferguson, he was as tough as they come. He revolutionized the tough-guy role by skating shotgun with Jean Béliveau—and keeping up. He could play the game with the best of them, but no one was going to take any liberties with Béliveau when Ferguson was on the ice.

Finally, one of the players convinced the guys to bring their families and meet at a restaurant so that they could all get to know each other. It pulled them together. They started to play as a team, not as individuals. And they made the playoffs.

When Ulf Nilsson and Anders Hedberg went over to the Rangers in 1978, the Jets' goalie, Joe Daley, said, "Bobby Hull lost the fingers on his glove." Bobby played only four games into the season that year.

In 1979, the Jets ended the season on April 18 in third place and were supposed to have a couple of days off before the first round in Quebec against the Nordiques on April 23. But Tom called the team in and worked them hard every day. It was not a popular decision. Still, they swept Quebec in four games and then got ready to play us, the Edmonton Oilers, for the WHA championship—the Avco World Trophy.

In that playoff series, four guys from Winnipeg really stood out for me. The first was their goalie, Gary Smith. When I signed with Indianapolis, Gary was the guy who took me under his wing. He was just tremendous to me. Then, when the Racers folded, the Jets signed Gary as a free agent. He walked into their dressing room with long hair, his shirt untucked, dragging his bag. Then he flopped down on the bench, looked around, and said, "Guys, my name is Gary "The Axe" Smith. They call me Axe because I've been axed from so many teams. My goals-against in Indianapolis was 5.51, but don't let that fool you. I'm not that good." Everybody laughed. But Gary went on to play very well for the Jets.

And like all goalies, Gary had some unusual habits. He wore seven pairs of socks in his skates, but depending on the day, he might pull on up to fourteen pairs. After every period, he'd go for a shower. But as soon as the fifteen minutes were up, he'd be back on the ice in time for the next period.

Kent Nilsson was another top player on the Jets. Kent was a natural. He was such a smooth skater, and his slap shot was unbelievable. He was once challenged on television to hit the crossbar from the red line. He tees it up, glances at the net a hundred feet away, then calmly cranks it off the crossbar. They called him the Magic Man.

Like Kent, Morris Lukowich was a great Jets forward. With Kent and Morris on their team, you knew they'd get a whole lot of points because Kent had incredible puck-handling skills and Morris had one of the quickest release wrist shots I've ever seen. A goalie had no time to adjust or square off, and his shot was deadly.

Terry Ruskowski was the Jets' natural leader. He was a tremendously hard worker. Unfortunately, though, he hurt his shoulder in Game Three and missed Games Four and Five. What happened was, he went against the boards with his elbow up and then someone hit him from behind and really stretched it. He couldn't lift his arm. But he was back for Game Six with his shoulder covered in heat and plastic. He had to skate to the bench in warm-up and pull the plastic off because his skin was blistering. Still, he went back out, finished the warm-up, and played very hard. Throughout the game Terry was giving his defenseman Barry Long these nice little saucer passes, and Barry scored twice on them.

It was do or die. Terry got four assists and the Jets beat us 7–3. We knew going into the series that it was going to be the last Avco Cup ever. I know we wanted to win and be part of that history. But Winnipeg was just better than we were in those six games.

The WHA and the NHL had been battling it out for seven years, and it was costing teams in both leagues. But while some owners thought it only made sense to stop the financial bleeding by joining forces, others couldn't let the hard feelings go. So it took a few years to work out a merger deal between the two leagues.

In 1977, two years before the merger, John Ziegler took over for Clarence Campbell as NHL president and discovered that the league was in terrible shape financially. So John pulled the hardliners together and got them talking. It was finally looking like four WHA teams—Edmonton, Quebec, Winnipeg, and New England (renamed Hartford)—would be joining the NHL. Thirteen of the seventeen teams had to agree in order for that to happen, and so a vote was held. Ziegler was sure he had the votes, but they lost by one. It turned out that Toronto, Montreal, and Vancouver had all voted against adding three new Canadian teams.

Once again, it was about television. Molson owned the rights to the Canadian teams in the NHL and didn't want to compete with other sponsors, especially in Quebec. They had lobbied the owners to vote down the merger, and it worked a little too well. Fans wanted to see the merger and there were calls for a boycott of Molson beer. Members of Parliament passed a resolution unanimously asking the NHL to admit the Canadian teams. It got ugly. A bomb threat was called in to the Molson brewery in Quebec, and someone fired a bullet through the window of the Molson facility in Winnipeg.

So another meeting was called, and the vote went through. The second vote wouldn't have been necessary if the owner of the Canucks, Frank Griffiths, had attended the first meeting. But he couldn't and had sent his team president, William Hughes, with directions to vote yes. For some reason, Hughes voted no—and when Griffiths found out, he fired Hughes on the spot. The two had been friends and business associates for years.

So the four WHA teams finally joined the NHL in the 1979–80 season, but the NHL owners wanted their pound of flesh. I think they were afraid of how well the WHA teams would do. How would it look if a WHA team won the Stanley Cup? So the NHL charged each of the WHA owners an expansion fee of $6 million. And then, in a dispersal draft, they reclaimed players that the NHL teams held rights to. The WHA teams could protect only two skaters and two goalies. That was it. And then they got the bottom four picks in the 1979 entry draft.

It was like turning very good teams back into expansion teams. But the new WHA franchises had no choice—it was a take-it-or-leave-it deal—and so they restocked their teams with fringe players available in an expansion draft. It would take until 1985–86 for all four teams to make the playoffs in the same season.

B obby Hull came back and played with the Jets in the first year they were folded into the NHL—but only for eighteen games.

Tom McVie insisted that his players be in the dressing room an hour and a half before the game. If you were late, even by one minute, you didn't play. So everyone was always there on time.

Saturday, December 15, 1979, was the very first time the Jets hosted the Montreal Canadiens. The game was scheduled for eight p.m. but got moved to seven p.m. for the CBC. An hour before game time, Bobby wasn't around, so Morris Lukowich got on the phone and called him. He said, "Bobby, where are you?"

Bobby said, "I'm just leaving for the rink."

Morris said, "You're late."

"What do you mean? I'm looking at the tickets and it says eight o'clock."

Morris explained that the hour had been changed for the CBC. He said, "Bobby, is there anything you need? Any of your equipment? Do you need your skates sharpened or anything like that?"

"No, no, everything's ready to go. I'll be right down there."

But when he arrived a few minutes later, Tom wouldn't let him play. Bobby drew a line in the sand and said, "Either the coach goes or I go."

John Ferguson said, "Well, we can't fire the coach. He just helped us win the WHA last year."

Bobby said, "Then I'm gone."

There are certain things that happen when egos get involved, and you wonder about them later. Tom McVie was a good coach, but it's hard to make your team better by driving Bobby Hull away.

T he NHL's amateur draft was renamed the entry draft so that the underage WHA players could be included, with the eligible draft age being lowered from twenty to eighteen. I wasn't selected in the entry draft because Edmonton protected me as one of their two skaters. But everyone else was going into the expansion draft, meaning that we'd lose guys like Blair MacDonald and Dave Semenko. Fortunately, Glen Sather was able to work out deals to keep those two.

Glen's very first pick in the draft was Cam Connor. Cam was in his mid-twenties and one of our strongest guys—he'd worked construction for cement companies in Winnipeg. Cam was a clutch player. He played with us most of that season, and was then traded to the Rangers. The Oilers' second pick was defenseman Lee Fogolin, who'd been playing for the Buffalo Sabres. Buffalo had a very good veteran team led by Gilbert Perreault and Danny Gare. They consistently came in at the top of the standings. But sometimes there's a fit for a player and sometimes there isn't. Lee wasn't progressing the way he wanted to as a player, and so he decided to move on. That's when the Oilers picked him up. We all listened when Lee said something— he commanded so much respect in our locker room.

The very first day Lee was in training camp with the Oilers, it was apparent to all of us that he was going be the spokesperson for our group. Nobody gives you leadership. You earn that mantle, and he earned it from day one. The Oilers had a lot of natural talent in our group—Mark Messier, Jari Kurri, Glenn Anderson, and Paul Coffey. Lee wasn't super talented, but we really respected how hard he worked each and every day.

In the late 1970s and early 80s, long hair was the style. All the guys wore it that way. Darryl Sittler, Bobby Clarke, even Bobby Orr. I don't mean long, long hair, but full and over the ears. Guys would come in and the first thing a team would do is shave your head. Lee Fogolin, who was our captain by that time, said, "Hey, we're not doing that. Everybody's the same here." He learned that kind of respect from his father. The tradition of the rookie dinner actually started in Edmonton. Rookies would take everybody out for dinner one night as initiation instead. It was a great introduction to the NHL, but no one said it was cheap.

Twenty-Five

THE SUMMIT SERIES

P hil Esposito has won just about everything there is to be won in the game of hockey. He scored almost 1,600 points in the NHL, won major trophies several times, and has had his number retired. But when he tried out for a bantam team in his hometown of Sault Ste. Marie, he was cut.

That's what family is for. His father drove truck for Phil's uncle, who owned a company called Algoma Contractors that used to remove the slag from steel plants. The company was doing well, so his uncle was convinced to sponsor a team so that Phil could play in the league that year. Phil went on to play junior in Sarnia, Ontario, which made him the property of the Chicago Black Hawks.

The Black Hawks' GM, Tommy Ivan, offered Phil his first professional contract, but because he held out for more, Ivan considered him a troublemaker. Billy Reay, who'd been a second-line center with the Canadiens in the late 1940s and early 50s, was the Black Hawks coach. (He was a player's coach. He didn't have to scream and yell—he'd just give the players a look. Billy would retire with a 516–335–161 record, the best in the team's history.) Billy wanted Phil to improve his skating. He also thought Phil was too heavy, and told him to lose weight. Phil was 215 pounds and Billy wanted him to weigh in at 190, so he started to fine Phil ten bucks for every pound he was over. But every time Phil tried to steam the weight off, someone would bring in a six-pack of beer and mess up his plans.

Phil was doing a great job centering Bobby Hull. For whatever reason, Reay didn't take him seriously, though. Maybe Reay and the Black Hawks just thought that every center should be a warrior like Stan Mikita. A year earlier, in 1966–67, Mikita had won the Art Ross, the Hart, and the Lady Byng trophies (and he did it again the next year, 1967–68). Reay didn't see Phil as that guy. And in a way, he was right. Phil didn't get by on hustle. His genius was being in the right place at the right time, and the right place was usually the slot. But Reay was spectacularly wrong in another way. A year later, in 1968–69, Phil would win both the Ross and the Hart.

The expansion trade deadline freeze was scheduled for May 15, 1967, at midnight. That afternoon, Milt Schmidt, the only man in Bruins history to serve as player, team captain, coach, and general manager, took a call from Tommy Ivan. All season long Ivan had been after hard-hitting defenseman Gilles Marotte. But Milt's GM, Hap Emms, had coached Gilles in junior and wanted to keep him.

Boston hadn't won a Cup since 1940–41. They hadn't even made it to the playoffs since 1958–59. They had the makings of a great team, with Bobby Orr as a rookie and Bernie Parent and Gerry Cheevers in goal, but they were missing the final piece of the puzzle: a top forward.

Schmidt thought Fred Stanfield might be the answer. Stanfield had grown up in Toronto, and Schmidt had seen him play enough to like him. The two GMs went back and forth. After five hours of negotiations, they agreed that in exchange for Marotte, goalie Jack Norris, and Pit Martin, Tommy would send over Fred Stanfield, Ken Hodge, and Phil Esposito. It turned out to be one of the most lopsided trades in history.

Stanfield did become a great top-six forward for the Bruins. But the key to the deal was the guy the Black Hawks wanted to get rid of. Phil Esposito was about to go on a six-year streak leading the league in goal-scoring. There was a popular bumper sticker in Boston that read, "Jesus saves. Esposito scores on the rebound."

By 1968–69, the Bruins finished with a then–franchise record, one hundred points. They'd also go on to win two Stanley Cups, in 1970 and '72. But I'd say that it was the 1972 Summit Series that was the highlight of Phil Esposito's career. It's probably where he played his best hockey.

The Soviet Union's national team had been dominating amateur hockey for a decade. They'd won seven world championships and three Olympic gold medals in a row. They also spent at least nine months of every year at camps away from their wives and children, working out three times a day, getting stronger, faster, and incredibly skilled. The amateurs from Canada and the U.S. had virtually no chance against the Soviets.

Canadian hockey hadn't changed much from the 1930s. Go after the puck, play physical, shoot every chance you get, and crash the net for rebounds. The Russians brought all kinds of innovations. Instead of three-man lines, they changed as five-man units.

They played in constant motion. Everyone seemed to know where his teammates would be. Wingers cycled the puck in the corners. Forwards looped back to start quick transitions. Rather than firing the puck in deep for a change, they'd pass it back into their own zone and hold on to it during the change. Every one of these strategies would be adopted in the NHL. The Oilers' Glen Sather was one of the first NHL coaches to bring in this kind of play.

The Russians didn't begin working on their game until 1946. But once they'd started, they wanted to win everything. Excelling at sports was political, a way to demonstrate that communism was superior to capitalism. Coaches started evaluating kids at an early age. They would pick out the most promising and put them in special programs to get them ready for the national team.

Anatoli Tarasov is considered the father of Soviet hockey. Using ideas from Canadian Lloyd Percival's *The Hockey Handbook*, he worked with the Russians on a new way to train and play the game. He concentrated on building up his players with dryland training—weights, jumping exercises, balance. They carried each other across fields. They played a game called Kill the Canadian (which involved smashing into the boards, dropping down to one knee, then smashing into the boards again). His drills in the 40s and 50s look like the drills today. Tarasov was sixty years ahead of his time— and he was also a great sportsman. The players loved him. After the 1960 Olympic final when the Americans beat the Russians, Tarasov came into the American locker room and kissed coach Jack Riley on the cheek.

But after winning gold in 1972, Tarasov—who'd coached the Russians to seven consecutive world championships and three Olympic gold medals—was fired, in part because he'd disobeyed an order to throw a game against Czechoslovakia that would have pushed the Czechs instead of the Americans to a silver medal. He was later replaced by Viktor Tikhonov, whose grandson played for the Coyotes (I coached him when I was in Phoenix). Where Tarasov had been grandfatherly, Tikhonov was an iron-willed general. He didn't want to lose, but I don't think he was much liked by his players. In fact, at the 1988 Olympics he punched Alexander Mogilny in the face right on the bench. Tikhonov became known for everything people hated about Soviet hockey.

But between Tarasov and Tikhonov, the U.S.S.R. tapped Vsevolod Bobrov to coach the national team. No matter what our thoughts were about the Russians, it would be pretty hard not to respect Bobrov. He was a truly gifted athlete. He started out as a soccer player and absolutely shone in international play. When his club, Moscow Dynamo, toured the U.K., he scored six goals in games against Arsenal, Chelsea, and Glasgow Rangers. He scored five goals for the U.S.S.R. in the 1954 Olympics. But as good as he was at soccer, he was even better at hockey—which he'd never even seen played until he was twenty-three years old. He led the Soviets to the gold medal in the 1956 Winter Olympics, and took the world championships in 1954. Incredibly, he scored eighty-nine goals in fifty-nine games wearing the famous CCCP sweater in international play.

It was Bobrov who was behind the Russian bench for the most famous series in the history of hockey.

For years the Russians had wanted to prove that they were as good as NHL players. Tarasov had been asking for a game against the Canadian pros since 1964 (he got permission from Khrushchev, who later changed his mind). But in December 1971, a Russian sports columnist put a small article in a Moscow newspaper suggesting some kind of "friendly" series. A Canadian diplomat read it and knew right away that its appearance in the paper meant that the idea had come from the Soviet government. Today, of course, the NHL has players from all over Europe, Canada, and the United States, but back in 1972, the league was almost entirely Canadian with just a handful of Americans. So the two governments started talking and set up a series of games to be played in September before the NHL season began. It would be four games in Canada, four games in Russia.

The Canadians put together a team of the best players in the league, led by Phil and Tony Esposito, Bobby Clarke, Brad Park, Yvan Cournoyer, Frank and Pete Mahovlich, Jean Ratelle, Guy Lapointe, Ken Dryden, and Paul Henderson. Bobby Orr couldn't play because he was injured. Bobby Hull couldn't play because he'd jumped to the new rival league, the WHA. Gordie Howe had retired. But still, it was an incredibly stacked team.

Canadian fans and Canadian sportswriters thought their team would dominate, maybe win all eight games. The players felt that way too. They figured they would roll right over the Russians.

On September 2, 1972, the two teams skated onto the ice at the Montreal Forum for Game One. Prime Minister Trudeau dropped the ceremonial puck. Phil Esposito took the faceoff for Canada. The Canadians scored in the first thirty seconds, and then scored again minutes later. But even so, the Canadians knew they had a game on their hands. Then the Russians settled into their game—and it was a revelation to Canadian hockey fans. The Soviets looked like they were toying with Team Canada. Circling with the puck, passing with a kind of craftiness NHL fans weren't used to—and doing it all at top speed.

As the night wore on the difference in the two teams' conditioning started to show. Canada had dressed only five defensemen, and during the last part of the game the Russians were all over the ice. By the end of the night, the Canadians were in a state of shock. They had been hammered 7–3.

The Summit Series continued across the country. In Game Two in Toronto, Peter Mahovlich scored one of the prettiest goals ever in hockey history. Canada was up 2–1 and the Russians were on the power play in Canada's zone. Mahovlich picked up a pass from Phil Esposito and skated all the way down, deking Vladislav Tretiak. Canada won that game 4–1. It seemed to make people think, "Okay, it's going to change. We're going to win seven out of eight games now." But then Game Three ended in a tie.

Team Canada was booed at the beginning of Game Four in Vancouver, and booed again at the end. In between, they lost 5–3. And the score actually flattered Canada. Coach Harry Sinden called the game a "beating."

When Phil Esposito, who'd been chosen as the Canadian star of the game, skated over to accept the honor, the fans booed him too. Canadian sportscaster Johnny Esaw later interviewed Phil, who was really upset. What I remember is the sweat pouring off his face from the effort he'd put into the game. "Some of our guys are really, really down in the dumps," he said. "We know, we're trying like hell. I mean, we're doing the best we can, and they got a good team, and let's face facts. But it doesn't mean that we're not giving it our 150 percent."

I really believe a speech can turn a team around. You would think that highly trained professionals shouldn't be swayed one way or another by a few words. But hockey is a game of emotion. All the skill in the world won't help you if you don't have passion. It's hard to have that kind of passion if you're expecting an easy win. Phil's emotional outburst, and his acknowledgement that Canada's biggest stars were in deep against the toughest competition they had ever faced really changed the way Canadian fans looked at the series.

The players didn't hear Phil defending them, because they were back in the locker room. I've heard Phil Esposito say that a side trip to play the Swedish national team during a fourteen-day break between the four Summit games in Canada and the final four in Moscow united the team because the Sweden games were so physical. Wayne Cashman was cut for fifty stitches by a high stick that actually split his tongue. Phil has said that up to that point, the Canadian team was more or less of a collection of all-stars, but in Sweden they gelled.

But I've had an opportunity to spend some time with the great Serge Savard, and he says that it wasn't until they got to Russia that the team really came together. That's when coaches Harry Sinden, who'd come out of retirement, and John Ferguson decided to shorten the bench from thirty-five to twenty. Sinden had said that before the series he was "just a guy from Rochester with a million friends. Now I can count them on one hand."

Sinden made some tough decisions and gave some pretty good hockey players news they didn't want to hear. Take Vic Hadfield, a left-winger on the Rangers' GAG (goal-a-game) line along with right-winger Rod Gilbert and center Jean Ratelle. Hadfield was the only fifty-goal scorer in Rangers' history. A month before the Summit Series, the WHA's Cleveland Crusaders had offered him a five-year, $1-million contract, and he used it as leverage with the Rangers to get the same offer. Sinden told Hadfield he wouldn't be playing. Hadfield didn't want to just hang around, so he left Moscow and headed home along with Buffalo players Gilbert Perreault and Richard Martin, and Jocelyn Guevremont of the Canucks.

Serge told me that the guys who stayed made a decision: "'To hell with them, we gotta do it together'—and to me that's where we became a real, real team."

E veryone was nervous going behind the Iron Curtain. When the team arrived there were guards with automatic weapons everywhere. The players felt they were being watched constantly. They were also pretty sure their rooms were bugged, so they were careful not to talk about their game plan. They even got calls waking them up in the middle of the night—and one night they had to leave their hotel while police investigated a bomb threat. Alan Eagleson didn't trust the food, so he'd brought in a shipment from Finland: 350 steaks, 350 cases of milk, 350 cases of soda, 350 cases of beer. By the time it was delivered to their hotel, half of it was gone.

All four games in Moscow were played at the Luzhniki Palace of Sports, which of course had the wider European ice surface. That would put the Canadians at a disadvantage against the puck-moving Russians.

In Game Five, when the players were introduced, Phil Esposito stepped out and fell down on his backside, feet sticking straight up in the air. His skates had caught on the stem of one of the flowers strewn on the ice. It could have been embarrassing, but Phil got up on one knee, bowed deeply, and blew a kiss into the stands. Though the stands were packed with Red Army officers in uniform and government officials (as well as the three thousand Canadians who had made the trip), he won the crowd over in that moment.

Canada jumped out to a 3–0 lead, but the Russians came back and won 5–4. Now there was no margin for error. To win the series, Canada would have to sweep the last three games.

In Game Six, the Canadians chased Russia's star forward Valeri Kharlamov all over the ice and took the body at every opportunity. Brad Park stepped into him a few times, and a number of other Canadians took a run at him. Kharlamov didn't shrink from it at all—in fact his temper seemed to rise throughout the game and he dumped a couple of Canadians to the ice, including Bobby Clarke. Clarke chased him down the ice and caught him with a hard two-hander across the ankle. But it wasn't exactly retaliation. Assistant coach John Ferguson admits he leaned over to Clarke and said, "I think he needs a tap on the ankle." And Clarke had some expertise in slashing. He did it so much that Serge Savard remembers wearing ankle guards whenever they played the Flyers. Bobby always said that if he hadn't learned to lay on a two-hander once in a while, he'd never have left Flin Flon. He got a two-minute penalty for the slash, and the Soviets scored on the power play, but Kharlamov was gone from the game. He missed Game Seven as well. He played in the final game, but he was not the same, and neither were the Russians.

The Russians had their way of doing things too. Canadians who played in '72 and '74 felt that while the media and the fans had branded *them* as mean and dirty, the Russians were probably worse. They weren't seen that way, though, because they didn't fight. The Russians were really good with their sticks. They were tough and they were mean and they wanted to win just as badly or worse than we did.

For them it was survival. Today we have a better sense of the life they lived back then under communism. In order to get ahead players had to be part of a successful team. If the team won championships or Olympic gold, they'd be rewarded with new cars or better apartments for their families, maybe even an extra week off during the season. Whether it was ice hockey, track and field, or soccer, they had to be successful as a group and make their nation proud.

Gordie Howe hated the Russians. Phil Esposito, too, has talked passionately about how he hated the Russians back then. Yet, when we went to Russia five years ago for a charity event with the '87 and '72 teams, you could see the bond that Esposito, Tretiak, and Alexander Yakushev had developed over the last forty years. It's pretty special.

Paul Henderson scored the Game Six winner with a slap shot from the slot. In Game Seven he skated through the entire Russian team, beat both defensemen, and whipped the puck past Tretiak with just over two minutes left. He was quickly becoming a Canadian hero, and left-winger Alexander Yakushev was doing the same for the Soviets.

At over 6'3" and 200 pounds, Yakushev was the biggest Russian—the Soviets' answer to Phil Esposito. He finished the series only two points behind Phil. When I was with the Oilers, if a guy scored a really pretty goal we'd say, "That was very Yakushevian." (A couple of years ago, Mark Messier and I had a chance to have lunch with Yakushev in Moscow and tell him how both of us—me from Ontario, and Mark from out west—were so taken with him back in '72. He got a real laugh out of it.)

The series came down to the final, Game Eight. The Canadians got into penalty trouble early in the final and they fell behind.

Phil Esposito tied the game, the Soviets went ahead, and Brad Park scored to make it 2–2 after the first. The Soviets scored early in the second, Bill White tied it midway in the period, but they scored two more, and now the Canadians were behind 5–3 going into the third period.

Phil Esposito was having an amazing game. In the second period, when Ken Dryden got caught way out of his net, Phil had dived across the crease to block a shot. Then, in the third, he caught a puck deflected out of the corner, knocked it down to the ice, and swatted it past Tretiak. Yvan Cournoyer picked up Phil's rebound, and on a second rebound he tied the game 5–5.

The Soviets wanted a tie. They'd scored two more goals in the series up to that point and felt they could claim victory. With less than a minute left, Cournoyer intercepted a clearing pass and sent it over to Paul Henderson, who was tripped and crashed into the boards. He jumped up just as Phil slapped a shot at Tretiak. Henderson whacked at the rebound. Tretiak made the save again. The puck popped out in front and Henderson was there. He found a hole and slipped it in.

Tretiak said later that Henderson must have gotten that puck from God himself.

Bobby Clarke's take on the '72 Summit Series was that it turned out to be one of those special moments in a hockey player's life that you don't plan for or anticipate—you just stumble in on it. Obviously the Russians wanted to win and obviously they tried very hard to win. But Bobby said that because Canada was desperate, they played a more physical, more aggressive, and nastier game than they'd ever played in their lives, and it paid off.

He thought the Russians learned from that. He also thought Canada had learned from the Russians that passing the puck was critical. Canada would shoot it in and go chase it and then try to pound the Russians, but they learned the hard way that this wouldn't work against a team that could pass like the Soviets. Canada knew they'd have to change their game. The grinding game that we'd played for so long and that we excelled at was ending.

That was it. That was the Summit Series. When it was all over the team went back to the hotel. There was a knock on Bobby Clarke's door. When he opened it, there stood Valeri Vasiliev, the Soviets' most punishing defenseman. The Russian said, "Come on." So Clarke followed Vasiliev into his room, where the future Soviet captain pulled out a big bottle of vodka, filled two water glasses, and handed him one. Bobby took a little sip. Vasiliev laughed and said, "Nah!" Then they both tipped back and shot eight ounces. It was a pretty neat way of showing good sportsmanship.

Twenty-Six

INSIDE THE MIRACLE

O
ne of the greatest stories in sports history almost never
happened. When Soviet troops invaded Afghanistan in
1979, U.S. president Jimmy Carter called for a boycott
of the 1980 Moscow Summer Olympics in protest. A lot of people
expected the U.S.S.R. to pull out of the Lake Placid Olympics in
response. But the Russians were probably just like anyone else.
They had put too much work into preparing for the Games to pull
out at the last minute. (They boycotted the 1984 Los Angeles
games instead.)

Nowadays, the Olympics is a huge production, but back then
Lake Placid was just a small ski town of twenty-five hundred people.

The Americans had won gold at the Squaw Valley Olympics in
1960, but the team hadn't been very successful since then. They'd
placed only fifth in the 1976 games. Meanwhile, the Soviets had
won twelve of the previous fifteen world championships and four
Olympic gold medals in a row. In 1979, instead of an All-Star
game, the NHL invited the Soviets to play a three-game series to
be called the Challenge Cup. In the deciding game, the U.S.S.R.

crushed the best players in the NHL 6–0. So they looked like a good bet to beat a bunch of amateurs at Lake Placid.

To fall within Olympic rules, the Soviets were called amateurs, but in reality they were beyond professional, paid to train and play year-round. Their record since Squaw Valley was 27–1–1. When the U.S.S.R. collapsed in 1991, one of the most incredible streaks in hockey history came to an end. The Soviets had won a medal at every single International Ice Hockey Federation tournament they had ever entered. Not exactly what you would expect from a bunch of amateurs.

There were only two countries in the world that had true amateurs, Canada and the U.S. Everyone knew that. The Europeans were pretty much all getting paid to play, whether it was Sweden, Finland, or Czechoslovakia. At world championships, people would see European players with fistfuls of hundred-dollar bills after big wins.

In the United States, the goal was to build a team that, while not having much chance of winning, would at least not embarrass the country.

Herb Brooks was hired as coach. If there was one guy in the program who wasn't playing to avoid embarrassment, it was Brooks. Twenty years earlier, Herb thought he'd made the national team as a player. He was even in the team picture. But he was cut just one day before the team left for Squaw Valley. He missed out on one gold medal, and he had no interest in letting another slip away.

Herb Brooks was an innovator. He studied offensive hockey and was always trying something different. On the power play, for example, he tried putting two players behind the goal line rather than out on the blue line in order to flip the rink into two. He had a lot of ideas that worked, and some that didn't. Brooks had played on the Minnesota Golden Gophers men's hockey team from 1955 to 1959 and then coached the team from 1972–73 to 1978–79. College teams play only on the weekends, Friday and Saturday, and practice Monday right through to Thursday, making college hockey the ideal place to try new ideas. In fact, some players specifically go to college to develop because they practice so much. Others go to junior, where they play twice as many games and where it's a lot more like the NHL.

Centerman Craig Patrick—the son of Bruins GM Lynn Patrick and grandson of hockey innovator Lester Patrick—figured his playing career was coming to an end, and he was looking around for work. He'd played with Brooks in the early 1970s on the U.S. teams. And when Brooks was coaching in Moscow at the world championships, he'd made Craig captain. One day Brooks said, "I offered the assistant coaching job for the Olympic team next year to somebody else, but I don't think they're going to take it. Would you be interested if he turns it down?" Craig said, "Sure." Two weeks after they got home, Herb called and said, "Are you still interested?"

Craig's grandfather Lester had died of a heart attack on June 1, 1960, just after Craig had turned fourteen and moved from his home in Massachusetts to Montreal and would eventually play junior hockey for the Montreal Junior Canadiens in the OHA. Frank Selke Sr., the Canadiens' GM at the time, gave Craig a set of equipment and told him that he could skate at the Forum any day he wanted. So after school Craig would take the bus to the Forum and practice by himself on the ice. One afternoon he was skating toward the net, and as he was about to shoot he looked up and saw his grandfather sitting in the stands, just watching him. Craig shot the puck, and when he looked up again Lester was gone. Craig circled the net and skated back, trying the same move again and again, hoping his grandfather would return, but he never did.

Craig played for the Pioneers at the University of Denver, where they won two NCAA championships in 1968 and 1969, and then on the U.S. national team in 1969–70 and 1970–71. He was up and down in the NHL on a few different teams until he retired at thirty-three and joined Herb to put together the U.S. Olympic team.

Eighty of the best college players from across the country were invited to Colorado Springs in July 1979 to be evaluated for the team, but Brooks had already pretty much decided on the twenty-three guys he was going to take. He'd won three NCAA champion-ships coaching Minnesota, so he knew all the college players.

He took Craig aside and said, "A lot of these guys hate each other, and the only way I can think to make them a team is for all of them to hate me. You're going to have to keep all the pieces together and be the guy they can lean on, because they're not going to be able to lean on me. I'm going to be the same to all of them, and I'm going to be tough on them all." That was his game plan.

Training camp started in August 1979 with an intense program of team-building exercises, strength and conditioning sessions, and on-ice practices. Herb worked the guys hard. Craig had never seen a coach teach so many different systems, and each guy knew each one intimately. Herb would change the system right on the bench, saying, "Okay guys, we're going to play it this way now," and they'd change their game. Next to the Soviets, they were by far the best-conditioned team in the Olympics that year.

Just before Herb recruited their goalie, Jimmy Craig, Jimmy's mother passed away. She'd been his biggest supporter. When she was dying of cancer she told Jimmy that when you die your strength isn't lost forever. It just goes to others. Jimmy felt that he'd picked up some of her strength and took it with him to the Olympics.

Herb talked a lot about puck possession. He'd tell the guys, "Don't dump the puck in. That went out with short pants." His philosophy was more European—when the opposition had the puck everyone on the team was a defenseman, and when Team USA had the puck everyone was a forward. He didn't believe in two-on-ones, either. He called them two-on-twos since the goalie is a player too.

Team USA's first game against the full Olympic Russian team was at Madison Square Garden just before the Olympics. The Russians beat them 10–3. The U.S. players were in awe of them. Craig said his players didn't play that game, they watched it.

Brooks had spent a lot of time in Russia learning some of their systems. (He studied a lot of systems elsewhere in the world as well.) Herb discovered that when the Russians played hockey, they didn't shoot the puck unless they thought they could score, and so although it might look as if they had fewer than ten shots on goal, they were shots that counted. Jimmy Craig referred to their play as "poetry"—totally selfless and completely in tune with one another.

Again, it was all about puck possession. The Russian team didn't have to work as hard in defense because they had the puck so often. When a lot of people watch hockey, they don't think to focus on that. A big part of my game was the forecheck—chasing a defenseman down, lifting his stick, and taking the puck. If you take the puck off a defenseman or a player in his own end, you don't have as many players to beat in order to score or to make a play.

I remember Scotty Bowman once telling me that when we were playing any of his teams, he'd continually harp at his defensemen, "Get away from Gretzky. Don't be trying to beat him individually." Pavel Datsyuk was a player who could steal pucks—in 2010 he had 54 percent more takeaways than anyone else in the NHL. Detroit's Nick Lidstrom was another perfect example, even though he was a defenseman. When Lidstrom got the puck, the team usually kept it on the next play. And that's the difference.

Herb thought his players had too much respect for the Soviets. He started to chip that away. He'd tell his players over and over that someone was going to beat those guys, that they thought they were better than they were. He started joking about the Soviet captain, Boris Mikhailov, saying that he looked like Stan Laurel from the old Laurel and Hardy movies.

Jimmy Craig came up with a strategy to play the Russians. For him, playing one period against them was equal to playing a whole game against anybody else. So he decided to break each period into four five-minute segments. After each segment he'd start all over again. And at the end of each period he'd go to the locker room to get completely undressed so that he could mentally and physically prepare for the second "game." That way, if he was playing great he wouldn't get too comfortable and if he was playing badly he wouldn't carry that into the next period.

The first medal-round game had been scheduled months before for Friday, February 22, at five p.m. At that time no one had expected that it would match up the world's two superpowers. American television asked to have it moved into primetime, but the Soviets refused. So ABC taped the game at five p.m. and broadcast it at eight. One of the most memorable moments in American sports history would be watched by most Americans three hours after it happened.

In the locker room just ahead of the game, Herb Brooks gave the most inspirational speech of his life. He told the guys, "You were born to be a player. You were meant to be here. This moment is yours."

The players skated onto the ice and looked up. The arena was packed. People were waving American flags everywhere. In the first minutes, the Americans surprised the Soviets with how fast and emotionally they played. Still, the Soviets scored first. Then the unexpected happened. Buzz Schneider raced down the left wing, took a slap shot just over the blue line, and beat goaltender Vladislav Tretiak, tying the game. The Soviets scored again, and it looked as if the period would end 2–1.

Then, with only five seconds left in the first, Dave Christian picked up the puck in his own zone and shot it up the ice. The Soviets had already let up, thinking the period was basically over. But Mark Johnson chased that puck down, deked Tretiak, and slipped it in with one second left. The period ended 2–2.

In the second period, Soviet coach Viktor Tikhonov pulled a surprise move. He replaced Tretiak—a guy known as one of the best goalies of all time—with his backup, Vladimir Myshkin. I've had the opportunity to sit down with Tretiak and hear his opinion about it. Tretiak was the biggest star in Russia—and maybe still is, thanks to what he did in '72 as a twenty-year-old goalie——and I think it used to drive Tikhonov crazy. Tretiak was also a huge star in Canada. Tikhonov was very egotistical. He wanted to show everyone that his coaching was the reason they were winning the Olympics, not Tretiak's goaltending. And to this day, Tretiak thinks that's why he was pulled.

With a new goalie in the net for the Russians, Herb didn't want his team to adjust. He wanted them to play with the same intensity, the same way they'd been playing from the start, so he went up and down the bench saying, "Don't change a thing. Don't change a thing because they changed goalies. Don't change a thing. Play the same way."

In the third period, the Soviets looked dominant again. Then on a rush, a shot from Dave Silk slipped through a Soviet defenseman's skate right onto Mark Johnson's stick. Before Myshkin could move, it was in the net and the score was tied. A minute later, the American captain, Mike Eruzione, scored.

Now the Americans were leading, just ten minutes away from a shot at a gold medal. Brooks kept walking up and down the bench saying, "Play your game. Play your game." He repeated it a thousand times at least.

Jimmy Craig was in the zone. He wasn't going to get scored on. When a goalie is in that kind of zone, especially in playoffs, his ability to anticipate the shot is as good as the rest of his skill set. And Craig wasn't alone—the whole team was flying out there. When you go into a series without the sense of entitlement the Russians had, it gives you the intensity you need to get to that extra level.

The game ended 4–3 for the U.S. The Americans swarmed the ice. They could hardly believe it—they had to keep telling themselves, "We beat them. We. Beat. Them." It was the first time the Russians had lost an Olympic game in twelve years. The celebration spread right across the country. No sporting event had ever stirred that much emotion from coast to coast.

B ut the Americans still had to beat Finland for the gold. Brooks came into the dressing room before the game with a very short speech. "If you lose this game, you will take it to your effing grave." He took a couple of steps, turned around, and said, "Your effing grave."

In the second period in the game against the Finns, the U.S. was down 2–1 and Brooks was so angry he didn't want to go into the dressing room. He said, "Craig, you go in there and you get them going." But when Patrick went in he discovered he didn't have to say anything, since all the guys were already saying it. "Don't worry, Craig, we're not going to let this one go." And so Craig turned around, walked out, and said to Brooks, "Don't worry. We're not going to lose." They were all winners, they all knew how to win. The final score was U.S. 4, Finland 2.

As Jimmy Craig stood in his crease looking for his dad in the crowd, an American from Syracuse named Peter Cappuccilli Jr. jumped over the glass with the U.S. flag in his hands and draped it over Jimmy's shoulders. Jimmy held it tight around him because it would be disrespectful to let it fall to the ground. Once he made eye contact with his dad, then he would celebrate.

T here are so many intangibles in the game of hockey. Skill will get you only so far. Strength and speed get you only so far. In some sports, the player can focus on one job, and put everything into going out there and executing. But in hockey, there is so much going on, so fast, that even the most skilled player is going on instinct. Ever notice that a guy on a breakaway almost always scores, but the same guy will be shut down over half of the time in the shootout? When you're on a breakaway, all you see is net. When you're in a shootout, you're thinking about the goalie. That's because when you're in the flow of the game, you are fueled by desire. You are running on instinct. Without that passion, you're not really in a hockey game.

There is no denying that the 1980 Soviet team had as much skill as anyone could handle. They had dominated international play for years heading into the Olympics, and they continued to dominate in the years ahead. They took the gold medals in 1984 and 1988. And in 1981 they got their revenge on Team USA with a 4–1 win in the Canada Cup. Then they absolutely smoked the very best players Canada could assemble in the final. That team included guys like Ray Bourque, Mike Bossy, Marcel Dionne, Denis Potvin, Larry Robinson, Bryan Trottier, and many other future Hall of Famers, myself included—and we were thrashed 8–1 by the Russians.

The Big Red Machine, as Soviet hockey was known back then, was truly intimidating. They had one five-man line known as the Green Unit. Sergei Makarov, Igor Larionov, and Vladimir Krutov were the forwards, and Alexei Kasatonov and Viacheslav Fetisov were on the blue line. They were always on the ice together, and when they were, pretty much no one else in the world could touch the puck. It took us years to figure out how to defend against them.

But in 1980, the American team brought something to that game that the Russians didn't. They were so focused, so passionate, that they weren't thinking about the Russians. They were just playing their game. And when you play that way, most of the time the puck bounces your way.

If it hadn't been for the U.S. beating Russia and winning gold on home ice, you have to ask yourself, Would there be hockey in Dallas? Would there be hockey in Florida and in L.A.? Because that win was a defining moment for hockey. It was the moment the game started to grow in the United States. The sport wasn't big in the United States at that time. It had its cities—Boston, New York, Philadelphia—but there was very little interest in the South, for example. The realization that Americans could be the best in the world inspired young people across the country. They wanted to be one of those players who achieved a miracle.

Twenty-Seven

THE 1984 CANADA CUP

We had a lot on the line going into the Canada Cup in 1984.

We were a mix of older and younger guys, but one thing a lot of us had in common was that we were looking for revenge for the beating the Russians had given us in 1981. We knew it wasn't going to be easy. Canada's weakness in 1972 was overconfidence, but we certainly weren't suffering from that in 1981. We had six weeks of training camp before the 1984 Cup. That meant a two-hour skate in the morning, a two-hour skate in the afternoon, and then on the bike for five miles. Every guy did this every day for four weeks. The theory was that because the Russians took no time off, and we took June and July off, we had to catch up in August.

I knew personally how tough it was going to be. My first experience with them one-on-one was at the 1977–78 world juniors. We had a really good team—all twenty guys on our team went on to play in the NHL. But I remember watching the Russians in warm-up and thinking, "Wow. These guys are going to be tough." I was sixteen, and in particular I was watching Sergei Makarov and defenseman

Viacheslav Fetisov. The way they skated put them in a whole different league from us. It was a great game, but we lost 3–2. They won gold.

By 1981, most of their national team veterans—Mikhailov, Petrov, Kharlamov—were gone. The Soviets had a new regime: Fetisov, Krutov, Larionov, Shepelev, Khomutov. It's easier to intimidate younger guys, so we felt it was important to put a lot of pressure on them to try to get them back on their heels. We thought that was the key. If they were coming at you brimming with confidence they were going to make you look bad, so the only way to beat them, we thought, was to dent their armor and push forward with physical play and offensive pressure. It didn't exactly work out that way.

Their goalie, Vladislav Tretiak, was one of the greatest goaltenders ever. People in North America didn't get to see him very often. He was way ahead of his time, a hybrid butterfly and stand-up goaltender. A big, big man and stick strong, similar to today's NHL goalies. He had a training workout that was unheard of back then, and he had an outstanding read of the game. Back in the 1970s and 80s goaltenders worked off pure talent and a lack of fear. I'd love to see guys like Glenn Hall or Tretiak playing today in the bigger, lighter goaltenders' equipment. They'd be unbeatable.

One of the biggest thrills for me back in 1981 was playing on a line not only with Guy Lafleur but also with Gilbert Perreault. When I was a kid back in Brantford, skating on our backyard ice, I was Gordie Howe for a number of years, and then, because we got a lot of Buffalo Sabre games on TV—every second week or so there'd be a midweek game—I was Perreault for a while. I loved how he handled the puck, but I couldn't skate as well as he could, and so at some point I decided that maybe I wasn't Perreault after all.

Gilbert broke his ankle four games into the tournament, so Marcel Dionne replaced him on the line. Marcel was so hungry around the net. Nothing came between him and a loose puck. He was absolutely tenacious about it.

We felt confident in the first few games, but the Russians cured us of that. We just unraveled. We simply had no answers for the Soviets' talent. We were outshooting them for a while, but that didn't mean a lot against the Big Red Machine, because they didn't take a lot of shots. Or they didn't take a lot of shots that missed. They just moved the puck around until they saw the shot they wanted, and then the red light was on.

When we got down 4–1, we had to open up to get back in the game and the Russians just fed on that. They capitalized on every mistake we made. I think we fell into a real trap with them. Tretiak was standing on his head. And we were running around, while the Soviets' positioning seemed to be perfect. The moment when we knew we were beaten came when we were on the power play. We got the puck deep and were trying to get set up down low when the puck squirted out to the high slot—right onto the stick of Vladimir Krutov, of all people, who was already moving up-ice. It was turning into a one-on-two, and he had his choice of Denis Potvin and Guy Lafleur, who was playing the point on the power play. He wisely came in on the left, where he froze Lafleur with a fake windup, then stepped around him and picked the corner on Mike Liut. At that point Liut kind of gave up. You could just see it.

We lost to the Russians 8–1. Mike Liut wears it, but it certainly wasn't his fault. We had only four shots in the third period. No goalie in the world is going to save you if you can't get shots on net. We could have had Jacques Plante in net and they would have won. I say this sincerely—they were so much better than we were that night. It was devastating. We felt that we'd let people down and let the country down.

S o now the stage was set for the '84 Canada Cup. This time we were a lot less confident.

Glen Sather was coaching. But we were really bad. I mean, just awful. The best players on the team, guys like Mike Bossy, Mark Messier, Paul Coffey, and Brent Sutter, were a little bit physically and mentally tired. The Oilers had been in the Stanley Cup final two years in a row and the Islanders had been to five finals in a row. We'd played a lot of hockey. On top of that, there were twelve guys from the Islanders and the Oilers on that team. So although it was born out of respect, there was friction. We'd spent two years at war with each other, and here we were sitting side by side in the locker room. Some guys were understandably gun-shy about the prospect of gelling together.

We lost a few games at the start. We got booed too. On September 6 we were playing against Sweden in Vancouver at the Pacific Coliseum. It wasn't a sellout crowd—just nine thousand fans in a building that holds sixteen thousand. Not only that, Sweden had a couple of guys playing for Vancouver, Patrik Sundstrom and Thomas Gradin, so it's likely that more than half of the fans were cheering for the Swedes. But we needed to win that particular game. Coff made an unbelievable defensive play on a two-on-one and then turned it back up-ice, brought it into the zone, and got a shot on goal. Bossy just tipped it in. They won 4–2, but I think it was one of the key moments in that series because it showed what we were capable of.

On September 7, we were in Calgary for a game against the Czechs the next day and had a team meeting at Yosemite Sam's restaurant. Bob Bourne, John Tonelli, and Mark Messier—two guys from the Islanders and one from the Oilers—stood up and basically got everybody on the same page. We were at risk of bombing out of the tournament altogether. After that, we pulled it together.

After we were smoked in 1981, Alan Eagleson, who was running the Canada Cups, came up with a plan to protect Team Canada from the kind of meltdown we had against the U.S.S.R. in 1981. After the round robin, the teams that placed first and fourth would play in one semifinal while the second- and third-place teams would play each other in another. The winner of the semis would meet in the final in a best-of-three series. Eagleson thought Canada might play one bad game, but no way could the Soviets beat us twice.

We finished fourth, with a record of 2–2–1. And who finishes number one, with a record of 5–0? The Russians, who had beaten us 6–3 in the round robin. It was going to come down to a single-game knockout after all.

There were probably only twelve or thirteen thousand fans at Calgary's Olympic Saddledome. I think it was a late afternoon game, so the timing wasn't perfect. Plus, tickets weren't cheap and we hadn't been playing well. I hadn't had a great tournament in '84. I just played okay. And I understood that because I wasn't playing great, my role had changed. I was on the third line. Brent Sutter's line with Bossy and Tonelli was playing really well, so Glen Sather was double-shifting them. (That's where your responsibility as a player comes in. In '84, the third line was where I fit during that game. And the only reason I bring this up is that when I was executive director for the Olympic team in 2002, I sat down with one of the players who was concerned about his ice time. Guys who make the Olympic team are used to playing their twenty-two to twenty-three minutes a night. I said, "Listen, it's not about how much ice time you get. Nobody remembers how much I played or didn't play. What they remember is that we won.")

I thought we played great that game. It was a very physical game, and very emotional. John Tonelli was a bulldozer along the boards all night, and he scored the first goal on the power play. But the Soviets scored to tie it up again, then Makarov went end-to-end, split the defense, and buried a backhand to take the lead. Vladimir Myshkin was standing on his head. But late in the third I found Doug Wilson drifting in from the left point and he sent it to overtime.

Paul Coffey and Doug Wilson were out on defense. Vladimir Kovin was coming in on a two-on-one with Mikhail Varnakov. It looked dangerous for Canada. But when Paul saw Kovin dip his shoulder, he knew the pass to Varnakov was coming. What followed was probably the most famous poke check in history. Paul snagged the puck and went racing back the other way. He shot, and the puck went into the corner, where Tonelli and Mike Bossy were scrumming with the Soviets. Tonelli would not be denied. He came out with the puck, fed Paul Coffey at the right point, who uncorked the shot. Mike Bossy tipped it in. So it was an Islander to an Oiler to an Islander. But in that particular game, we were all Team Canada.

During the handshake after the game, Igor Larionov quietly asked me to meet him back at his hotel. So a bunch of us tracked him and Vladimir Kovin down in the lobby and snuck them out to a restaurant on Calgary's Electric Avenue to talk about hockey and life in general. I was struck by how intelligent Larionov was—he lived his life the way he played the game. That is, he saw the big picture. He had long-term plans to come to the NHL, as long as he could do it properly. But what impressed me was how much English he understood. (As I was talking to him I kept thinking, "So when our guys talked to each other about where to stand and what to do on the faceoff, he understood us all along . . .") That's one of the amazing things about sports, that players from opposite sides of the deepest rivalry in the game could come together and talk about all the things they have in common. That is something I will always remember about that tournament.

W e met Kent Nilsson and the Swedes in the best-of-three final after they surprised the Americans 9–2 in the semis. But we had shaken the monkey off our backs by then, and there was no way Sweden was going to slow us down. We swept them pretty decisively. It was great to be back on top, but we knew that the Russians had given us all we could handle. We had to dig pretty deep to come out with that overtime win. And there was more white-knuckled hockey still to come.

Twenty-Eight

THE 1987 CANADA CUP

A lot of people think the 1976 edition of Team Canada was the best ever. And it was an absolutely incredible roster. In fact, just about every guy on that team ended up in the Hall of Fame. Bobby Orr, Bobby Hull, Bobby Clarke, for starters. Guy Lafleur, Larry Robinson, Phil Esposito, and on and on.

I don't want to say that the 1987 Canada Cup team was better than those guys. But I think the best-of-three series for the championship was some of the best hockey ever played. For one thing, the Soviets were stacked. They were always good, of course. They were always skilled and disciplined, and ruthless. But the 1987 squad may have been their best ever. Certainly the famous KLM Line of Krutov, Larionov, and Makarov has been called the most dangerous line of all time. But so many of those guys were just so good, and so strong. Viacheslav Fetisov, Valeri Kamensky, Alexei Kasatonov—they were all incredible players individually, and they played even better together. There is no doubt in my mind that they were the best team in the world in September 1987. Just looking at the roster, they were better than Team Canada.

During an exhibition game in the pre-tournament I asked Igor Larionov whether he'd like to bring some of the guys over for a barbecue at my dad's place. They were staying near Hamilton, about half an hour away. He said they'd love to, but that his coach, Viktor Tikhonov, and about three KGB guys had to come too. When they got there, Tikhonov wouldn't allow any of them to have a cold beer, and so I took them downstairs to show them the hockey memorabilia my dad had in the basement. While my dad's friend Charlie Henry guarded the door at the top of the stairs, we passed around some beers. Today it sounds kind of silly, but they weren't allowed to drink at all.

The Soviet guys would pick my brain on how to get to the NHL, although they were adamant about not defecting. They were too proud of their country. They didn't even like to mention the prospect because it was really dangerous to even whisper about it. In the late 1930s, Igor's grandfather had said something about Stalin, and as a result his family had been exiled from Moscow to Voskresensk, a factory town so dirty with soot that the snow fell black.

In the mid-1980s, under Mikhail Gorbachev's perestroika policy, Soviet sports had to self-fund. So by the end of the decade, the Soviet Hockey Federation decided to sell a few players to the NHL, which paid $3 million in total for Sergei Makarov (Calgary Flames), goalie Sergei Mylnikov (Quebec Nordiques), and Krutov and Larionov (Vancouver Canucks). Fetisov's dream finally came true. He and fellow defensemen Alexei Kasatonov and Sergei Starikov signed with the New Jersey Devils. Each player was paid about $100,000.

Things were going to be different in '87. There were more games played back in the east. Glen Sather had coached so much hockey that he stepped aside and pushed for John Muckler to be assistant coach along with Jean Perron. Mike Keenan was head coach. He made some controversial choices in the way he put the team together—when Scott Stevens is cut and Normand Rochefort is playing, try to figure that one out—but it worked. Cam Neely, Wendel Clark, Steve Yzerman, and Patrick Roy were all late cuts, which just shows you the depth of the talent available.

At the beginning it was a déjà vu of 1984. We started crappy. We weren't losing, but the team was not gelling whatsoever and every game felt like a slog. It was really awful. We had a big team meeting with the management side—Bobby Clarke, Serge Savard, and Phil Esposito—with everyone trying to get to the bottom of what was wrong and what we needed to do. Just as in '84, the conversation was about the top players who'd played so much hockey. The Oilers especially were physically and mentally tired. Mike had us wearing full equipment at a couple of the practices while going hard, and so one of the things the management and coaching staff agreed to do was to back off a little bit and let us regroup.

There was a pre-tournament game in Hamilton where we got clocked pretty good, and then we were really flat in the tournament opener in Calgary. Mike was steamed. He told me to make sure that everyone made the team meal at the hotel because wanted to speak to us. Some of the guys weren't happy because we were hoping for a chance to go out and relax. After we ate, Mike got up and said how ticked off he was. But then he said, "As a result, I want everyone to get their butts back on that bus. We're all going out together. Everybody!" That night we shut down a little country-and-western bar.

The next morning we got on the plane and started playing one of the longest card games I've ever been involved in—and one of the most fun. In the days before laptops, iPads, and iPhones, cards were a time-honored hockey tradition. We were flying commercial from Calgary to Toronto and then to Hamilton. As soon as we boarded we started playing a game called In Between, or Acey Deucey. In Vegas they call it Red Dog. That game lasted for the entire ride. The player on the left is the bettor. Using a double deck, the dealer puts down two cards face-up. The player bets. The dealer puts down another card between the two cards. If the card ranks between the two cards, the player wins and takes equal money from the pot.

We were screaming and yelling and guys were betting quite a bit of money. I was partnered with Paul Coffey. We started going big and kept losing, so the pot got bigger. When we got to Toronto, the pot was still alive, maybe $20,000, and so we picked up the game again on the bus.

Claude Lemieux, who was just a kid at the time, had pretty much left a full paycheck on the table. If you didn't have the money you had to bail out because it was cash only. Claude looked down and saw that he had great cards, a two and a king. He needed his money back. So he looked over at Mario Lemieux and said, "Will you back me up?" Mario winked and said, "Go for it." Ray Bourque was dealing. He pulled a five and Claude was whole again. We had just a great, great time.

I liked the way Mike Keenan coached. I think it was pretty smart the way he was able to find the right chemistry in such a short period of time. We had so many good players that Keenan would mix up the lines a number of times. He liked a physical presence on all the lines, so he spread it out and I think it served him well. The guys had a lot of respect for him.

The best coaches all have different styles, but they all let the players play to their strengths by adapting the game to those strengths. That gives players confidence. And as that confidence builds, the players become harder to beat.

A good coach also knows how to handle the ups and downs. When you win, players can get overly confident and that can be a problem too. So a coach has to be able to manage both overconfidence and underconfidence.

Mike put Mario and me together for the first time. We hadn't played on the same line because we were both centermen. But Mike had seen us score on a power play in the middle of the tournament and decided to leave us together. Still, when Mike first put us out there together we'd skate in the same place, side by side in the offensive zone. That's because we both saw the ice the same way. But after a couple of games we could read each other and I didn't have to adapt my game in any way. We started as linemates when we played against the Swedes, then the Soviets, followed by the Czechs. We tied the Russians and won the other two games, and everything propelled forward from there.

Hockey used to have a lot of famous lines. I've already mentioned the late 60s' GAG (goal-a-game) line in New York, with Jean Ratelle, Rod Gilbert, and Vic Hadfield. The Bruins' Espo Line, with Phil Esposito, Wayne Cashman, and Ken Hodge, was big. The Canadiens had the Dynasty Line, with Guy Lafleur, Jacques Lemaire, and Steve Shutt. And the Kings' Triple Crown Line, with Marcel Dionne, Charlie Simmer, and Dave Taylor, was another big one. But in my era there weren't too many famous lines.

Selfishly, helping Mario become a better player made me a better player. Mario was just a kid, but he had so much God-given talent. He was so big and yet so fluid on his blades, almost like a figure skater. Some guys can elevate their game to a greater level, and that's what I saw Mario do. The older guys helped get him ready in training camp and all through the round robin. Learning from some of the great players on the team meant that he not only had a lot of new moves in his arsenal; I think it also lit his fire. I advised him to do two things. First, I wanted him to watch what the others were doing and then follow their lead. I told him to look at Mess, who was always the first guy on the ice at practice, never late. Second, I wanted him to let me be the passer so that he could shoot. He had these tremendous wrists. As for accuracy, he was an atomic clock.

Mario and I were part of the big offensive production, but the guys in the dressing room who grinded it out were every bit as important. I look at impact players like Michel Goulet and Dale Hawerchuk. They were put in a position to do whatever had to be done in order to win. Goulet, who was the number-one gunner on his team, described himself as a plumber during that series, but it didn't discourage him at all. He was just proud to be part of the group. Everyone felt that way. Craig Hartsburg was probably sixth defenseman. He was vocal on the bench and in the room, a great motivator. Every guy tried to find a way to help—Rick Tocchet, Brent Sutter, Brian Propp, go down the line. They accepted different roles from what they had on their own teams.

The 1987 Canada Cup may have been one of most skilled hockey series of all time, but it might have been the most vicious hockey too. If some of the stuff that went on happened today there'd be huge suspensions for both sides. The Russians may have been a little subtler about it, but they certainly had a fierce competitiveness. They were so strong physically that every battle was very tough. And remember, these were two teams with a lot of pride on the line. A passion to win and hating the other team feel a lot alike. That year at the world juniors, a stacked but chippy Team Canada had lost its shot at a gold medal because of a bench-clearing brawl against the Soviets. Theo Fleury said that Valeri Zelepukin, the guy he scrapped with in that game, was the strongest he had ever played against. Those Russians weren't just good. They knew how to handle themselves.

We won because Mike Keenan outcoached Tikhonov. Mike was really one of the best bench coaches ever. Still, I thought Tikhonov was a really good technical coach and that the system they played was tremendous: the way they broke out, how they took their time, how they killed penalties. Their five-man units and their power play. And it was all so special because of their patience. They'd hold the puck for two full minutes just to get one good shot.

In this day and age, the key to success is to get people moving around so that you get the puck back to the point. You might get eight shots in on one power play. The Russians never did that. If they didn't see what they wanted, they'd go back and restart.

Where Tikhonov was weak as a coach was his stubbornness. He was very predictable and he didn't change on the fly. He thought his athletes were better than our athletes, and so he never shortened his bench. He would roll six defensemen and four forward lines. Every player was thought to be as good as the guy in front of him, so the rotation never changed. At the beginning of the period the first line would start, then the second line and the third line, and then the fourth line would go. Soviet hockey may have been a machine, but there was a downside to that. They didn't adapt as the game went on.

It's only fairly recently that they've even pulled the goalie if they're down one goal. It wasn't that they didn't know how. It was just that they were confident that they were going to score with only five attackers. It started to change a little in the late 80s. You'd see the Big Five get double-shifted every now and then, but it was rare. Over the years, Soviet players got a bad reputation for not having heart. I've talked to them, and I know they cared about the game just as much as any Canadian. It's possible they cared even more—for them, every game was an audition. I can see why people might think they didn't play with passion, but it has more to do with coaching than with the players' personalities. They were just forced to stick to the script.

Glen Sather or Mike Keenan might start Messier's line in the second period and my line in the third to get the matchup they wanted, but Tikhonov would start his best five guys every period. If they got a power play he'd put out the next unit up in rotation, whereas coaches like Mike, Glen, or Scotty Bowman would double-shift players, with Lafleur, Bobby Orr, and Denis Potvin playing every other shift.

Our bench coaching was always better than theirs, all the way back to '72. Had we played the Russians in the way they're coached now, where they double-shift guys like Alex Ovechkin and play three lines and go down to four defensemen, history might look different.

The best game I ever played in was the second of the 1987 finals against the Russians. The level of competition that night in Hamilton was so high. It was an emotional game too, because we'd just lost 6–5 in Game One in Montreal after Vyacheslav Bykov threw a shot in front of the net and it deflected off my skate for the tying goal. I'd come out afterward to see my dad standing there looking angry. He was rarely critical like that, but he said, "You know, that loss was your fault. You stayed on the ice too long and that goal cost you guys." I'd just told him that I'd gotten permission for him to fly with us on the charter to Hamilton. So I only looked at him and said, "You're welcome."

On our way to Hamilton for the next game, I thought about what my dad had said and started feeling pretty grumpy. I kept thinking, "Hamilton? Why Hamilton?"

My favorite arena to play in other than Edmonton at the time was Maple Leaf Gardens. I always played well there. In those days the glass behind the players' bench was only a few feet high, meaning that if someone stood up behind us they could reach out and touch us. At Maple Leaf Gardens and the Montreal Forum we were practically sitting in the stands. It was wild, and players loved it. I remember thinking, "Wow, this is so cool." There were two seats next to the end of the bench at the Gardens and my dad used to sit in one of them. I'd even be able to talk to him during the game. But he was so nervous that I'd say something like, "Hey, how you doin'?" and he'd barely be able to answer.

No one had ever really played in Hamilton, so we didn't know what to expect. It wasn't an NHL city. In those days the games started at ten after eight, which was really late. I always got to the rink around three-thirty because once I was in the locker room no one could bug me and I could sit and have a coffee and talk to the trainers. But when I walked into Copps Coliseum it was dark and quiet, and again I thought, "Why not Maple Leaf Gardens?"

Anyway, I was wrong. Once we stepped onto the ice after the warm-up, the electricity in the arena was amazing. It charged us up. And because it was a smaller arena, the sound stayed inside. That kind of atmosphere virtually changes your gravity.

The game started off with a bang, back and forth. It felt like one of those nights when the puck just seemed to follow me around.

Mark and Mario and I played every second shift. The Russians were playing four lines. The tempo was extreme. We were in the zone, but the Soviets were fresher. I remember coming to the bench and looking at Mark and saying, "Mess, I don't think I can go." We'd almost fall down on the bench. But twenty seconds later Mike would walk behind us and give us a little kick in the arse—"You're up again"—and we'd jump over the boards.

I had five assists, and Mario got three goals. We headed into double overtime. It was a pretty spectacular night. I was feeling very confident. I'd take my chances in overtime with Grant Fuhr in net any day. And he didn't let us down.

He made some saves that were incredible. We won the game and the jubilation was electric.

I was staying at my folks' place that night because Brantford's just twenty minutes from Hamilton. I drove home with them. It was two a.m. We ordered pizza and I sat back on the couch, looked up at the ceiling, and thought about what a great night it had been and just how important this series was. Losing would mean letting the country down. And then I exhaled for about five minutes.

When we skated on in Game Three, Copps Coliseum was vibrating again. The fans were all standing and cheering. But the tempo of Game Two had been so fast that Mario, Coffey, Messier, and I were a little tired. Sure enough, Makarov scored less than a minute in, and by eight minutes in we were down 3–0. The high-energy electricity was dying in the stands like burst balloons. A lot of the fans sat down.

And this is why I said earlier that Mike Keenan outcoached Tikhonov. He gave Mario, a couple other guys, and me a breather for about eight minutes while he double-shifted Brian Propp, Brent Sutter, and Rick Tocchet. Tocchet put the Russian defense back on their heels, especially along the boards. All of a sudden things weren't so easy for them. They were looking over their shoulders. Then Tocchet banged in a rebound on the power play, followed by a goal from Brian Propp. We gave up one more before the end of the first, but we were much happier trailing 4–2 than 3–0. We were back in the game.

When we went into the locker room, everyone was waiting for Mike to kind of blow up. Instead he walked in very calmly and said, "You guys will be part of one of the greatest comebacks in Canadian hockey history today." Then he left the room. It just seemed to relax us while at the same time it fired us up. And it worked. Larry Murphy scored from the right point. Then Sutter got another. When Dale Hawerchuk shoveled in his own rebound, we were back in front.

Mike idealized Scotty Bowman. I don't think there's any secret about that. Scotty had this reputation for being unreadable. He'd do things that were abnormal. People would be watching the game and saying, "Why is Bowman doing that?" He liked the surprise element. Like a card player, he didn't like to tip his hand. And he'd ask a lot of questions to try to find out as much as he could about the other team. He'd rather surprise than be surprised. And like Scotty, Mike kept some ice cubes in a little cup and would chew on them. But he had his own tricks too. Sometimes, when he wanted to give us a break, he'd throw pennies on the rink and the refs would have to stop the game to clean up the ice. He wasn't obvious about it; it's just that there were holes in his pockets. And I think

Mike really relished it when, as they did with Scotty, people would say, "Geez, what's Mike doing?"

So when it was 5–5 with a minute and a half to go, Mike put Mario, Dale, and me on the ice for a faceoff in our own zone. The three most offensive players in hockey for the most important faceoff of the series. As we went over the boards, Dale asked, "Are you gonna take the draw?" "No, no, Dale," I said, "you take it." So Dale was at center, Mario was on right wing at the hash marks, and I was just to his right. Larry Murphy was behind and Paul Coffey stood to the left of the hash marks.

Dale kind of lost the draw and Mario raced into the middle and grabbed the puck. Two Russians came toward him, but when they fell over each other, Mario chipped the puck toward the point. Mike Keenan's philosophy in hockey was always "Two guys on the puck," and so both Mario and I immediately went toward it. Mario did a pirouette to dodge a check. Now we had three Russians out of the way.

Mario feathered a soft pass to me up the left boards. I picked it up at the red line and carried the puck into the zone. Larry Murphy saw everything developing and just took off toward the net. The Russian defenseman, Igor Kravchuk, now had to cover me and Mario and also be in position to take away the pass to Larry, who was headed for the far post for a possible tap-in. Meanwhile, Hawerchuk got his stick on one of their backcheckers, Slava Bykov. This meant that when Mario came up as a trailer he was wide open. I dropped the puck back to Mario, and with 1:26 left in the game, he took two strides and ripped it over Myshkin's glove hand into the top corner.

So it wasn't so much what Mario and I did. Had Larry not gone to the net and had Dale not taken the backchecker out, we may never have scored. It goes back to Mike. Mike had enough confidence in Dale, Mario, and me—three offensive guys—to make the play.

Seeing the puck go in the net, we all had a feeling of elation. You could feel it right through that whole building. Larry Murphy called it the last of the "good versus evil" games.

Twenty-Nine

THE 1991 CANADA CUP

T hree things about 1991 stand out for me: the first is Eric Lindros, the second is Mark Messier, and the third is the strength of the American team.

Mike Keenan was now coaching in Chicago. I think there are only four players who played together in three Canada Cups from 1984 to 1991: Mess, Paul Coffey, Brent Sutter, and me. Three of Mike's guys made the team: Eddie Belfour, Steve Larmer, and Dirk Graham. We had one of the biggest camps ever, fifty-four guys. And even without Mario, Ray Bourque, Stéphane Richer, John Cullen, and Mark Recchi, we had some tremendous players.

Midway through training camp, Mike came up to me and said, "You know, Gretz, I want Eric Lindros to be on this team." Who wouldn't want Eric on their team? Even as a teenager he was a truly intimidating hockey player. At 6'4" and 235 pounds, his size alone made him someone you'd have to watch out for. But he could skate with anyone, he could stickhandle in close like a much smaller man, and his shot was a bomb. He could go through you, or he could go around you, and an open-ice hit from Eric Lindros was like stepping in front of a bus. Ulf Samuelsson found that out in our round-robin game against Sweden. Samuelsson is a big boy, but Eric absolutely rocked him. That was the end of the tournament for the Swede. Then Lindros knocked Martin Rucinsky of Czechoslovakia out of the tournament as well.

Mike Keenan told me that Eric would be captain of Team Canada someday, and so he wanted him to be around the guys on our team. I thought, "Wow, you're the coach, whatever you think, it's fine by us."

That 1991 team was stacked—possibly the most talented Team Canada I ever played on. We were deep. We were defensively dominant. If there was a weakness, it was up front, particularly with Mario Lemieux out of the lineup with a bad back. Toward the end of training camp, Keenan took me aside and told me he thought we needed Mark Messier if we were going to win. I told him I'd give Mark a call. When I reached him, he said, "I'll be there tomorrow."

That year, for the first time ever, the Russians weren't as much of a factor. It was the middle of the dissolution of the Soviet Union and so everything was up in the air. One hundred Soviet players had left for the NHL, teams in Europe, or North American minor leagues. Tikhonov was still in charge, but he left some of his best players, like Pavel Bure, Valeri Zelepukin, Evgeny Davydov, and Vladimir Konstantinov, at home because he was worried that they'd defect. In the end, the U.S.S.R. didn't even qualify for the playoff round.

The team that had the best chance of beating us was Team USA. The kids who had been inspired by the American victory at Lake Placid were just coming of age, and they were an impressive group. Players like Chris Chelios, Tony Granato, Brett Hull, Brian Leetch, Joel Otto, Craig Janney, Jeremy Roenick, Pat LaFontaine, Kevin

The NHL changed forever in 1967, and learned a lot about how to grow the game. The California Golden Seals had some strong hockey people in the front office, but never had much success on the ice or at the box office. The Minnesota North Stars did a lot of things right, and had a bona fide star in Bill Goldsworthy, but their best draft pick—Mike Modano—wouldn't win a Cup until the team was in Dallas. The Pittsburgh Penguins struggled early, but thanks to drafting the likes of Mario Lemieux, Jaromir Jagr, Evgeni Malkin, and Sidney Crosby, they are easily the most successful of the 1967 teams. (Seen here on the left is Kim Clackson. I always wanted to know where he was on the ice.)

The first expansion team to win the Cup was Philadelphia. They had balanced scoring, team toughness, and possibly the best goalie in the league in Bernie Parent, but the heart and soul of that team was their captain, Bobby Clarke. Over the years, people have asked me how I started using the space behind the net as my "office." I always tell them—from watching Bobby Clarke.

When the WHA came along, it gave players all kinds of new options. For a kid like me, who was too young to enter the NHL draft, it meant I could play pro hockey. Here I am in Junior B. In a couple of years I would be in Indianapolis. For a superstar like Bobby Hull, it meant the kind of negotiating power he could only have dreamed of earlier in his career. Here he is, holding a mock check for $1,000,000 as he arrives in the WHA.

I didn't last very long in Indianapolis, and to be honest I wasn't mature enough back then to be a major part of a new organization. I was traded eight games into the season, along with Eddie Mio and Peter Driscoll. When we hopped on this plane, though, negotiations were still in progress. We didn't even know where we were going to land, Edmonton or Winnipeg. Below, here I am in my first game as an Oiler. You can tell it's my first, because that was the only game I wore a CCM helmet. I switched to Jofa the next game and that was all I wore until I retired.

People often say that the Canadian roster at the 1976 Canada Cup was the best team ever to skate together. And it's tough to argue against that—Bobby Orr, Bobby Hull, Bobby Clarke, Marcel Dionne, and Denis Potvin would be pretty tough to beat. Still, Canada was smoked 8–1 by the Soviets at the next Canada Cup five years later. That was my first time facing the Big Red Machine, and I was impressed. Here I am with Guy Lafleur.

Every team has to learn how to win—and when they do, they tend to keep winning. It's no coincidence that Montreal has won the Cup so many times. They've had great players, and a culture of excellence. Here Guy Lafleur is coming over the boards to celebrate winning the 1979 Stanley Cup, followed by Yvon Lambert, Doug Risebrough, Mario Tremblay, and Pierre Mondou. Scotty Bowman coached that team, and brought some of that same culture to Detroit, where the Red Wings, led by Steve Yzerman, became the standard by which NHL organizations were judged.

We had a great team in Edmonton, but we were just kids. Here I am joking around in the dressing room with Dave Dryden and Brett Callighen. Below that is Mark Messier showing off his ping-pong skills. Even when we started getting serious, we never stopped having fun. Here are Jari Kurri and Glenn Anderson joking around with the Campbell Bowl. Some players think it's bad luck to touch it, but that never stopped us.

Every game in the old Smythe Division was a battle. Winnipeg always played us tough—here's Dave Babych hauling me down by my face. And our relationship with the Flames went beyond the word "rivalry." We knew that the road to the Stanley Cup ran through Calgary, and they knew the same about Edmonton. Here I am making my way into the Calgary zone, a step ahead of Rob Ramage and Jim Peplinski, thanks to a little interference.

One thing we learned from our first trip to the Stanley Cup final against the Islanders was that talent was never going to be enough to win a championship. To win, you need heart and a willingness to sacrifice. Mark Messier had all that (seen here on the left against another true competitor, Joel Otto). But you only win the Stanley Cup as a team. Everyone has a role. When we won our fourth Cup in 1988, we savored that more than ever.

Canada's roster in the 1984 Canada Cup was made up largely of Oilers and Islanders—and it took us a long time to come together as a team. One guy I really enjoyed playing with was Quebec Nordiques gunner Michel Goulet. And the 1987 Canada Cup was even more intense. I believe the Soviet team we played in the three-game final series may have been the best team ever to hit the ice. Even with players like Mario Lemieux, we had no business beating them. But we found a way. On the top right is Glenn Anderson getting position on Igor Larionov, one of the most complete players I've ever seen.

Two things stood out for me from the 1991 Canada Cup. The first was the arrival of Eric Lindros. The other thing was the emergence of the United States as a new rival. The Russians were quiet that year, but Team USA gave us all we could handle. That's me looking to pass around my future teammate and good friend Brian Leetch. By the time the 1996 World Cup rolled around, the Americans were ready to take us on. And they wanted to show it. Here Keith Tkachuk squares off against Claude Lemieux in the opening seconds of our first game against them. Canada won Game One of the three-game final, but the United States beat us in the next two to claim the title.

There will always be a spot for Dave Semenko and Marty McSorley on my team. They were good teammates, and they could play the game—they weren't just out there to fight. The role of the tough guy is changing, and fighting won't be in the league forever. But hockey is a rough game, and it's not easy to create space out there. So guys like Jarome Iginla, who combine toughness and skill, are never going to disappear.

You always want to win, whenever you step on the ice. But respect for your opponents is part of the game. When the L.A. Kings ran into the Toronto Maple Leafs in the 1993 conference final, both teams gave absolutely everything. We won in Game Seven, but to this day the performances of Doug Gilmour and Wendel Clark stand out as some of the most inspirational playoff hockey I've ever seen. In the end, we fell short against the Montreal Canadiens in the final, and I have to respect that too.

It's harder to win the Stanley Cup now than it has ever been, and harder still to build a dynasty under the salary cap. Those Montreal, New York, and Edmonton dynasties are probably a thing of the past. The closest we may come are the perennially elite teams, like the Blackhawks and Penguins, who manage to hold on to core players like Toews, Kane, and Keith, and Crosby, Malkin, and Letang. But I've still got a soft spot for Edmonton, and anyone who has seen Connor McDavid play knows it will be hard to stop him.

On the day of Gordie Howe's funeral, I heard someone say, "There were only three players who could turn a hockey arena into a cathedral—Jean Béliveau, Maurice Richard, and Gordie Howe." We have some special players in the league today, but I don't think we will ever see players who could lift their whole teams on their backs like that again. I am just glad that when I met my idol, he was even greater than I dreamed he would be.

No hockey player, no matter how good he is, accomplishes anything alone. We've all got teammates, and coaches, and all kinds of other people who help out. But family is most important of all. I wouldn't have got far without my parents, and I can't even imagine my life without Janet. I wouldn't be here without you.

Miller, Joey Mullen, Gary Suter, and Mike Modano had all grown up wanting to play hockey. Team USA was going to be a powerhouse.

Just a glance at that list tells you the American team in 1991 wasn't going to have a problem putting the puck in the net. Imagine Pat LaFontaine, Brett Hull, and Mike Modano on the power play. And they weren't going to be any fun to play against either. The U.S. was a tough, tough team. Midway through the round robin, after Czech right-winger Tomas Jelinek checked an American player, fracturing the guy's shoulder, Chelios knocked out Jelinek's front teeth with a cross-check.

But we had a really good tournament, moving through the round robin undefeated because our team was so deep. We rolled four lines and six defensemen. It was maybe the best hockey team I've ever played on as far as overall strength goes. We had chemistry, size, skill, commitment, and goaltending. Our six defensemen, Paul Coffey, Al MacInnis, Eric Desjardins, Scott Stevens, Larry Murphy, and Steve Smith, along with our goaltender, Bill Ranford, made it almost impossible to score against our team, simple as that.

We played our final game of the round robin against the U.S.S.R. in Quebec City. Keenan told me that Eric would be my roommate while we were there. No offense to Eric, but he was the last guy I wanted to hang out with in that particular city. A lot of people there were upset with Eric. Before the draft, he warned the Quebec Nordiques that he wouldn't report to camp if they chose him. They picked him anyway, he refused to report, and the two sides were locked into a battle of wills. His agent, Rick Curran, said that he'd talked to Bobby Orr, who advised Eric not to lose his late teenage years by playing somewhere he didn't fit. But the Nordiques' fans were furious that Lindros seemed to think that he was too good for their team. To make matters worse, an Associated Press article said that Steve Yzerman wouldn't report if he was traded to the Nordiques, either. But in fairness, it wasn't anything against the French for either of those guys, and it wasn't about the team. In 1991, the Nordiques were a young, exciting team with young guys like Joe Sakic, Owen Nolan, and Mats Sundin on the roster. It was about exchange rates and taxes. (Yzerman could fill up for $17 in Detroit, while a tank cost $44 in Quebec.)

I could see both sides of the argument. But I was also aware that Eric was getting bomb threats and that people were threatening to shoot him—and now Mike wanted me to share a room with him. I did not relish the prospect. I mean, I don't even like driving fast. I owned a Ferrari and drove it in second gear—to this day I've never had a speeding ticket. And I don't like heights, either. So I told Mike, "No way. Listen, I'll talk to the media. I'll calm people down. I'll do everything I can to protect him, but I am not going to risk getting blown up." I think Mike thought I was kidding, and so he put us together anyway. I didn't sleep a wink.

We tied the Russians 3–3, and Eric may have endeared himself to fans in Quebec City by scoring on the power play in the first period to tie the game up. We went on to beat Sweden in the semi-finals in what was Borje Salming's farewell to Maple Leaf Gardens. And then we faced Team USA in a best-of-three final.

I talked earlier about how, just before playoffs on March 22, 1990, I injured my back in a game against the Islanders. As a result I'd missed three out of ten playoff games that season. And now, in the first game of the Canada Cup final, on September 14, 1991, I was checked from behind by Gary Suter. That started up my back spasms again and I was out for the rest of the tournament.

With me gone, Mess and Coffey stepped in. Everybody loves the "Win one for the Gipper" moment in the dressing room. Guys really rally around it. But Mess did something different. He knew that the team had to get back to a levelheaded kind of focus at the drop of the puck. He didn't want guys looking for revenge on Suter, and he didn't want anyone thinking about how things might have been different if I had been in the lineup. So between periods, Mess told the guys to play as if I'd never been on the team. That way there wouldn't be a hole. The guys responded, and Canada won the first game 4–1.

Game Two was a couple of days later, and the media was all over Gary Suter for what a lot of people thought was a questionable hit. I can't say it was fun, but if I had been a little closer to the boards it probably would have been just another bruising hit. I have never believed it was Gary's intention to injure me. Trust me, I've been hit harder than that, and I guarantee that a few American players were hit harder than that by our guys.

In Game Two, the score was tied at the end of the second period. The coaches were in the dressing room and everyone was upset. Mike's Chicago guys took over the room and calmed things down. And when they got back on the ice, Steve Larmer scored a shorthanded goal, making Suter the goat. Dirk Graham got the insurance goal.

It was a big win for us, but still, it was scary how well the U.S. played. The difference between them and the Russians was that the Americans played our game. Their coach, Bob Johnson, was just a very positive, great guy. He'd coached the Flames during some of the biggest battles against the Oilers, and he'd just coached the Penguins to their first Stanley Cup that year. Sadly, he was diagnosed with brain cancer during training camp, and his assistant, Tim Taylor, had to take over. But right to the end, Bob saw it as his mission to develop U.S. players. In a letter, one of the last things he told his players was that "U.S.A. hockey needs identity. This is our chance to reach out for some." It was just a matter of time before the Americans had the same number of great players we had.

The Canada Cup had been an Alan Eagleson project from the very beginning. At one time he was arguably the most powerful guy in hockey. As an agent he represented the best player in the world at the time in Bobby Orr, as an executive he ran the players' union, and as a businessman he rubbed elbows with the owners. He was so close to the Canada Cup that when the Soviets packed up the trophy to take it home in 1981, Eagleson personally wrestled it back as they were getting on their bus. But complaints by agents Ron Salcer and Ritch Winter and the former director of the NFLPA Ed Garvey led to an investigation by a reporter, Russ Conway, which found that Eagleson had been embezzling money from the NHLPA and the players he represented.

The FBI and the RCMP got involved, and Eagleson was forced to resign from the Hockey Hall of Fame. He lost his Order of Canada. And in 1998, he would be sentenced to eighteen months in prison. As he read out Eagleson's sentence, the judge said, "Power corrupts."

So in 1996, as he was being investigated, Eagleson was out of the picture. The Canada Cup became the World Cup of Hockey. The tournament was split into two divisions, with the Czechs, Finns, Germans, and Swedes in a European pool and the Canadians, Americans, Slovaks, and Russians in a North American pool.

This time, we knew we had to be ready for the Americans. And we knew they would be coming for us. I'd just finished the season with Brett Hull in St. Louis and then signed with the Rangers as an unrestricted free agent on July 21, 1996. Both the U.S. team's captain, Brian Leetch, and their goalie, Mike Richter, were my new teammates. But when you play international hockey, you play for your country. So no matter how much money you make or who you play for professionally, I think most guys will agree that your country comes first.

People ask me who the most underrated hockey player is, and I'd have to say Brian Leetch. Yes, he's won the Calder (1989) and the Conn Smythe (1994) and the Norris (1992, 1997), but he was such an incredible teammate. With his energy and abilities, along with his willingness to block shots and do everything possible for the team, he had the heart of a lion.

Leetch, who was from Connecticut, had been in the bantam playoffs in Massachusetts, staying at a hotel with his team, when the tape-delayed Miracle game came on TV. He remembers running around the hallways with the other boys, doing what eleven- and twelve-year-olds do at a hotel, when the parents and coaches rounded them up and gave them a little background on the political climate and what a big underdog the U.S. was. Leetch told me that every time the U.S. scored, they'd jump up and down on the beds and throw pillows around.

By the 1996 World Cup, the Americans had guys like Brian who'd played through different Olympic teams and had experience in Canada Cups. Added to that, they had Mike Richter, who'd given their first great goaltending performance since Jimmy Craig. Mike had been the U.S. backup goalie at the '88 Olympics, and since then he'd continued to get better. He was always searching for a way to get the most out of himself, whether it was through nutrition, or training, or psychology. He'd worked on positive thinking and imagery before it became mainstream for athletes. When the Rangers let John Vanbiesbrouck go to the Florida Panthers in the 1993 expansion draft, via a trade with Vancouver, they'd obviously decided that Mike was their guy. And then of course he won the Cup in '94. In '96 he was not only the best goalie in the United States, he was possibly the best in the world.

Team USA added more and more players to the mix, guys who were not just good NHLers. These guys were the stars on their teams. They had speed to burn in Mike Modano and Dougie Weight, and they had a pure sniper in Brett Hull. But they could also play what we thought of as the Canadian game: the Hatcher brothers on defense and guys like Keith Tkachuk, Billy Guerin, and John LeClair up front. And they had a warrior in Chris Chelios. He was the Americans' answer to Mark Messier. Every game was a Game Seven when Chelly pulled on the Team USA sweater. They didn't just want to beat us—they wanted to beat us at our own game.

Mind you, we brought a very physical team to that tournament. We had a lot of big boys, led by Eric Lindros, who by then was dominating the NHL, but they were also guys who played to intimidate, like Scott Stevens and Brendan Shanahan. The stage was set for fireworks. And the teams didn't disappoint. Keith Primeau and Bill Guerin scrapped in the pre-tournament, then went at it again only twenty seconds into the round-robin game, as Claude Lemieux and Keith Tkachuk also squared off. We won Game One of the finals in Philadelphia, but we needed overtime to do it.

Then we lost Game Two. I think it's safe to say that we outplayed them in Game Three in Montreal. We'd bombarded them in the second period, but Mike Richter kept them in. Then we scored early in the third to go ahead 2–1. But we did not manage the lead well. You could feel the Americans gaining confidence. Brett Hull made a great tip, reaching behind and deflecting the puck down, and so we were 2–2 late into the third. And then less than a minute later Tony Amonte scored again. Suddenly we had to open up to get back into the game, and the Americans buried two more. And all of a sudden it was over. They'd won. It was kind of stunning.

I think what hurt us was losing Mark Messier in the second game. Mark was the guy who brought us all together. He was back in Game Three, but everyone could see he was not 100 percent. Especially in the third period, when we were holding on to a lead, Mark was the kind of guy who could really make a difference.

They scored four goals on us in just over three minutes in the third, and that may be why it felt so disappointing to us. After such a close, hard-fought series, it was tough to see the team come apart like that, even for just a few minutes. I've said it before: hockey is a game of emotion. You can let that carry you to victory, but when you lose, it can be crushing. I am not surprised when I see guys cry when they lose a long playoff series. It's not that they're feeling sorry for themselves. It's that the emotion can carry you down as quickly as it carries you up.

But hockey players also learn how to move on. And as disappointing as that loss was, there were a lot of positives in that tournament. The game was growing. It wasn't just Canada and the U.S.S.R. in the final every year, with Sweden and Czechoslovakia playing for third place. Finland was coming on, and now the United States had beaten a strong Canadian team. Honestly, it would be boring if Canada won every year.

Now we had a true rival right next door. It didn't feel good at all at the time, but that was a good thing.

Thirty

THE 1998
WINTER OLYMPICS

I n 1988, the Winter Olympics were held in Calgary. Canadians couldn't help thinking about the American home-ice victories in 1960 and 1980. They wanted a "miracle" of their own. But Canada didn't even finish in the medals (despite having Andy Moog in net).

For years, Canadian hockey fans would watch as everyone else celebrated gold medals and grumble that if only we could send our best players, we would show them how it was done. In 1998, we were going to get our chance. Back in 1992, when the NBA put together a dream team for Barcelona, Summer Olympic basketball changed. And in 1998 at Nagano, Japan, the same thing happened in hockey. The NHL was finally going to allow pros into the Games. We were going to get our Dream Team.

I was probably the last player chosen. After our World Cup loss two years earlier, Team Canada was going with a younger crop. I understood that, but it meant no one really knew where I fit in. I was the old guy. In fact, I ended up playing only one more year of professional hockey after that.

Philadelphia's GM, Bobby Clarke, was the new guy in charge—and just as Glen Sather had built his Canada Cup teams around the Oilers, Bobby was building his Olympic team around the Flyers: Eric Lindros, Rod Brind'Amour, and Eric Desjardins.

We all met in Vancouver, and then traveled as a team on a charter flight to Japan. Remember the top part of 747s? That's where all the coaches and managers were holed up. They were bringing the players up one at a time to meet with the guys and to explain the rules, roles, and responsibilities. Assistant coach Wayne Cashman and I were good friends, so he let me know that I'd be playing a little bit on the power play, and was probably sort of going to play on the fourth line, and was I comfortable with that? I basically said, "Yes, that's how I was raised. You earn your ice time. If I'm playing well I'm sure I'll get on the ice, so I'm not worried about it."

There was a lot of chatter in the media and behind the scenes about how the hockey guys were going to get special treatment—that we'd run roughshod over the Olympic Village and stolen the limelight from the other athletes. That didn't happen. I don't mean this to sound egotistical, but our team actually helped bring all the Canadian athletes together. In the Canadian common room, we got the CBC TV feed with Ron MacLean and Brian Williams. We made plans with the other athletes to hang out together: "All right, what time are we meeting in the common room? What are we going to watch tonight? Who's playing ping-pong?" When snowboarder Ross Rebagliati came in after he'd won gold for the giant slalom, Brendan Shanahan was the first guy to jump up and shake his hand. It was such a cool moment—his win was our win. We were one big team for Canada.

The NHL guys loved the whole Olympics package. It took us back to our roots when we were twelve, thirteen, fourteen and used to get billeted with families at hockey tournaments. The players ate it up. I loved that we had three or four guys to each dorm. My roommates were Martin Brodeur, Rob Brind'Amour, and Steve Yzerman, and I think that, for all of us, being away from the distractions of friends, family, and the media brought us back to what hockey was all about. Our dorm had one room with two beds and then two rooms each with a single bed. It wasn't fancy by any means, but it was cool. We really liked it. And since goalies work on different schedules, we all said, "You know, Marty, since you're a goalie, you take a single." That's when Brodeur said, "No, it's okay. I'm not playing."

We were all shocked—"What do you mean you're not playing?" Marty was possibly the best goalie in the world at the time, and he went on to set several records, including most wins in the NHL. He had incredible reflexes, and he handled the puck so well that he was like a third defenseman when the other team dumped the puck in. The NHL finally decided to bring in the "Brodeur Rule" to prevent him from quarterbacking the breakout. Any team would want Marty in the net.

But he was fine with sitting. "In my meeting on the plane they told me. I'm the third goalie, I'm not going to play." He hadn't said a word about it, and he wasn't complaining. "Hey, listen, don't tell anyone," Marty continued. "This is not a big thing, and I don't want it to be an issue in the locker room. That's just the way it is." He was such a team guy, and so professional about it, that it was unreal.

We had a really good tournament. We were undefeated in the round robin, and even handled Team USA without much trouble, beating them 4–1. We gave up only four goals against in the first four games. Team Canada usually starts slowly, as guys from different teams take time to figure out how to play together. But we were firing on all cylinders from the beginning.

And in the semis we had a great game against the Czechs. We were controlling the play and skating them into the ice. They were just trying to hang on, and they did. We were going into overtime, tied 1–1.

The problem was, we didn't know what came next.

We'd been so well prepared for the entire event. We had a big meeting on the airplane on the way over, and then more meetings about practice time, sleep, rest, when we'd have our meals, the system we were going to play, and who was going to play. But the one thing we didn't know was that there was a ten-minute over-time, followed by a shootout. The players had all just assumed that, as in the NHL playoffs, we'd settle it in sudden death, so we were caught off guard. It's possible that the coaches knew and didn't want to tell us. Sometimes as a coach or management you don't want players to have that option in the back of their minds.

In this day and age it's different because shootouts are part of our game. Back then we never did them. Ever. The European teams always had shootouts, though—whether it was in minor hockey, junior tournaments, club championships, or the league, it was part of their repertoire. So, without wanting to sound arrogant, if we'd kept going in overtime, we would have beaten them, no question. Our guys knew how to play sudden death because it was part of *our* repertoire.

When we went into the first minute of overtime, I remember thinking, "Oh my God, they're playing for a shootout." They'd get to center ice, dump it in, and no one would go get the puck.

It was the craziest thing I'd ever seen. It was almost as if the Czech goalie, Dominik Hasek, had told them, "Listen, just get us into the shootout."

We used to do a breakaway thing at the All-Star games' skills competition. And that year, Hasek had given up only two goals in thirty-two shots. Both were scored by Joe Sakic. I looked up at the stands and saw Joe sitting there with his crutches—he'd sprained his knee when Rob Blake crushed a guy in the Kazakh game and the guy fell over Joe's left leg. Joe was so great on the breakaway. He'd come in with speed, then fake a shot and slip it in the five-hole or low blocker, or follow the fake by roofing a backhand. Joe could put the puck in a coffee cup. If a goalie's glove was down a bit, he could find an inch and go high glove. When you're in a moment where there's that much pressure, you don't worry about the other guy, you worry more about what you're comfortable doing, and those were his moves.

But Hasek wasn't like other goalies. He was awkward and always seemed to be sprawling the crease without his stick. But he didn't quit. You would think you had him beat, but he'd find a way. If you had him beat wide, you'd still have to put it under the bar because if you tried shooting low he'd find a way to kick it or to do something with his body to make a save. He was unreal. He could make saves even when he looked out of position. You'd have to surprise him, shoot before he was ready, and it had to be quick. Because if he was ready, forget it. On top of all that, Dominik was such a hot hand that day. Sometimes a goalie is just unbeatable.

I remember sitting beside Steve Yzerman and him asking me who was shooting. I had no idea. But that meant it wasn't us. Coach

Marc Crawford called up Theo Fleury, Joe Nieuwendyk, Eric Lindros, Brendan Shanahan, and Ray Bourque. Incredible talent in that group, and all clutch guys. Plus I knew that Patrick Roy was just as good as Hasek at the other end. My first thought was, "We're going to win this over the five shots." Then Hasek stopped Theo. And their first shooter, Robert Reichel, scored. Roy could shut the door, but we still had to get one. Bourque was stopped. Then Nieuwendyk. Lindros was up next for us. He went in at full speed, head-faked Hasek to the ice, then hit the post with a backhander. Two shooters left, one for each team. Jaromir Jagr had a chance to put it out of reach, but he hit the post too. That left Shanahan. He tried to pull the puck to Hasek's glove side, but Dominik outwaited him and he ran out of space.

We were crushed. Such an empty feeling. We hadn't even lost the game. We were knocked out of gold-medal contention because of an *event*.

If you lose in the NHL, you go home. And when you go to world tournaments, you go to win a gold medal. And now here we were, playing the Finns for third. That game, playing for bronze, was the worst game ever. It was so bad I used to joke that I'd rather have played in an All-Star game. In a way that's a good thing. Because from midget hockey through to World Juniors, Team Canada is taught that it's gold or nothing. I think that puts a lot more pressure on Team Canada than other countries have to handle, though. You need guys who can handle that pressure. In my view, we should have taken Mark Messier to Nagano. His experience and his ability to play his best under pressure would have been huge assets. But I know why we went in the direction we did in

1998—we had lost in 1996. And when you lose, you adjust and get better. That's why the decision was made to take one of us, but not both. And yet, when the margin between defeat and victory was so close, there is no doubt in my mind that Mark would have made the difference.

It was such a hard game for us to play. It was so miserable—it really was. Throughout my entire career I tried to win every single game I ever played. I hated losing, but it was better for hockey when Jari Kurri and the Finns beat us and won the bronze medal because it meant way more to their country. Finland is smaller, and winning that medal helped build their hockey program.

Obviously the team was very depressed after that game. The question was do we charter home Saturday or do we stay for the closing ceremony on Sunday? All of us voted to stay. If we'd won the gold medal we would have stayed, and so it wouldn't be right to leave just because we lost.

We'd played so well all the way through—and then to lose on a shootout? It doesn't keep me up nights, but it still bites.

After the tournament ended and I retired, Bobby Clarke sent Bob Nicholson a letter saying that I should be the director of the 2002 Olympic team.

Bob and I met a few times and I talked about my thoughts and ideas. I told him that I wanted a smaller management group, and that I wanted to hire a head coach who understood the importance of being on the same page as the players, because you really only have ten days to win gold. The coach has got to be the kind of guy who'd not only give his assistants things to do, but give them actual responsibility. I also told him that I thought Pat Quinn would be the perfect choice.

And so Bob Nicholson really took a big chance when he stepped outside the box, and instead of hiring an active NHL general manager, he hired me.

The first guy I hired was Kevin Lowe because we look at the game the exact same way. Then we hired Steve Tambellini and Lanny McDonald. What a great group.

When we picked the team, we picked it as a group. You choose guys on the basis of two really good years or eight good career years. Everyone had a say, but the one guy I pushed for was Theo Fleury. I'd played against him for years and had always found him to be a gutsy, big-game player. Theo was going through some hard times at that point, and so I called him up. I didn't have to ask him to make any promises. I knew he'd do what he needed to do.

I have to tell you, there were times when I was genuinely scared for our team. Not after our first game, when we lost to Sweden 5–2, but after Game Two against Germany. We'd been up 3–0, and then they scored two third-period goals. We won 3–2, but it was a really ugly game. Germany should have been a tune-up game for us, but it was a real struggle.

So we were in the car driving back from the Peaks Ice Arena in Provo, Utah, and I felt genuinely sick—as in physically nauseated. I thought, "Wow, we're in trouble here." Meanwhile, the Americans were flying, and that made it worse. I thought, "What's wrong with Canada? The Americans are taking over!" The only thing that kept me going was the thought that in '98 we'd been flying through too, and *that* had ended pretty abruptly. Lanny McDonald was so positive. He kept saying, "Don't worry. This is gonna be fine, we're gonna be fine, this team is good."

Curtis Joseph was a great goalie that year. Pat Quinn was coaching him in Toronto. He would end his season 29–17–5. There was no question that he deserved to start Game One, but Marty Brodeur was a really good goaltender too. So we came up with a plan. Curtis would play Game One, and if we won it, Marty would play Game Two and Curtis would play Game Three. But if we lost Game One and Marty won Game Two, he'd play Game Three, which is what happened.

When you're playing in the Olympics, you can't afford to make one mistake. You're playing with the best of the best. There are three to four hundred other players who want to be in your shoes. Sometimes there's a problem if you go with the hot hand and he gets injured in the third or fourth game. Where does that leave the second guy? His confidence will be down. And yet Curtis understood, because Marty had been his backup at both the World Cup of Hockey and the IIHF World Championships in 1996. So even though it was tough for Curtis not to be in net, he was really positive.

As the years went on, I got to know Curtis really well. He's one of the best people in the world—nothing but class. It can be hard when we all have such pride as athletes. Everyone wants to be a part of the game. A good team guy will say, "Whatever is best for the team." But deep down, a great athlete is saying, "I wish that was me." Back in '98, when I was sitting on the bench during the shoot-out, yeah, I wished I was one of the five guys tapped. But if you don't think that way, you don't make it.

Ed Belfour backed up Marty and Curtis. His attitude is pretty typical of most Canadian players, and it shows you why Canadians have been so successful in international competition. When we were putting the team together, I called up Ed and said, "Listen, you're going to be the third guy, and if that doesn't work for you, I get it. No one will know I asked you." Ed said, "Are you crazy? I'm definitely going to be there, and I'll be the team's biggest cheerleader."

He was so gung ho, scouting teams and helping our goalies. It was pretty remarkable.

Then we played the Czechs and tied 3–3—and that was the game where I took off on a spontaneous rant at the press conference. I was frustrated. When you're the guy running the show, if you don't win you take all the bullets, and rightly so.

But you know when you're shaving or in the shower and you have talks with yourself? When you take all the injustices and all the insecurities that have been swirling around at the back of your mind and you argue them out? We hadn't won gold since 1952, and here we were, one, one, and one. I was thinking (again), "What's wrong with Canada? The Americans are undefeated!" And so when Paul Romanuk asked me a silly question about our NHL guys taking so long to get rolling because they lacked respect for the international game, I started to heat up.

Our guys weren't just out there coasting. I thought about the game against the Czechs. They had a great team with Hasek and Jagr, but we'd played really well in the third period, outskating them while the Czechs were doing everything they could to slow us down. Plus, when Theo Fleury was standing in front of the net and Roman Hamrlik gave him a wicked cross-check in the back, there was no call. I got emotional. I said, "I don't think we dislike those countries as much as they hate us . . . they love beating us . . . and we gotta get that same feeling toward them."

And it just sort of manifested to a point where I remember saying that there was a spear and a cross-check in the same play, and that if we'd done that it would've been a big story. I kind of went off about how there were four or five blatant penalties that weren't called, and then I added, "I'm tired of people taking shots at Canadian hockey. When we do it we're hooligans, but when

Europeans do it it's okay because they're not tough or they're not dirty? That's a crock of crap." I really did feel the world was against us.

I didn't even realize it was a big deal until the next morning, when I got a bunch of phone calls from friends in Canada talking about what a great press conference it had been. I remember thinking, "What did I say?"

Typically, Canadian teams get better as the tournament goes along, and our team was no exception. We got really lucky that Belarus upset the Swedes. It was an eleven a.m. game, and I don't know if this is true, but someone told me that the Swedes were so confident about winning that Hardy Nilsson, the Swedish coach, had scheduled a practice earlier that morning. So the players were really tired when they played that game.

They lost 4–3 on a shot from center ice that hit Swedish goalie Tommy Salo in the mask and bounced over his head.

I was sitting in my hotel room in Salt Lake City when Vladimir Kopat scored that goal for Belarus with about two minutes left. I was so excited that I jumped up on the couch and almost hit my head on the ceiling. We wouldn't be seeing the Swedes again! We went on to beat Belarus 7–1 in the semis, and then we got to the final game against the Americans.

When you're a player going into a final game you're excited, but parents, family, friends, and coaches are really nervous. In my position, what could I do? I had to just sit there and sweat. It's so much easier when you're on the ice. When someone asked me, "How do you think the game will go today?" I said, "Well, if Mario, Sakic, and Yzerman are the best three players, we're gonna win."

I went down to the locker room about two hours before the final just to wish the guys good luck and to say hello to the coaches. I was chatting with Stevie Yzerman, who was on the trainer's table. Ken Lowe was icing down his knee and working on his leg. As I left the locker room I said, "All right, well, good luck today." I was halfway down the hallway when Ken came running after me. He said, "Wayne! Wayne! Can I talk to you?" I said, "Yeah, what's up?" And he said, "I gotta tell you this. Yzerman's knee is so bad that if this was Game Seven I wouldn't let him play." I said, "Well, tell him thank God this is only a gold-medal game." That's the kind of guy Steve was. And just as Bobby Clarke wrote to Bob Nicholson about my taking over the 2002 team because, as Bobby put it, "It's time to sort of let someone else do it," I felt the same way about Vancouver and Sochi. I met with Bob and told him that Stevie was a first-class guy who knows hockey. Stevie Yzerman was the right guy.

Nothing was going to keep him off the ice for that game. Stevie ended up playing on one leg. That's the kind of leader he was. There was no way he was going to miss the opportunity to play a role in that game. It was a hugely emotional game. The rink was buzzing with both the home crowd and Canadians who had made the trip. And the fact that the women's team had just won gold over the Americans in an epic game also gave the guys a lift.

Both teams came out on fire. Everyone played great that game. When the Americans scored first, we didn't panic even though it was a clean breakaway. We just harnessed that emotion and kept playing our game. Paul Kariya scored a classic for us, taking a pass from Chris Pronger that went right between Mario's skates. Then Jarome Iginla, who had a huge tournament for us, banged in another. Brian Rafalski tied it for the Americans off a point shot, but we kept coming. Sakic scored from the high circle with one of his famous wristers, and we never looked back (though Brett Hull cranked one off the post). Iginla scored another, then Joe Sakic finished it off.

Afterward, American Jeremy Roenick gave one of the classiest post-game interviews in the history of the game. Even though the two teams were bitter rivals, and had fought hard, he tipped his hat to the Canadians and generously conceded that the better team won. But he made a more important point as well. He called the two teams possibly the best collection of players ever to be on one sheet of ice, and that he was just proud to be a part of a game like that. I felt exactly the same way.

I love the Olympics, having been a part of three of them, one as a player and two in management. It's just such a great way for the game to come to nontraditional hockey people. And I know the players love playing. When I was growing up, honestly, most professional hockey players could not have cared less about the Olympic games. And I say that not to be mean-spirited but because when we were kids, our dream was to play in the National Hockey League, and we knew from day one that if you played in the NHL you couldn't play in the Olympics. So very few guys set their sights on being part of the Canadian Olympic team. Now, though, hockey is such a big draw that it spills over to those people tuning in just to see ski racers and curlers and skateboarders. The Olympics in turn have a much bigger profile because of the game of hockey. And being in the Olympics really helps to sell our sport worldwide. We're up front and center for three weeks. Still, I'm worried that hockey might end up like soccer, where only U23 teams compete. It's true that the Olympics are bigger than the athletes, but shouldn't the best athletes be competing?

But it's a catch-22 situation. On the management side, I do respect and understand the risks for owners and cities. An NHL owner knows that if he loses his best player, it can put a dagger through his chances to win the Stanley Cup. If Ted Leonsis loses Alexander Ovechkin, what does that do to his franchise and his franchise's value? One solution might be for the IOC to help with making sure that the players are adequately insured in the event of a temporary or permanent disability.

I think that, as a league, the NHL looks at it like this—the IOC benefits from having its players compete. In fact, the hockey games make the IOC hundreds of millions of dollars. So the NHL wants some insurance, a bit of a safety net in exchange for offering up their number-one assets. Yes, they're getting satisfaction because the players enjoy doing it. And yes, they're getting some exposure internationally. But if you ask the owner of a team in, say, the southern United States, "Does having your players play in the Olympics help out in your market?" I think he'll say no.

And I will tell you that, after we'd gone to Japan in 1998, it was very difficult for the players when we came back. All the best players in the NHL—not just from Canada and the United States, but from the Czech Republic, Sweden, Finland, and Russia—were mentally and physically drained, and as a result they weren't quite as good. Going back to regular-season games in the NHL isn't going to give players the same rush as wearing their national colors. A lot of guys slump a little when they get back, especially from somewhere as far away as Japan or South Korea, where the next Olympics are going to be held (or China, for that matter, where the Games after that will be).

Getting NHLers to the next two Olympics is going to be a big challenge, but having been there, I can say that it is worth the effort of finding a way to make it work.

Thirty-One

THE CULTURE
OF WINNING

Y ou hear people say it all the time—whenever you put on a
Team Canada sweater, you expect to win gold. That's not
always true, and it's not always fair. It's ridiculous to think
you're going to win 100 percent of the tournaments you enter.
Sometimes the bounces don't go your way. And sometimes you just
run into a better team. It has happened to me more than once.

But that belief that you *can* win every time you step on the ice
is important for every team. And so is the expectation that you
should. If you don't hold yourself to very high standards, there is no
way you are going to be able to dig deep enough to beat the guy
you're lining up against.

Perpetual winners don't win by accident. You just have to look
behind the curtain to see why they've been successful. It's a culture
that they've created in the locker room and that players pass on to
the next generation.

If you consider the most successful organizations in every team
sport—and I don't mean one-year wonders, but strong organizations
like the New England Patriots or the St. Louis Cardinals—there's

a defined culture that runs through every part of them. Trust, teamwork, accountability, sacrifice. They put in place the pieces that follow the culture and they live within it.

Part of it is who they sign as players and coaches. A winning culture is often passed along from veterans to new players when they arrive. They mentor by example. You see it in Detroit—from Yzerman to Lidstrom to Datsyuk and to the great group of young players they have now. For teams that have a lot of talented young players but haven't found success, there may be an absence of that kind of leadership.

In all of pro sports, the NBA's San Antonio Spurs may represent one of the best examples of this. It goes back to May 17, 1987, when the Spurs won the NBA draft lottery and picked David Robinson as center. Then they put in place a continuity of management. Peter Holt joined the ownership group in 1993 and was CEO for twenty years. Gregg Popovich has been head coach since 1996.

This builds trust. They know that the team isn't going to get blown up if they ever have a bad year. New players who come in grow to greatness and stay productive for long, highly successful careers.

I think the Spurs took an intellectual approach to defining the culture they wanted in that organization. Every decision made was based on it—how they train, how they have their players recover, how rookies are treated, how veterans are treated, how the veterans treat the rookies, all the way down the line. There's a way for all that to be done and there's an expectation that it will continue to be done the right way.

When Robinson retired, he'd already passed his beliefs on to Tim Duncan, Manu Ginobili, and Tony Parker. They've continued that culture through five titles. Now that they're getting up there, Kawhi Leonard has come along, and you can take it to the bank that everything he's learned from those three veterans is going to be part of the leadership he demonstrates to the young players the Spurs bring in.

When Craig Patrick was GM in Pittsburgh in the early 90s, he traded for guys who turned a good team into Stanley Cup winners— Joey Mullen, Ulf Samuelsson, and Ronnie Francis. But he also made a trade with Calgary for Czech forward Jiri Hrdina in order to help out Jaromir Jagr. It was Jagr's first year and he was homesick, ready to go back to Kladno. Guaranteed that when Jagr walks into the Hall of Fame, one of the first guys he'll acknowledge will be Hrdina.

And when Darryl Sutter took over the L.A. Kings in December 2011, no disrespect to former coach Terry Murray, but they weren't in the playoffs. In a year's time Darryl brought them to a Cup win and another two years later in 2014. Same team. I think it was huge to trade for Jeff Carter and Mike Richards, but still, how does that happen? Well, Darryl changed the culture. He raised the expectations and brought out the best in each player. Mess said it best recently when we were in Edmonton for the closing of the Coliseum—"Every player on your team, man for man, is valuable." It's true. From your top player to your bottom player, all have to be pulling together. Darryl does that. He makes sure that everyone knows his role.

Like Scotty Bowman, Darryl is really prepared. There's a game sheet with the rosters that comes out before every game. Players are supposed to read it, but they never do. In the locker room on game day, Darryl will point out the name of a new kid playing that night. He'll say to a player, "Hey, So-and-So, what about John Doe there? What do you know about him?"

Well, So-and-So will have no clue, but Darryl can tell you what the kid had for breakfast that morning, what his mom and dad do for a living, what grade school he went to, and his shoe size. Everything there is to know about the kid.

His practices aren't long, but they're high tempo, and he has no tolerance for lack of effort. If you screw up, make a bad pass, he'll stop the play and call you out on it. He expects your best and loses his mind on guys who aren't giving 100 percent in games and practice. He'll run a drill three or four times if he needs to, saying, "Do it right!" Even though Darryl's hard on the players, he's hard for a reason. The best coaches seem to be that way. He's softened a little over the years. Back then he was little more intense.

For any team to be successful, management, coaches, players, everyone has to buy into what the coach is selling. And everyone bought into Darryl. Whatever leadership is, the Sutter family seems to have figured it out. Darryl is just one of six brothers to play in the NHL. (The others are Brent, Brian, Duane, Rich, and Ron.) Four of them went on to become coaches or GMs. Collectively, they've won the Stanley Cup six times and played nearly five thousand NHL games. Now the next generation of Sutters is coming into the league. That kind of success doesn't happen by accident.

And you see it with hockey clubs. Some have figured it out, and others are still working on it. It may look as though this or that team finally succeeded because it drafted well, but that is only part of it. The history of the league is full of stacked teams who never figured it out. The dynasties are the ones who did.

You can't talk about dynasties without mentioning the Montreal Canadiens.

From just after World War II until the late 1960s, each NHL team was allowed to sponsor Junior A and B clubs. In the 1960s,

Montreal's Junior A teams were the Peterborough Petes and the Montreal Junior Canadiens. NHL teams could also affiliate with minor pro teams, who could in turn each sponsor Junior A teams. The Junior A teams could sponsor Junior B teams, who in turn sponsored midget and juvenile teams, and so on. In short, NHL teams like Montreal's had a huge network of players and teams to develop them.

Until the 1967 expansion, Montreal spent twice as much as any other team on player development. In 1964, there were three hundred guys at Montreal's training camp, which was held at six different rinks. The Canadiens would separate players from their main team, which included Jean Béliveau, Claude Provost, Henri Richard, John Ferguson, Bobby Rousseau, Ralph Backstrom, Jacques Laperrière, and all the other guys guaranteed a spot. The main players would practice at the Forum, and then whoever was having a good camp at the other rinks would be brought up for a couple of practices. Only one or two spots would be open. If you didn't make the team, you'd be sent back to Rochester or Cleveland or Des Moines or Charlotte or Houston. There were so many great players in the 60s, including Yvan Cournoyer, Danny Grant, Rogie Vachon, and Mickey Redmond, who were sent back down.

In the case of Jean Béliveau, it worked the other way. He was playing in the Quebec Senior Hockey League, and had no interest in moving up to the NHL. He had a couple of brief call-ups with the Canadiens, but refused repeated offers to sign with them. In 1953, Montreal finally bought the entire league and turned it professional just to get Béliveau into their lineup.

When I was thirteen years old in 1974, we were in the dressing room about half an hour before Game One in the Quebec

International Pee Wee Hockey Tournament when Jean Béliveau came in. I couldn't believe how big he was. He looked down at me and said, "I heard there's this really good player and I just wanted to come in and say hello." Whenever I was in situations like that as a kid, I became tongue-tied. I remember just staring up at him. He laughed and said, "Now, don't let me down tonight." That night our team, Brantford Turkstra Lumber, won 25–0 against a team out of Texas. I scored seven goals and had four assists. When I saw my dad after the game, I said, "Gee, I hope I didn't let Mr. Béliveau down."

Frank Selke, who came from the Leafs and had been the Montreal Canadiens' GM since 1946, put hundreds of thousands of dollars into Montreal's farm system and player development. Selke also discovered Sam Pollock, the twenty-two-year-old coach of the midget Canadiens team. Pollock, who learned quickly and ended up replacing Selke when he retired in 1964, was GM for fourteen seasons. He was the architect of the Canadiens teams that won nine Cups and seven regular-season championships in the 1960s and 70s. But he was an even better forward-thinker. He was the first GM who traded veterans to expansion teams for draft picks.

In 1971, Sam Pollock wanted to draft Guy Lafleur number one, but at the last minute he hesitated. Lafleur played for the Quebec Remparts, and had finished the season with 130 goals and 209 points in 62 games. But Marcel Dionne was promising too, having scored 62 goals and 143 points for the OHA's St. Catharines Black Hawks in 46 games. At that time, the OHA was stronger than the Quebec league. It was a really, really tough decision. Pollock went with the Flower and Detroit got Marcel, who was later moved to L.A. and became part of the famous Triple Crown Line.

People have compared Lafleur's and Dionne's stats over the years, wondering if Pollock made the right decision. Listen, I think they were both great players, both Hall of Famers. Marcel played 1,348 games and scored 1,771 points. His career plus/minus is 28. Flower was on five Stanley Cup teams. He played 1,126 games and has 1,353 points. His career plus/minus is 453. Eighth overall. But he was playing on one of the greatest teams of all time.

The Canadiens teams of the 1970s changed hockey. This was an era where rapid expansion, from six teams in 1966–67 to thirty-two in 1974–75 (eighteen in the NHL and fourteen in the WHA), had thinned out the talent. There were no Russian players yet, and very few Americans or Europeans. The lack of skilled talent explains why there was so much violence in that era.

More than any other coach, Sam Pollock wanted to sign players who were tough but who could also skate and handle the puck. In 1971, he brought in Larry Robinson in the second round. He turned out to be one of the top Montreal defensemen of all time, but when Larry started out, his coach with the Nova Scotia Voyageurs, Al MacNeil, made it clear that he could either fight or play in the International Hockey League. He was a big, strong guy, and that advice served him well over the years. Even legendary heavyweights like Dave Schultz were known to turn down an invitation from Larry. He could hit hard and he could fight, but that's not really who he was. Serge Savard once told me, there was no meanness inside Larry. He was a good, clean hockey player. Better than good—he was outstanding. And as I've got to know Larry over the years, I agree. He's a big, tall, gentle giant.

S cotty Bowman, who joined the team for the 1971–72 season, was the coach of the second Montreal dynasty. In 1972 they added Steve Shutt, fourth overall. The next year they drafted Bob Gainey, and then Doug Risebrough the year after that. The Canadiens were so dominant by 1976–77 that they won sixty games and lost only eight. That's still a record for fewest losses in an eighty-game season.

From St. Louis to Montreal, and then to Buffalo, Pittsburgh, and Detroit, every team improved when Scotty brought in a change of culture or built on the culture already in place. And in Montreal's case, that culture had been established back in the Toe Blake years.

Scotty had strong beliefs about how to put a team together. Although there are three forwards on a line, he always tried to think of a twosome first. Two compatible players, and then you add a third component. (When I was with the Oilers I played with Jari Kurri just about exclusively while Glen Sather would send different guys on and off our left wing. Because the game is so fast and physical that you don't have time to think, in my mind, the most important thing about line combinations is chemistry with a linemate. You need to know where he's going to be. Kurri hardly spoke any English and I didn't speak Finnish, but when we stepped on the ice, we played the same game. He saw the game exactly as I did. If someone was coming at him, he knew where I'd be for an outlet pass. We had that chemistry from day one. And when I look at guys today I see that certain players have that same chemistry—Perry and Getzlaf in Anaheim, Ovechkin and Backstrom in Washington, and Benn and Seguin in Dallas.)

When Scotty was in Montreal he put Guy Lafleur with Steve Shutt, and a couple of different centermen played with them. The third player was chosen depending on the team they were playing against. Sometimes they needed defensive strength, and sometimes Scotty would add an offensive player.

It was the formula of that era. Mike Bossy and Brian Trottier played together with the Islanders. Mark Messier teamed with Glenn Anderson on the Oilers. The Flyers' Bobby Clarke and Reggie Leach were linemates going all the way back to junior in Flin Flon. Scotty did the same thing with defensive forwards. In Montreal, he liked Doug Jarvis with Bob Gainey. In Detroit, he put Kris Draper with Kirk Maltby, maybe the best checking tandem in the league at that time.

In Detroit in 1995–96, Bowman broke his own rule a little. He took a page from the Soviets' playbook and built a five-man unit. The Russian Five—Larionov, Fedorov, Kozlov, Konstantinov, and Fetisov. They didn't play the North American style of hockey. And it helped Detroit, because the other teams had never seen that kind of system. Scotty played them as a group about half the time and moved them around the rest of the time. He didn't want other teams to figure out what they were doing. By moving them around a little he wanted to make it more difficult to defend against them. Of course, five-man units mean too many defensemen and don't really work for an NHL team. It's fine if you're rolling six defense, but no NHL team does that. But still, a few times a game, the Red Wings could basically send out a line plucked from the Soviet national team, and their opponents would have no idea what to do. The Wings set a record of sixty-two regular-season wins, beating Montreal's 1976–77 record of sixty.

Igor Larionov was a terrific playmaker because he saw the ice so well. He was pretty small, about 160 pounds, but he was strong and a very agile skater. He could spin on a dime. He was an artist on the ice, very creative. Larionov believed that if you had the puck you shouldn't be getting rid of it and chasing it. He was adept defensively too. That was the most underrated part of his game. And like most of the Russians, he was a very unselfish player. He didn't shoot the puck a lot. He'd rather set guys up. And he was a clutch player.

I always thought an awful lot of Sergei Fedorov too. I was just amazed that he could play at such a high level. One year Detroit was short—they'd had some injuries—and so they put him on defense. There are very few players who could switch to defense like that. Most of us couldn't do it, and I'm including Mario Lemieux, Jaromir Jagr, and myself. But for a good six weeks, Fedorov played back there like an all-star. He was such a powerful back skater. In 1994, he was the first European-trained player to win the Hart.

Vyacheslav Kozlov wasn't as big as Fedorov or Fetisov, but you don't have to be huge to play hockey. He was a goal scorer. He had great hand-eye coordination and an above-average shot. Kozlov's car was hit by a bus in 1991 while he was going to a practice in Russia. He suffered brain damage, but made a miraculous recovery. Kozlov would end up playing until he was forty-three—1,182 NHL games, 853 points.

Vladimir Konstantinov was drafted in the eleventh round. He was a very tough guy, among the most physical Russian players ever. Anyone who thinks Russians are soft should have been paying more attention to Vlad. Konstantinov never scored a lot of goals, but he was probably one of the best defensive defensemen. His teammates would feed him the puck and he'd shoot through the middle and create a lot of scoring chances. He loved the contact and would play a really hard-nosed game.

Viacheslav Fetisov was regarded as the best defenseman who ever played in the Russian system. I mean, no one can compare to Bobby Orr, but Fetisov liked to carry the puck and had been an exceptional skater in his youth. When he was twenty, around 1978, he was one of the best in the world. Detroit got him when he was thirty-seven. He wasn't the skater he'd been in his twenties, but he could still skate out of trouble, and if he saw daylight, he was gone.

There's been some controversy lately because Fetisov is on the Kontinental Hockey League (KHL) board of directors in Russia and he's talking about keeping the most talented players in the country until they turn twenty-nine. That doesn't surprise me, and I'll tell you why. I know Fetisov pretty well, and there are a couple things he loves in life, and one of them was playing in the NHL. The other thing about Slava is that he's a very proud Russian. There were opportunities for him to leave illegally, but he wouldn't do it—he wanted to do it properly. He wanted to be able to go play in the NHL and still say, "I'm Russian and Russia is my home."

Now that he's part of the KHL, which is the top professional league in Europe and Asia, he wants to develop kids who'll play in and expand the league. Fetisov wants to make Russia what North America is. I don't think that's hypocritical. I think what he's trying to say to them is, "I want you to go play in the NHL, but I want you to brand our country first and build our league first." And in some ways I agree with him. Russia is losing so many good players at a young age that the sport of hockey isn't growing as much as it used to there. And it costs a lot of money to develop players. So they're putting a ton of resources into developing these kids only to have them leave as soon as they get good. And more importantly, he wants those young players to take pride in the system that groomed them. There was a time when no one could touch the Russians. He wants to build that pride back into the system.

Now, will Fetisov be able to pull it off? I don't know, but I give him full marks because I know he's speaking from his heart and that he wants those kids to stay for the right reasons. No question in my mind.

Of course, Detroit also had Stevie Yzerman and Kris Draper. They were really strong at center ice. And they had such big, strong forwards—Darren McCarty, Marty Lapointe, and of course Brendan Shanahan. For a good, skilled team, they were also very tough. After Bob Probert left, they didn't dress an enforcer—and Probert was a lot more than an enforcer, since he could play the game and put the puck in the net. Detroit was ahead of its time by building a team around high-end skill guys who knew how to handle themselves.

Ask anyone on Detroit's Cup-winning teams of 1996–97 and 1997–98 whether it was the Russians who won those two Cups for Detroit, and he'll tell you, "It was the Red Wings."

That's one thing that every good team has in common—everyone has a role. What really made them winners was the way they came together. They were the United Nations of hockey. They had Tomas Sandstrom, Tomas Holmstrom, and Anders Eriksson from Sweden, and Mathieu Dandenault and Martin Lapointe, who were French Canadian. They were all really proud of their cultures—cultures that the team showed a real interest in. During those years, certain guys like Stevie and Mike Vernon would step up and buy dinner for everyone on the road, and they all had to show up. And once, on a road trip to L.A., the Russians took the team to a great Russian restaurant. The entire team ate together, drank together, and hung together. They really got to know each other.

They also once played paintball, with the Europeans and French-speaking guys against the English-speaking North Americans, and they just had a riot. Those are the types of things that helped unify the players. At the team dinner after they captured their first Cup, Steve Yzerman said in his speech that one of the reasons they won was the way they stuck together.

That sort of thing doesn't happen by accident. That takes the kind of leadership that a guy like Steve provides. But the thing those Montreal and Detroit teams had in common was Scotty Bowman.

Coaching is a unique part of hockey. It's different from coaching baseball or football in that when hockey teams struggle or experience lulls in the season, players start questioning the coach more than they do in other sports. Does he know what he's doing? Is he practicing us too hard? Are we using the right systems?

When things go off the rails, all pro athletes in a team environment will start looking to save themselves: "Hey, it's not my fault." But a coach like Scotty Bowman will keep the emphasis on the player, never allowing him to deflect responsibility onto others. And because Scotty wouldn't tolerate crutches or excuses, he minimized distractions.

His teams would stay in nice hotels and had as good a travel schedule as possible. He drilled into his players that every decision they made had to be for the team. Individuals were important, they could win trophies, but the number-one goal for everyone was to win as a team. When you've got a guy like Bowman, the team stays strong because players don't dispute or revolt. The ship is never rudderless.

I didn't always agree with every coach I played for, but I respected what he was trying to accomplish. I understood that if I followed whatever direction he was taking the team, it would be easier for everyone else to hop on board. I might sometimes debate the coach, talk to him about it, but ultimately I went along. My focus as a player was on one thing only—getting myself ready to play. I had to be the best I could be every night.

When I started coaching the Phoenix Coyotes in August 2005, I found it to be a completely different experience from playing. Coaches have to get twenty guys ready and on the same page. I loved it, I truly did. I knew that financially we couldn't afford the caliber of players other teams had, and that we'd be a young team. Winning was going to be tough.

At first I'd tell my players, "You need to play with your instincts more." I assumed that they all understood the game as well as I did, but I should have taken into account the number of years I'd studied the game. It didn't take long to realize that, like everything else, instincts have to be developed and taught. So I put more structure into the details. I might say, "You can't go below the top of the circles on your forecheck," whereas early on I might have been looser about it and said something like, "Hey, when you come up and pressure that guy make sure you force him to one side or the other." Most players need parameters.

Listen, we're hockey players and professional athletes. We all have egos. The biggest challenge for me was that most guys thought they should be starting on the power play and doing the penalty killing and playing twenty-two minutes a game. Which is actually a good thing, as far as it goes, because as a professional athlete you need to believe in yourself.

I discovered that I wasn't only coaching games. I was managing people's lives. Some guys you have to build up and maybe coddle a bit, while other guys you have to bring into your office and get on them.

I knew Viktor Tikhonov's son, Vasily, really well. I coached Vasily's own son, also named Viktor, on the Coyotes. You wouldn't even know young Viktor was from Russia, or that his grandfather was one of the most terrifying coaches in the history of the game. Viktor is a really outgoing, nice, and fun young man, very North American. He grew up in San Jose, where his dad was the Sharks' assistant coach. Vasily was a very, very intelligent hockey man and very concerned for his son. When I had Viktor in Phoenix, Vasily would come down to the locker room and talk to me, and that was okay. I had concerned mothers calling me too. I understand that. I'm a father. Parents like to hear what's going on right from the horse's mouth: "Okay, what can my son do? How can he be better? How's he doing?"

And we had such a young team. Adam Kostis—who played for the East Bridgton Academy Wolverines in Maine and was the son of Peter Kostis, a famous golf coach and a friend of mine—was a pretty good goalie. I saw Peter at a game once and I said, "I'm going to give Curtis Joseph the day off tomorrow. Why don't you bring Adam and he can play goal at practice?" The next day, when the kid got on the ice, I blew the whistle and said, "You go down to that net."

And Adam said, "Well, I gotta stretch."

"Stretch? You're seventeen! Get in the net!" I'm old school.

Later we were doing breakaways, and a guy came down and shot it hard, hitting Adam high in the upper chest. I blew the whistle and said, "Hey, listen you guys. This kid is seventeen years old—take it easy on him. Just take it easy."

Eddie Jovanovski looked at me and said, "Well, Gretz, the kid who just shot on him is eighteen."

Glen Sather was a big believer in families being around. He didn't have many rules, but one was that everyone had to bring a date to the team Christmas party. He didn't want eight single guys sitting at a table only to have everyone leave before dinner ended. Half the guys would bring their mothers. I took my mom and so did Kevin Lowe.

Now, would Glen Sather have taken those calls from concerned parents? I don't think so, but hockey has changed a lot since the 1980s, and Glen did really like the family scenario. We'd be in Toronto getting on the team bus at Maple Leaf Gardens with Mr. and Mrs. Coffey and my mom. That just wasn't done in the hockey world at that time. If we were in playoffs in Calgary, I'd walk out for the morning skate and my dad would be standing there. Glen would fly him out because he always felt that I played better with my dad in the arena.

Glen reached out to all the dads—including Jack Coffey, Bill McSorley, and Doug Messier. Now teams organize father trips and mother trips, but there were times in the 1980s when, if we were struggling in playoffs, he'd let your family get on the plane. He was really good about that stuff, way ahead of his time. When I coached I learned from that. If a player came to me and said, "Hey, my wife's going to Vancouver, can she fly on the charter?" I'd agree to it, and even encouraged it. Allowing only the team on the plane is dinosaur thinking. I always felt that if the players are happy, they play better.

Managing your players on the bench is just as hard. I'd coached only a couple of games when the ref came over, staring at the roster sheet. He looked as if he didn't want to say anything, and I wasn't sure what was going to happen next. Finally he blurted out, "Hey, umm, there's a player missing here." It was one of our young guys, Freddy Sjostrom. We'd had a couple guys coming up and down, and I'd forgotten to put his name on the sheet. Freddy had to leave the bench.

Coaches like Glen Sather and Scotty Bowman and Joel Quenneville and Darryl Sutter win so much because of great bench sense. They get the right players on the ice at the right time. More often than not, that means your better players, but when your better players aren't working, a great bench coach can tap into the next group of guys and get the most out of them too. He can give the lineup a shake when the team is flat. He can add some grit if that's what's called for, and he knows who has the best chance to win a faceoff.

The guys on the ice win or lose the game, there is no way around that. But by determining who is on the ice, and guiding what they do, a coach can have a huge effect on the outcome of a game. In the 1976 finals, the Canadiens were up against Philadelphia, the defending champions who had just won consecutive Cups in '74 and '75. The Flyers' top line—Bobby Clarke, Bill Barber, and Reggie Leach—had played the whole regular season together. They allowed only twenty-eight goals against, at even strength all year. Bobby Clarke led the league in plus/minus at eighty-three, Barber was second at seventy-four, and Leach and Montreal's Steve Shutt were tied for third at seventy-three. At the time, there wasn't another line in the NHL that could match up. The Philly line would eat any other line for lunch.

Bowman designed four lines to neutralize them. He started with his usual checking line—Doug Jarvis, Bob Gainey, and Jim Roberts. But he didn't want to just play defense. He wanted to give that big Philly line something to worry about. So he used his scoring line—Peter Mahovlich, Lafleur, and Shutt—and then added another line that could do both—either Yvon Lambert or Rick Chartraw as grinding checker, Yvan Cournoyer, an offensive threat, and Jacques Lemaire, a great forechecker and playmaker. His fourth line was young and aggressive—Doug Risebrough, Mario Tremblay, and either Murray Wilson or Yvon Lambert. And it worked.

For the next two years the Canadiens faced the Boston Bruins, and those '77 and '78 finals saw some of the toughest games ever played. From 1946 to 1987, Montreal won eighteen straight playoff series against Boston. They had a bitter rivalry and have played each other more than any other two teams.

In 1970, when he was coaching the St. Louis Blues, Scotty had lost to the Bruins in the Stanley Cup final. At the time, the Blues and Bruins weren't in the same class. Boston had Orr, Esposito, Bucyk, McKenzie, Hodge, and Stanfield—six guys with more than twenty goals. As an expansion team, St. Louis didn't have the wherewithal to play any kind of offensive game against guys like that. So they countered with a close-checking shutdown defense and the unheard-of strategy of shadowing Bobby Orr, even though he was on the blue line. They lost, but losing to Bobby Orr doesn't make you a bad coach or a bad team.

By 1977, however, the Big Bad Bruins didn't have Bobby Orr anymore. (The Bobby Orr era came to an end when Number 4 went to Chicago as a free agent. But he played only twenty-six games over the course of three seasons as a result of the pain from his deteriorating knees.) Boston did have Brad Park, though, one of the best defensemen ever. He could skate the puck, he could pass it, and he was no fun to play against. (Win or lose, after a series against the Bruins, a star like Guy Lafleur would be pretty banged up.) Boston relied on their players' toughness. Coach Don Cherry's roster, dubbed The Lunch Pail Gang, included guys like Terry O'Reilly, John Wensink, and Stan Jonathan. Jonathan, a Mohawk, stood at just 5'7", but pound for pound, he was one of the toughest players ever. He could throw punches from either his left or his right. To this day, almost forty years later, Don still shows clips of his fights on "Coach's Corner."

Montreal never had many guys looking for fights, but Scotty would use the other team's positives to make his own guys feel more competitive. He'd talk about how aggressive the Bruins were, how they could get on guys and turn the puck over. Or he'd tell them that they needed to forecheck like Philadelphia. Larry Robinson said that praising the other teams hurt their feelings—and made them try harder. But unlike when Montreal played Philadelphia in 1976, when they went up against Boston in '77 and '78, Scotty matched up his players with the Bruins individually. Doug Jarvis and Bob Gainey were used in defensive roles. They played against Jean Ratelle, who was a very underrated offensive clutch player. Jacques Lemaire centered Steve Shutt and Lafleur, and they became a really strong, dominating two-way line. Montreal had a real edge on defense with three all-stars, Savard, Robinson, and Lapointe. The only defensive team that was maybe better was the first Canada Cup team in 1976, which included the Montreal guys along with Denis Potvin and Bobby Orr and Philadelphia's Jim Watson. Imagine having all of them on the same team.

The last Cup of the second Canadiens dynasty, the 1979 finals, was played against the New York Rangers, who were a miracle team. The Rangers beat out the Flyers in the quarter-finals, which was a big upset and a little controversial. They then defeated the Islanders, who'd finished first overall, in the semifinals. The Rangers had come in fifth overall. But they had Fred Shero, a great coach.

The Rangers had signed Shero—who'd won Cups in Philly in '74 and '75 and coached them to the '76 final against the Canadiens—at the start of the 1978–79 season. But because he still had a year left on his contract, the Rangers were worried about tampering charges, and so handed over their first-round draft pick to the Flyers.

(That pick turned out to be a guy who'd eventually play with us on the Oilers and become one of my best friends, Kenny Linseman. Kenny was the agitators' agitator in the NHL. He could really get under people's skin. He would slash and hack and just yap at you all night. Why do teams dress agitators? Because they help you win. Guys hate agitators so much that they get off their game, and they get sucked into taking stupid penalties. The truly great agitators can also put the puck in the net—nothing drives a team crazier than watching the guy who has been chirping at you all night bury a clutch goal. Kenny had over 800 career points.)

Now, the Rangers were supposedly under a curse. (They won the Cup in 1939–40, and the mortgage to Madison Square Garden was paid off shortly after. To mark that dual occasion, the Rangers president, General John Reed Kilpatrick, burned the mortgage papers in the bowl of the Cup, and they hadn't won since.) So in 1979, the Rangers were on a mission. They also had a good team. They'd signed Bobby Hull's WHA linemates Ulf Nilsson and Anders Hedberg, and they had Phil Esposito as well as a bunch of young guys—Ron Greschner, Dave and Don Maloney, Don Murdoch, Ron Duguay, and Mike McEwen. In short, they had three scoring lines and a mobile defense. But their goalie, John Davidson, was their key player (and is now president of hockey operations for the Columbus Blue Jackets). John, who was a big guy and covered a lot of net, was having a tremendous playoff season. He stood on his head game after game, even though he had injured his knee in the semifinals against the Islanders.

The Rangers won the first game of the finals in Montreal. For Game Two, Scotty Bowman was ready to start his backup goalie, Bunny Larocque, but in the warm-up Doug Risebrough hit Larocque right between the eyes with a shot, so Scotty started Ken Dryden instead. The Canadiens took the next four games.

The winner of the Conn Smythe Trophy that year really shows how important every player is. The playoff MVP was not a high-scoring forward, a star goalie, or a defenseman who logs thirty minutes a game. It was Bob Gainey, an incredibly hardworking defensive specialist. When his name was announced, his team-mates hoisted him up on their shoulders and carried him around the ice. It would be hard to think of a better illustration of what he meant to that team.

At the start of the 1995–96 season, Serge Savard, who by that time had been the Canadiens' GM for twelve years, was convinced they had a Cup-winning team.

Serge had been a great defenseman for the Canadiens. (Bobby Clarke has said that he was the toughest he'd ever played against.) Serge was bigger than a lot of players of his time and had a very long reach. He wasn't so much a body checker, but there was no way around him. He had a terrific stick, always active, always in the way. Sometimes he looked clumsy, but he wasn't. In fact, when people talk about the "Savardian spin-o-rama," they often assume that it was invented by Denis Savard (and not unreasonably—Denis could stickhandle in a phone booth). But Habs announcer Danny Gallivan actually coined the phrase to describe something Serge, not Denis, had done. Serge learned it from watching Doug Harvey and made it his own. I saw him use it in the Summit Series, and it's still a classic. Drew Doughty used it at the blue line against Russia at the 2010 Olympics.

But Serge didn't play a lot of offense at the time because he and Larry Robinson were a tandem. Both huge guys. Larry was a great two-way defenseman—he took the puck up—while Serge was more defensive. Serge won eight Cups in his fifteen years with the Habs, which ended in 1981. He played two more seasons with the Winnipeg Jets before returning to the Canadiens as GM in 1983. The teams he managed won the Cup in 1986 and 1993.

Ten days before the 1995–96 season began, at the end of training camp, Serge told Canadiens president Ronald Corey that he thought he was maybe one player away from a winning team, and Corey agreed. But the Canadiens lost their first four games, and Serge wanted to make adjustments. So he called up Pierre Lacroix—Montreal goalie Patrick Roy's former agent and now GM of the Colorado Avalanche—to discuss possible trades.

Lacroix wanted Roy, Savard wanted Owen Nolan. Savard mentioned he needed a goalie, and Stéphane Fiset's name came up. It sounded like a trade was possible. They agreed to pick up the conversation again. And then suddenly Serge was fired.

After Corey delivered the bad news, Serge went back to his office to clean it out. His phone rang, his private line. It was Pierre

Lacroix. Serge said, "Well, Pierre, I've just been fired, so I guess your next few calls have to be with somebody else."

Réjean Houle took over as GM and Mario Tremblay replaced Jacques Demers as coach. It's no secret that Mario and Patrick Roy didn't get along. There'd been rumors about Patrick being traded for years. In 1993, the slogan "Trade Patrick" was seen on billboards all over town. There was even a newspaper poll showing that 57 percent of people wanted to trade him. That really bothered Patrick. He didn't want to be traded, but two years later, with Mario Tremblay as his coach, he changed his mind.

Mike Vernon, who was playing for Detroit at the time, heard about it from Patrick himself. On the morning of December 2, 1995, the Wings were in Montreal getting ready for the game that night. Mike went to a little diner across from the old Forum. All the players went there. You'd walk in and go downstairs about five or six steps. There was a counter and a few tables. Patrick was at the counter. He and Mike had never said two words to each other, but when Patrick saw him he said, "Mikey, come over here. Sit down."

Mike sat down and Patrick opened up. He said he was thinking of quitting hockey. What with all the negativity from the coach, the fans, and the media, he was really feeling the stress of playing in Montreal.

But Patrick was the most sought-after goaltender in the league. Mike told him he was too good to quit. He said, "You're the best goalie in the league and we can't lose a guy like you." Mike said that he really loved playing in Detroit after the pressure cooker of playing as a hometown boy in Calgary. He added, "You're too valuable to just quit. Just go get traded and you'll have a lot more fun."

That night at the Forum, Detroit beat the Canadiens 11–1. Tremblay left Roy in for the first nine goals—until the fans were booing every time he even touched the puck. Mike watched as Patrick finally came off the ice. At first he went to sit down, but then he stood up, went over to Corey, and told him that he was done with the team.

Mike showered and dressed in record time and left. He worried that Patrick might say something about their conversation that that morning, and the last thing he wanted to do was talk to the media about what might have been going through Patrick's mind. (It wasn't until years later that Mike opened up about his conversation with Patrick, in an interview with Kelly Hrudey on *Hockey Night in Canada Radio*.)

Serge Savard had been watching that game, and the whole situation was hard for him. He felt that Mario Tremblay had made a major mistake. For Serge, Patrick was a player who'd worked so hard for the team and won so many games for them, and as a former player he knew that you never try to humiliate an athlete. You just don't. Serge felt that when a goalie has a bad night—having let in, say, three goals—you just pull him and say, "Hey, you've done enough. Take a rest and we'll start back the next game." Serge felt that forcing Patrick to stay in the net that night was the spark that went on to destroy the team he'd built.

Patrick and Mario had been roommates back in 1985. When guys get into management, the main thing they have to remember is that we're all human beings; the hockey element comes second. That's why you appreciate guys like Cliff Fletcher—and there are a lot of other general managers out there who treat guys with respect.

I don't know what was going through Mario Tremblay's mind. I imagine he regrets it now, because it's probably brought up a lot.

Four days after that game, on December 6, 1995, a deal was announced: Canadiens GM Réjean Houle had traded Patrick Roy and their captain, Mike Keane, to the Colorado Avalanche for wingers Andrei Kovalenko and Martin Rucinsky and goaltender Jocelyn Thibault.

Serge felt that they'd traded character away when Mike Keane left. And it's true that the Stanley Cup seemed to follow Keane around. It was even more demoralizing for him when the team went on to bring back players Serge himself had traded. They traded for Stéphane Richer. Then they got Shayne Corson and Murray Baron from St. Louis for Pierre Turgeon, Craig Conroy, and Rory Fitzpatrick. Pierre was a heck of a scorer, one of the best in the league, and at the time of the trade Conroy was Montreal's best player in the minors.

When he got to Colorado, Patrick was determined to stick his trade up Tremblay's nose. He was a fiery, fiery competitor. He hated anyone scoring on him, even in practice. Joe Sakic has said that it made him a better shooter. Colorado had a really good team. They finished in first place in the Eastern Conference as the Quebec Nordiques the year before but lost in the first round to the Rangers. A loss like that really schools you. And then suddenly they had the best goalie in the game, so now they could play both ways—shut down the opposition and score.

With Roy in net, Colorado won the Stanley Cup in 1996, but it's hard to win year in and year out. In the next four years, Colorado lost three conference finals, two of them in Game Seven. So they were close, especially in 2000, but they came up against Dallas, who were so deep. Dallas had Ed Belfour in goal—another guy who was very competitive. He never quit on anything. They had the offensive defensemen in Sydor and Zubov. They had Hatcher and Matvichuk, really tough defensemen, and they had Nieuwendyk and Modano up the middle. Their coach, Ken Hitchcock, had them playing as a stingy team, whereas Colorado was more of a skating, offensive team.

But in the next year, 2001, Patrick Roy again made the difference in Colorado's second Cup win. Montreal hasn't won a Cup since they traded him.

Thirty-Two

HOCKEY ON
THE ISLAND

One of the fun things about expansion and the arrival of the WHA back in the 60s and 70s was that truly no one knew how it would all come together. You had all these new players, new teams, new cities. It felt a little as though anything could happen.

But I would guess that no one predicted the kind of dominating success the New York Islanders had. The Islanders made the playoffs for fourteen straight years, winning four Stanley Cups and nineteen playoff series in a row. I'm not sure that record will ever be broken.

Along with the Atlanta Flames, the Islanders entered the NHL in 1972 as an expansion team—a defensive measure by the league to keep the WHA's Raiders out of the New York market. The team moved into Long Island's new Nassau Veterans Memorial Coliseum, built for the New York Nets. Meanwhile, the Raiders were forced into a difficult lease at Madison Square Garden and then left the city halfway through their second season. By 1974–75 they'd ended up in San Diego.

Bill Torrey, formerly of the California Seals, was the Islanders' new general manager. Torrey knew what Sam Pollock had done with the Canadiens, and he wanted to do the same thing—build from the draft instead of trading for veterans. He told his owners that they'd never win with other teams' castoffs.

Torrey was pretty sure they were going to end up in last place—and they did, with twelve wins, sixty losses, and six ties—but that meant getting first draft pick: Denis Potvin. He wasn't tall by today's standards, but he was 220 pounds. You don't have to be a big guy to hit hard. It's more technique than it is brute strength. Mike Peca was known as a devastating hitter, and he was not a big guy at all, maybe 180 pounds. Scott Stevens was maybe 200, and he put fear into guys' hearts. Potvin was a wrecking ball. He could bring down anyone in the league, and he had the hands and heart to match.

Every single general manager in the league offered Torrey something to trade Denis. Emile Francis from the Rangers offered him multiple players, and so did Sam Pollock. But Torrey knew that the only way the Islanders had a chance was if they drafted well for several years. So he held on to his future star.

In their first year, the Islanders led the league with 347 goals scored against. So there was still work to be done.

At the end of their second season, the Islanders were second last, ahead of only the California Seals. Torrey looked for a new coach—although in 1973, there weren't many who wanted to take on an expansion team, given how stingy the league had been in the way they'd distributed players to the two new franchises. The Islanders had about three players of NHL quality, and the rest of them were all minor leaguers. Still, Al Arbour agreed to take the job, and one of the reasons was that he could see the Islanders had put some pieces in place. Arbour knew a thing or two about creating success on an expansion team from his years in St. Louis. He would spend as much time teaching his young team as coaching.

The league made a change in the rules in 1974 because the WHA was signing all the best juniors. Halfway through the season the NHL board of governors decided that each team could draft one underage player between the ages of seventeen and twenty. Torrey's western scouts wanted his first pick to be Bryan Trottier, an underage kid who played for the Swift Current Broncos. But Torrey had his eye on Clark Gillies, a high-scoring left-winger fresh from his Memorial Cup win with the Regina Pats.

No one used the phrase "power forward" back then—that came up around the time Cam Neely joined the Bruins. But if it had existed then, that's what people would have called Gillies. Torrey called him "a grown man amongst boys." He was 6'3½" and weighed 220 pounds, and when the occasion arose he could really handle himself. He intimidated guys.

Torrey's luck held in 1974. Bryan Trottier was still available in the second round. Trottier was still in his first year of junior and playing on the third line. He wasn't yet a star, so teams weren't sure what they would be getting with him. In the end, anyone who let him slip by were kicking themselves very soon. Trottier became just a fabulous two-way player—exceptional defensively, great on faceoffs, and an excellent playmaker. He'd been mentored in Swift Current by Tiger Williams, and was so tough to play against. Bryan won the Calder as rookie of the year with a record 95 points in 1975–76. In 1978–79 he was the first player from a post–Original Six team to win the league scoring title, with 134 points. He also won the Hart as league MVP. Then, a year later, he won the Conn Smythe as playoff MVP when the Islanders won the first of four consecutive Stanley Cups. He'd become the most successful First Nations player in NHL history.

The Islanders had picked up three future Hall of Famers— Potvin, Gillies, and Trottier—in just two amateur drafts. And when you include the 1972 expansion draft, Billy Smith was the fourth.

In their third season, 1974–75, the Islanders took their biggest step yet by making the playoffs. They won the first round, beating the Rangers eleven seconds into overtime in the deciding game. That year, the circus was at the Garden. Billy Harris thought that was lucky, and so he shoveled some elephant dung into a bag—and the team kept it with them throughout that series. When they came back to beat the Penguins after being down three games to none, their good luck charm seemed to be working, but they threw it away after they lost to the defending-champion Flyers in the semifinals. The Flyers went on to win their second Cup in a row. But a bit of playoff success gave the Islanders confidence. It was their first whiff of victory.

I n the 1977 draft, Bill Torrey had the fifteenth pick and was looking at taking Mike Bossy. Bossy had played four years of major junior and averaged seventy-seven goals a year. No one had ever done that before, and no one's done it since.

When Torrey talked to his Quebec scout, Henry Saraceno, who'd coached Mike as a bantam, he said, "Henry, there's no way we can get him. Mike Bossy will be taken in the top eight or ten." Fortunately for the Islanders, though, Mike was a right-winger— and there were a number of right-wingers up for the draft that year. Cleveland took Mike Crombeen, the Rangers picked Lucien

DeBlois, Montreal got Mark Napier, Toronto got John Anderson, and Buffalo picked Ric Seiling. Torrey couldn't believe his luck when he got Mike. Five right-wingers were taken before he was. Hard to believe, but it's true.

Bossy would become the most dangerous forward in the league. He was able to disappear on the ice and get himself in the quiet areas where he could shoot the puck, a lot like Brett Hull. I played with him in the '84 Canada Cup, where he lined up about ten pucks on Grant Fuhr. I was shocked at how many he scored on Grant. He never shot the puck high—a lot of Mike's goals were in the bottom third of the net, twelve to fourteen inches off the ice above the pad. Billy Smith used to say, "Bossy's shots hurt you when they hit you." I'd seen Mike play in junior. I saw him play as a pro. He was one of the great, pure goal scorers. After Potvin and Trottier, Mike would become the third Calder Trophy winner as rookie of the year on the Islanders. He was the fifth Hall of Famer acquired by Torrey.

In that same 1977 draft, Torrey also managed to pick up John Tonelli, the thirty-third overall pick. A lot of teams didn't want to touch him because he was in the WHA, but Torrey knew that he had only one more year to go on his contract and figured it was worth the gamble.

John Tonelli was one of those guys you didn't like to play against. He was unpredictable. He had this high-energy approach to the game—his arms and legs would be going a hundred miles an hour all the time. In the corners or going to the net he was impossible to contain. And he was a very strong guy and tenacious on the puck. He was a tank along the boards. I'm not sure Johnny has been given the recognition he deserves. He was an integral part of the Islanders' success.

In the next two seasons, 1975–76 and 1976–77, the Islanders made it to the semis but ran into the Canadiens. Two years later, they swept Chicago in the quarters but then lost to the Rangers in the semis.

The Rangers were the Islanders' number-one rival. No question. That had been the case right from the get-go, when Rangers fans from Long Island would buy tickets to the Coliseum because it was closer and tickets at the Garden had sold out. At the 1979 training camp the Islanders played the Rangers twice in exhibition—and each game took about six hours because there were so many brawls. During playoffs at Madison Square Garden, Billy Smith used to hide in the net during "The Star-Spangled Banner" because Ranger fans would buy fish in the nearby markets and throw them at him.

In 1979–80, Al Arbour decided he wouldn't worry so much about regular-season standings. After four straight hundred-point seasons, the Islanders dropped to ninety-one points. But Torrey didn't tear it all apart. He stuck with his players, his coach, and his plan. I think that's the big secret. A lot of teams keep changing everything up, meaning that you can never get any traction.

Ken Morrow, who'd been part of U.S. Miracle on Ice, joined the team right after the 1980 Olympics. And as soon as Ken got on the ice against Detroit in his first game with the Islanders, Arbour knew he'd have a big impact on the team. The other big change was acquiring Butch Goring, a great two-way second-line center from L.A., in exchange for popular and longtime right-winger Bill Harris, along with defenseman Dave Lewis.

Butch Goring wasn't a big guy, but he was smart, a great skater, and incredibly fit. He'd been in the NHL for a long time—and without him, there might not have been any Islander Stanley Cups. He brought an element to the dressing room that was really good for the team. One of the first things he did was stand up in the locker room and say, "You guys don't realize how good you are." The team finished the season on a twelve-game undefeated streak. Butch kept the room loose, but when the puck dropped, he was everywhere.

Butch was also a character. He didn't have laces in his skates. He had Velcro straps instead—because as he saw it, tying skates was wasted energy. He wore cowboy boots and no socks with every suit he owned, which were all made out of corduroy. When the Islanders were on the road in Butch's hometown of Winnipeg, they'd come back to the dressing room after the pregame skate and there'd be only one or two sticks left for each player. The Goring family had gone home with the rest. And Butch is the guy who everyone says started the playoff beard tradition. He'd been playing well and didn't want to make changes, so he went into the playoffs with it and everyone on the team kind of followed along. A beard made guys look ready to fight it out.

When Butch came in, he was put on a line with Clark Gillies and Duane Sutter as his wingers—making for a heavy line with a smaller center who had savvy and skill. Another line, with Bobby Nystrom, Wayne Merrick, and John Tonelli (all of them big, 205–210 pounds), was counted on to check, to create energy, and to contribute offensively. The top line was Bryan Trottier, Mike Bossy, and Bobby Bourne. They had skill, speed, and two-way play. Finally there was Anders Kallur, Lorne Henning, Garry Howatt, and Steve Tambellini. That team had just incredible depth.

In the 1979–80 Stanley Cup finals, the Islanders beat the Flyers in six games. Bill Torrey would address the room once a year. He was a very positive guy. He'd echo what Al had been saying all year long and would talk about guys' roles on the team, how important they were. Are you a penalty killer? Are you a checker? Are you a power play specialist? Are you a guy out there playing against the other team's top line and ready to shut them down? Just like Scotty Bowman, he always emphasized that everyone on the team had something to contribute.

He always tried to talk about the teams that won Cups. He'd say, "Yeah, they had stars, but what the perennial Cup winners like the Montreal Canadiens have always had is balance. If you want to win you can't just be a one-man band. Every guy is important. Mike Bossy's a goal scorer. But shutting down their goal scorer is just as important."

What Bill Torrey told his players is still a huge part of what it means to come together as a team. Many players go unnoticed, and yet they're important. And when you win a Stanley Cup, everyone is rewarded.

At the Coliseum on May 24, 1980, the Islanders were leading 4–2 at the end of the second period, but Philadelphia evened it up in the third and the game went into sudden-death overtime. The locker room at the end of the third period was silent. But then one of the guys said, "Who's going to be the hero?" and each guy all the way down the bench said, "I am. I am. I am. I am. I am . . ."

They went out and Bobby Nystrom deflected a John Tonelli pass into the net. In just eight seasons of existence, the Islanders had won the Cup.

In their third run for the Cup, in 1981–82, the Islanders had Bryan Trottier, Butch Goring, Wayne Merrick, and Billy Carroll as their centers. In mid-season they brought in Brent Sutter and moved him into third-line center behind Trottier and Goring. He scored forty-three points in forty-three games that season. In the playoffs, Game One against the New York Rangers, second round, Brent was leaving his own zone with the puck when he tried to beat Rob McClanahan on a one-on-one. McClanahan stripped the puck from him, and the Rangers scored.

That was it for Brent: Arbour moved him to the fourth line. He didn't get much ice time after that, and it was frustrating. He knew he'd made a mistake and that it had cost a goal, but at the same time it was Stanley Cup playoffs! Brent didn't play a regular shift in the next ten playoff games (five more against the Rangers, four against the Nordiques, and one against Vancouver), but then, in the third period of Game Two in the finals against Vancouver, all of a sudden Al sent him out on a regular shift. He was also killing penalties and playing on the second power play unit.

Al played him a ton in Games Three and Four—and they ended up winning the Stanley Cup. The guys were all celebrating in the dressing room when the Islanders' equipment manager, Jim Pickard (who passed away recently), came in and said, "Brent, Radar wants to see you outside the room." Radar was Al Arbour's nickname.

Brent waited, and then Al came up to him and looked down. Al was over six feet, broad-shouldered, and wore big glasses. He said, "Did you learn anything from this?"

Brent, who was nineteen at the time, didn't know what to say. He was a little worried about his mom and dad and his brothers, Duane, Ronnie, and Richie, who were all back in the dressing room. So he just kind of mumbled something. Al grabbed him by the shoulders and said, "I just made you one of the stars of the Stanley Cup, and you're going to have a long, long career."

Brent has carried that with him ever since—not the party, or the dressing room, or the skating around with the Cup on the ice, but that moment with Al. Here was a kid who'd come into the show and everything was rosy. He was playing on a team that had won three Stanley Cups. By sitting him through most of the playoffs, Al was building Brent's mental toughness and making sure he didn't get too far ahead of himself. It was a great, key moment in his career. Al was a firm coach, a hard coach, but most of all, he was fair.

The Islanders made it through to the finals the next season, 1982–83, and even though they'd won three in a row, the media were calling them the underdogs. Against the Oilers.

Thirty-Three

ONLY THE GOOD
DIE YOUNG

P eople often say that when you expand the league, you dilute the talent. And that is partly true. But I don't think talent is a finite resource. I think talent is developed. A good team can grow talent, and a bad situation can damage it. So by bringing new teams into the league, I think the NHL created more opportunities for talent to thrive.

One reason I think that is the way the Oilers came together. In 1979, Glen Sather selected Kevin Lowe with the Oilers' first-ever pick. The four surviving WHA franchises picked at the bottom of the twenty-one NHL teams. (The last thing the NHL wanted was for a WHA team to jump into the league and start winning, so they dispersed the WHA talent, then gave the new franchises the worst draft positions.) The Oilers had the last pick of the first round and got a building block of the franchise.

In the second round, we could have added Neal Broten. But Glen had traded that pick for a pivotal guy in our lineup, David Semenko. In the third round, we got Mark Messier, 48th overall. In the fourth round, we got Glenn Anderson. The next year, 1980, we added Paul Coffey sixth overall, Jari Kurri at sixty-ninth, and Andy Moog at 132nd overall. In '81 we added Grant Fuhr at eighth.

That's three years and five Hall of Famers—Messier, Anderson, Coffey, Kurri, and Fuhr. I would have been in the '79 draft if the Oilers hadn't been able to protect me as part of the roster from their last season in the WHA. That would have made it six. It's hard to make the case that talent was thin when one team could draft that much raw talent that fast.

The key word is "raw." Those Oiler teams were not destined to be a dynasty. We could have messed it all up. In fact, when we started out, we had no idea how much work it was going to take.

The team had a lot of fun together in those early years. Wrestling was a part of that. The early 80s was its golden age in North America, and a lot of people would watch the WWF on TV. It was huge in Edmonton. When he was a teenager in Winnipeg, Cam Connor, one of our tougher wingers, had been good friends with Rod Toombs, later known as Rowdy Roddy Piper, one of the all-time great wrestling personalities. Thanks to what he'd learned from Piper, it was Cam's opinion that wrestling was an outstanding conditioner—as good as lifting weights. So after practices, he and Lee Fogolin (Cam's roommate and a man I will always admire) would team up to take on Dave Semenko and Mark Messier. They'd go into our little players' lounge and wrestle for real. And although Mark was just eighteen at the time, he was so strong that Cam had to dig pretty deep to pin him. That's how strong Mark was even then.

We'd give each other the gears—a lot. Kids and dogs were the only things that were sacred in our locker room. Dave Semenko always kept it loose there—which is what you need in a hockey club. When we were struggling as a group, Semenko would play a little prank or do something funny and it would just lift the weight right off our shoulders. Fans never got to experience that side of Semenko. They'd look at him and think, "That's just a real tough guy." But I'll tell you what, he was very witty and very intelligent. That's how I'll always remember Semenko.

He'd come in early in the morning and use a sewing needle to poke holes in the bottom of the Styrofoam coffee cups. Our shirts were always covered in coffee drips. Dave himself would never drink out of Styrofoam—he always had a heavy stoneware mug. So one day Lee decided to fix him. He went down to the hardware store and bought a 1/32 carbide bit, made it to the rink early in the morning, and drilled a tiny hole into the bottom of Dave's mug. A couple of hours later, Dave was sitting there reading the paper, coffee dripping down his shirt. He started looking around because everyone was laughing and he didn't know what was going on. Suddenly he saw that his shirt was all wet and he said, "Fogie, I know this was you—you're the only guy in this dressing room who knows how to work a drill!"

Whenever you walked into our locker room, you'd hear rock and roll. It had to be turned off thirty minutes before the start of the game, and someone was always delegated to do that. But you didn't shut it down hard. You'd fade it out. Paul Coffey had a big impact on the music because he had an absolute man-crush on Bruce Springsteen. He loved the Boss. One night, Andy Moog heard Stevie Ray Vaughan play "Mary Had a Little Lamb" and decided he must be the coolest person in the world. (Still,

Vaughan would get on the playlist only once in a while because his music was a little too off the beaten track.) There was also some pop, a little bit of electronic, like Devo. Canadian bands were popular, Rush and April Wine. We listened to a lot of Cheap Trick too. Guitar rock.

The booster club in Edmonton used to make signs for us all and hang them way up high in the Coliseum rafters. One night we stepped on the ice for a game and the sign in the rafters said "Penticton sent us a real peach." Paul Coffey knew that our goalie, Andy Moog, was the only Oiler from there, and so from that point on Andy was Peach. When I told Paul that I hadn't seen the sign, he said, "Really? You should skate with your head up."

Andy had a signed Gump Worsley hockey card in his locker. When Andy was very young, for Christmas one year he was given a hockey book full of spectacular color photos. One of the photos was of Worsley, the great Rangers/Canadiens goalie, getting ready to stop a shot with his face. (Worsley didn't wear a mask.) His nose is wrinkled and his lip is curled up. Young Andy had looked at the photo, seen Gump's courage, and thought, "Okay, that's what a goalie is."

Andy had been up and down to the minors a couple of times. Sometime during the 1981 season, Glen called Andy into his office to tell him that he'd be going down again, and Andy was not happy about it. No one is happy getting sent down—you'll never make it to the NHL if you don't believe you can play. But Andy was probably unhappier than most. So Glen gave him a stern lecture and told him to toughen up. "The NHL is no place for a sensitive guy. Get tough or get run over," he said. Glen leaned on all of us, especially early on, because we were all so young. He cared about each guy, he really did. But he could be hard on us.

It was quiet in the dressing room back then. We didn't have nearly the responsibilities after the game that players do today. The media weren't allowed back there, so you could be elated about a victory or frustrated about a defeat. The team even had a sort of post-game tradition where we'd take a bit of time after every game. It might be only five minutes, but it gave us a chance to decompress. Those few minutes talking about the game were special for me. We didn't say anything earth-shattering or mind-blowing, but we said enough.

By April 1981 we'd clinched a spot in the playoffs, but we didn't know who we'd be up against first. Billy Joel was playing at Northlands on April 5, and on the night of the concert we were in the locker room having hors d'oeuvres and cocktails with him when we found out that we'd be playing the Canadiens. Billy Joel was a hockey fan, and having been born in New York, he loved the Rangers and the Islanders. We went into that first game against Montreal with the ghetto blaster turned up full, playing Billy Joel songs like "You May Be Right," "It's Still Rock and Roll to Me," "Big Shot," and "Only the Good Die Young."

Eddie Mio was our number-one goalie, Ron Low was his backup, and Andy Moog was the third. But going into the first round against Montreal, both Ron and Eddie were out of action, each with a broken hand. Andy hadn't played much. He'd had only four starts, but they were all in the final few weeks that spring.

Earlier in the season we'd been at Maple Leaf Gardens, and during the morning skate, Glen told Andy that he'd be making his first start with the team that night. But thirty minutes before the game, right after warm-up, Andy came off the ice and Glen said,

"Andy, we're making a change. Eddie's going to start tonight." Glen's rationale was that if he told Eddie he was playing at Maple Leaf Gardens that night, Eddie would be nervous all day. He wouldn't rest or eat properly. Believing that Andy was going to play allowed Eddie to relax. And so, at his first NHL start, Andy was pulled in the warm-up.

On the way to the airport the next morning, Andy was sitting next to Paul Coffey, who'd been on the team only since the start of the season. They were talking about how frustrating it was not to get the chance to establish themselves. Each of them was saying, "Just give me a chance and I'll show you what I can do." Of course it doesn't work that way. You have to bide your time. But the guys were impatient to contribute.

The first day of the playoffs against Montreal, we were having a morning skate when Glen skated over to Andy and said, "How do you feel?"

"I feel pretty good." Andy was cocky and ignorant—a good combination.

"How would you like to start tonight?"

"I think I'd like that."

Glen said, "Okay, you're in," and skated away.

At that time, the first round of playoffs was a best-of-five series, so you wanted to get off to a quick start. We beat Montreal 6–3 that opening night. Andy was solid in net. Lafleur got some really good shots off, but Andy laughed and said he couldn't believe he'd made the saves. He told me that the puck came off Lafleur's stick differently—it exploded off his blade like a slingshot, but with greater accuracy.

Dick Irvin asked to interview Andy after the game. Dick said, "Andy, are you unhappy you didn't receive a star tonight?" Andy was green, not cocky, when he answered, "Well, maybe I'll get one tomorrow night." And sure enough he had forty stops the next night. We won 3–1 and he got his star. The headline in the Montreal paper the next day was "Andy Who?"

Toward the end of that second game, the Montreal fans let their team know they were unhappy. The whistles went up in the Forum non-stop. It was like another bit of ammunition we could use to try to beat them.

We were still flying commercial at that time, so we flew back to Edmonton the next morning, and when we landed we were met by cheering fans holding up signs. That took us all by surprise. And then about forty-five minutes before warm-up, we could hear screaming, foot-stomping, and cheering. Once we got out onto the ice, it was incredible. The fans stood and clapped and cheered for over three minutes. Northlands was actually vibrating from the noise.

Andy had to block out all that excitement or he'd overreact. Like a lot of goalies, his nerves showed up in his eyes. It's a hard one to explain, but Andy put it this way: "When you're calm, relaxed, and confident, your eyes stay focused on the puck. You're into the puck, you're on the puck. But high-energy games can distract you and make your eyes twitchy."

Andy's dad, Don, had been a goalie for the Penticton Vees, back when guys didn't wear masks. As a result he had no teeth and a nose made out of rubber—it was like a ball in that it could move all over his face. By the time Andy was thirteen, he was at a level where the technical parts of the game had gotten past his father. So for Andy's birthday he bought him a sports psychology book about mental preparation by Thomas Tutko. By the time he was fifteen, Andy had read it through a dozen times. It gave him an advantage in mental strength.

That night, I looked over at Andy. His head was down. He was staring at the ice in his crease, using the visualization and focus skills he'd studied. Moving back and forward. Slowing it all down.

The Montreal Canadiens were thrown off. They did not look like the team everyone knew from the late 70s. We were all over them. When we scored to make it 6–2, I looked over to the bench and saw my teammates' faces and started to realize that it was real. It had been twenty-nine years since the Canadiens had been swept in a playoff series.

The first guy to the net to throw his arms around Andy was Paul Coffey. He was just so incredibly happy for Andy's success. Coff would get his chance too. Within four short years, he'd win the Norris Trophy as the National Hockey League's best defenseman.

When I played for L.A. a few years down the road, Bruce McNall would sometimes tease me and say, "Hey, Wayne, why don't you tell us about the Miracle on Manchester?"

We thought 1981–82 might be our year. We'd come first in the Smythe Division with 111 points, 48–17–15. Vancouver was second, but they were thirty-four points behind us. We ran away with it.

We had the Kings in the first round. They had sixty-three points and a losing record, 24–41–15. And yet despite the point spread, we were both high-scoring teams. They had some great firepower on the Triple Crown Line with Marcel Dionne, Charlie Simmer, and Dave Taylor. Larry Murphy had scored sixty-six points on defense, and they had a great captain in Dave Lewis. These were really proud men. And when we went into the semi-finals to play them, I think we got ahead of ourselves and lost sight of that.

To this day, Bernie Nicholls, who would eventually become my friend and teammate on the Kings, says that they had absolutely no business beating us. In hockey, though, anything can happen. The Kings came into Edmonton and out-gunned us 10–8.

We took the second game 3–2 in overtime and headed to the Forum on Los Angeles' West Manchester Boulevard. In Game Three we were up 5–0 in the third period. Their owner, Jerry Buss, had gone home in defeat, and Glen Sather was behind the bench with a big grin. The Kings scored two goals early in the third. Suddenly, you could sense the momentum kind of turning. They scored their third just before Garry Unger took a five-minute major. They scored two more with Unger in the box, the last one tying the game with only five seconds left in regulation time. Now we were into overtime, and Kings' winger Daryl Evans scored off the faceoff to win it. That game became the Miracle on Manchester.

We took Game Four, but the funny thing is the Kings had just assumed we'd win the series and so they didn't even have a flight booked to Edmonton for Game Five. That meant we shared a plane, which took off at one-thirty a.m. The Kings asked for the front of the plane because we had to play that night and they thought that if we got off first and made it through Customs, Immigration might keep them there the rest of the night just to help us out. They beat us in the final game, 7–4. The hockey world was stunned. Every time I see an interview with their play-by-play guy, Bob Miller, he still talks about it.

But we learned from it.

There was a tremendous amount of pressure from media and fans to break up the whole group because they thought we were too offensively minded. But Glen never gave in to that pressure. What he did was very smart. He hired John Muckler, who came in and molded the group. He was really stern on the direction of each and every player. That freed up Glen to focus on being a bench coach, which meant he didn't have to be as hard on the players as he'd been in the past.

As much as the Oilers had some great players, we really weren't a great *team* in the 1982–83 season. We had a lot to prove. And we'd just learned that if you don't do well in the playoffs, the regular season is forgotten.

We finished our sweep of Winnipeg on April 9, 1983. On April 20 we eliminated Calgary in the fifth game of the second round, and then we swept the Black Hawks. Everything was a little too easy in those first three rounds. What I mean is that, if you're an experienced team, it's great to just walk through each series because it's not as hard on your body and it gives you an advantage, especially if the other teams go deep in their rounds. But if you're an inexperienced team, as we were, you get the wrong message. You think, "Wow, this is not all that difficult. This is going to be our year!" Not that we weren't thrilled. When we were handed the Campbell Bowl for winning the conference, we carried it around like it was the greatest trophy ever—until we got our hands on the next one. For a while, there was a tradition that it was bad luck to touch the Campbell Bowl or the Prince of Wales Trophy. But Sidney Crosby made a point of touching the Prince of Wales in 2016, so maybe that superstition is coming to an end.

Then we ran into the New York Islanders. We were at a point they'd been at a few years before. A disappointing playoff exit, followed by a solid season and a chance at redemption—and a Stanley Cup. The Islanders went through it, we went through it, and I think a big part of the stability for both teams was that neither Torrey nor Sather panicked. Torrey kept his core—Trottier, Bossy, Potvin, Gillies, Smith, and Bob Bourne—together. As I talked about earlier,

Torrey felt that stability was a big factor. Constantly changing coaches and players can lead to overkill in those areas, and by the time you get to the playoffs, you've almost got another team.

In both cases, the Islanders and the Oilers had to learn how to win. We had a real hatred for them and they had a hatred for us, but the one thing I will tell you is that we respected the Islanders more than any other team in hockey and we wanted to be like them.

But we had a long way to go before we could realistically take on the Islanders. Through three games they were simply the better team. We brought all of our speed and energy, and they just found a way to neutralize it. It wasn't that they embarrassed us or ran us out of the building or anything. They just had an answer for everything we could throw at them. The first three games weren't close.

Game Four was held in Nassau County Coliseum. You had to descend to the dressing room through the bowels of the arena. There was a fair bit of nervousness at that point because we were up against a very strong team. And we were down three to nothing. But when we walked into the dressing room to get ready for the game, there at the front of the room was a large blackboard where Kevin Lowe had written, "We've got them right where we want them." We all kind of laughed, and it broke the ice a bit. New York would beat us again to win four straight, but I think it was that kind of philosophy, the attitude Kevin had conveyed in his scrawled comment, that made us a stronger team later on. It was like saying, "They don't have us yet. Let's go out and do what got us here."

I tell this next story a lot because it was a turning point. A lesson that helped us through the next season and playoffs. As we were leaving the Coliscum, dressed up in our suits, Kevin Lowe and

I walked down the hallway past the Islanders' room where their management, wives, and families were celebrating, and we saw some of the old vets sitting there having a beer, relaxed but not in a really festive mood.

They were battered and bruised and had ice bags and heat packs all over their bodies. Meanwhile we were in great shape, ready to go another playoff round. Seeing them like that told us, "Okay, we learned a lot from the previous year—how hard the playoffs are, and how disciplined and focused you have to be. But to win the Stanley Cup, you have to take it to another level."

The time between losing that game and the first playoff game of the next season, 1983–84, seemed an eternity. All we kept thinking was, "We're gonna get back to that final, and when we do get back to that final, we're not gonna lose."

Thirty-Four

THE LAST DYNASTY

M ark Messier provided a lot of leadership in the locker room. He took the team seriously, and he made sure everyone else did too. One of the young players from the minors came in to practice once, and afterward he took his sweater off and threw it at the hamper. He missed and the sweater landed facedown. Mark got up, walked over to this young guy, looked him square in the eye, and in a quiet voice said, "That crest never touches the floor." He was saying it not just to the kid but to all of us. The message was clear. "If you don't respect what that logo stands for, then how can we ever become champions?" It resounded in the hearts of all the players, and the environment in the dressing room seemed to gel.

In 1983–84, the Oilers entirely transformed their thinking. Up till then we played so-called "firewagon" hockey. In other words, we just wanted to score the other team into submission. That's just the way things were in the Clarence Campbell Conference in the west, which was fast and high-flying—and distinctly different from the Prince of Wales Conference in the east, where teams like the Islanders and Bruins and Flyers played a more grinding, methodical game. (The contrast between the two exactly mirrored what was going on in the NBA at the time: the Celtics and the 76ers in the east were physical and the Lakers in the west were fast. Actually, for a number of years there were incredible similarities between the NBA and Stanley Cup playoffs.)

But now we were becoming focused as a team, defensively and offensively. Our assistant coach John Muckler, who was a real strategist, brought the guys together to form a team that could take on the Islanders.

Kenny Linseman was a big asset on the team. He was a smaller guy, 175 pounds soaking wet, but played with a big chip on his shoulder. He'd make a point of going after the tough guys so that they wouldn't come after him. (When winger Kevin McClelland joined the Oilers that year—if we made it to the final against the Islanders, we'd need that kind of muscle and grit—the first time he came into our dressing room he shook Kenny's hand and said he was sure glad Kenny was on our team because he wouldn't have to go through Kenny's stick anymore.)

Kenny could get very intense. He would get whipped up into a blind rage. His mom, Hazel, was a redhead with an unbelievable temper like his, and so they clashed. He was the oldest—Hazel had five kids after Kenny in just eight years. But when Kenny was seventeen, Hazel got sick and died of cancer. It was hard, especially given all the words they'd had between them. That always seemed to ride with Kenny.

I first saw Kenny when I was fifteen. I was playing Junior B hockey with the Toronto Nationals, who were affiliated with the

Peterborough Petes. My next-door neighbor, Paul Goulet, was the chief scout for the Petes (this was when Roger Neilson was coaching the team), and once a month, beginning when I was eight, he'd take me to a game. The next season they had some injuries, and so I got to play three games for them. By then, the Petes were coached by a guy named Garry Young, who was really good to me. My second game we played Kingston. Before the warm-up Garry called me over—I was small, probably 5'9", 125 pounds max. He said, "When you get out there, look over at Number 14."

I nodded.

"Every time 14 is on the ice tonight, you get off."

I got on the ice for warm-up, and saw this little guy wearing number 14. He was so small that I thought, "Why?"

I came back to the bench after warm-up and said to the coach, "You want me to get off the ice for that little guy? Is he that good?"

The coach shook his head. "No, he's the dirtiest guy in the league. He might cut your eye out, and I don't want that to happen." Number 14 was Kenny Linseman. To this day I still tease Kenny and say, "I wasn't allowed to play against you."

In Philly, Bobby Clarke nicknamed him the Rat. I always called him Kenny. I was funny about nicknames. I had a few of them: in the Soo it was Pretzel, early on in the Oilers' locker room it was Wheezy. I just like being called Wayne or Gretz. Not all guys were happy with their nicknames, and I know Kenny wasn't proud of his. I didn't think it suited him anyway. I mean, he played the game ferociously, as tough as anyone who's ever played in the NHL, but from his point of view he was just trying to do whatever it took to be successful and to be a champion.

When we made it through to the Stanley Cup finals, a lot of people perceived our matchup with the Islanders as the new against the old. Actually, the average age difference between the two teams was only a little over a year. Not as much as everyone thinks. (Although it's true that when you compare some of the key guys, they were a little older—Mike Bossy, Bryan Trottier, and John Tonelli were twenty-seven and Denis Potvin was thirty, whereas Oilers Andy Moog and Jari Kurri were twenty-four, Messier and I were twenty-three, and Coffey was twenty-two.) Kevin Lowe had a theory that every full playoff season you play makes you an extra year older—like doggy years. And in 1984, the Islanders were battle-worn. They'd gone through to the finals for five years straight.

Their goalie, Billy Smith, was one of the oldest guys on both teams. He was thirty-three. To call him a competitor would be an understatement. A year earlier, in Game One, we outshot the Islanders thirty-five to twenty-four and yet they won 2–0 on an empty-net goal. Billy did not fit the Islander mold, and in some respects that helped balance things out. He was on the wild side, which took them to another level. There's an old biblical saying, "An angry man stirs up fights," and that's what Billy did. We were in wars with him throughout the entire season and the playoffs. If he had the chance he'd cut your head off. He didn't even pretend he wasn't trying to hurt you if you came near him. I was particularly focused on Billy because I knew he would've loved to bring me to my knees. He hated me, and I didn't like him. Today, though, we have a mutual respect. I know how good he was and how much he wanted to win. Besides Ron Hextall, he was probably the best goaltender I ever played against. Each of them could wield his stick pretty good to protect his crease.

Billy was fearless too. I remember seeing him jawing with Dave Semenko and wondering, "What could Smith be saying to Semenko?" And more importantly, "What was Dave saying back?" Whatever it was, I'm sure it was witty and mean. But in general, tough guys don't get enough credit for being funny. It takes a special kind of coolness to come up with good one-liners in the heat of battle.

A lot of people don't know this, but during the nine-day break after we beat the Minnesota North Stars to make it into the final against the Islanders in 1984, Roger Neilson had just been released by Vancouver. He was a good hockey man and a very creative thinker, so Glen hired him as our first video coach. Very few teams used video back then, but Roger spent his entire career trying to find ways to win.

Before he started coaching in the NHL, Roger was coaching for the Peterborough Petes. In 1968, there was a penalty shot against his team, so Roger put a defenseman in net. When the shooter picked up the puck, the defenseman charged out. As a result, a rule was established that you had to have a goalie in net on a penalty shot.

Roger once pulled his goalie when the faceoff was in his own end. The puck dropped, a forward stepped on the ice and skated to the red line, and the guy taking the faceoff passed it up-ice for a breakaway. So, again because of Roger, there's now a rule that requires you to have all six guys on the ice unless there's a penalty.

Glen Sather never tried to snuff out our creativity, but he wanted to review the tapes and watch what was going on. Interestingly, the Islanders were doing then what a lot of teams do now: collapsing into the slot on defense. All five Islanders would protect the middle in front of their own net. They would let you wheel around the perimeter all night, passing back and forth and taking bad-angle shots. Then they would grab the rebound and go the other way.

You can't pass if no one is open, so it was really hard for us to make the kind of plays we were used to making. We were such a good skating, passing team. So we'd try it anyway—and we'd just end up turning the puck over and they'd go back on a two-on-one.

Our new game plan for the finals was to take the puck wide, take the shot, and have guys driving to the net. We weren't supposed to try to make any plays in the slot. The coaching staff said, "Forget trying for beautiful plays. Don't even bother looking in the slot until we're safely ahead and the Islanders are taking risks. Then, if you outman them, obviously make a play."

The Islanders were a really businesslike team. They had every element—skill, smarts, and some really tough guys. But they weren't bullies. The Flyers were bullies, and the Bruins were bullies, or tried to be. The Islanders were like Wall Street. They were like a corporation: everything was in place, everyone had their job. We knew that passing was a huge part of their game, but the video helped us with their patterns. Roger's videos were like that.

The thing about going up against championship teams like the Islanders is that they've got great forwards you have to defend against, tough defensemen you've got to get through, and then a top goalie you have to outmaneuver. They could beat you offensively and defensively and they could beat you up. They had it all. We did too, but they were a dynasty team, and once you win, you know what it takes to win.

People always say to me, "Who was the hardest player to play against? Who was the best defenseman?" There were a lot of good defensemen I played against—among them Larry Robinson, Ray Bourque, and Brian Leetch. And the Islanders had a Kim Clackson–type player named Gordie Lane who was flat-out dirty, so I didn't like being out there with him. You never knew what he was going to do.

But I have to say that Denis Potvin was the hardest. I played every shift against him, Butch Goring, and Bob Bourne. Matchups were a big part of the NHL, and still are, I was always conscious of where he was on the ice because he'd be looking to run the crap out of you. I even knew when he was drinking Gatorade on the bench—that's how closely I watched him. He wasn't dirty, but he was mean, very mean. I say that in a hockey way, not in a bad way. He used to like to step up at the blue line and he'd either stick his big hip out or lay his shoulder into you. He didn't want to let you get any momentum. It was like running into a parked car.

They really outplayed us in Game One, but we won it 1–0 because goaltender Grant Fuhr stood on his head and they couldn't score. As well, the video had shown us where to be when the Islanders moved the puck, so we were able to constantly intercept their passes. For instance, Brent Sutter and Kevin McClelland took a faceoff to the right of Billy Smith. Sutter won the draw for the Islanders, but our left-winger Dave Hunter followed him into the corner. Pat Hughes picked up the loose puck and passed it over to McClelland. Glen always preached, "Hit the net with a quick release," and sure enough, it worked in that situation.

McClelland was a guy brought in to provide some grit up front, and he ended up with the game-winning goal. Teams love it when guys like that score big goals. (In fact, Kevin chipped in a lot that spring.) But Grant was the hero that night. He turned away thirty-four shots to become the first goalie since the great Frank McCool in 1945 to get a shutout in his first Stanley Cup final game. Grant would never complain about the fact that he was often left alone to fend for himself defensively. And yet without him we wouldn't have won.

Because we'd shut out the Islanders in their own building, we had a lot of confidence. We thought, "Oh, things are going to be different this year." And then they beat us 6–1 in Game Two. I sat next to Lee Fogolin for the five-hour flight back from Long Island that night and I don't think we said two words to each other. We all had this "Oh man, it's going to happen again" feeling of dread.

The next day we called a lunch at this little dive in downtown Edmonton called Swat Headquarters, where we all went for pickled eggs and draft beer and to shoot pool. You could feel the intensity level. Everyone had it in their eyes: we were not going to let them beat us like last year.

Mark Messier could lift the team up on his shoulders sometimes. In the second period of Game Three, Clark Gillies scored to put the Islanders ahead 2–1. Then came a turning point. Lee Fogolin was on the blue line when the puck floated back to him. Mess came back and circled, and Lee just pushed it to him. Mess spun around, headed down the boards, cut across, skated around their defenseman Gord Dineen, and then put it in on Billy Smith's stick side.

It was a great goal. And not only did it regenerate our bench and our crowd, but it also seemed to deflate the Islanders. We ended up winning that game 7–2. In the dressing room afterward, Kenny Linseman said, "Once Mark smelled victory, man, it was over."

Near the end of Game Three, Grant got banged up in a collision with Pat LaFontaine outside the net. Back then the rule was "Hit the goalie, no big deal." Grant had also been nursing a sore shoulder, and the hit made it a lot worse. Andy stepped in for the last eight minutes.

The next day when we headed to the rink, everyone was wondering, "Is Grant going to be healthy enough to play?" Once we got there it was pretty evident that he wasn't, but we couldn't let that information out to the Islanders, so we kept it quiet until game time.

Andy Moog didn't like getting wound too tight. He thought his energy might take him all over the place, and then he'd over-challenge in the net or go way outside the crease and overhandle the puck. We knew he needed to relax and settle into his game, so we were pretty low-key with him. It was a "How do you feel? Are you ready to go? Let's get it done" sort of thing. Very much "another day at the office" kind of attitude.

We took Game Four with the same score, 7–2. Andy was still in goal for Game Five. He was so steady and focused. You've got to have goaltending or you're not going to lift the Stanley Cup.

No one was saying much once we got out on the ice for Game Five. Conversations were really brief. We had to stay in the moment because the Northlands was coming unglued. But when we scored an empty-netter with only a few seconds left on the clock to make it 5–2, I started looking around and seeing the faces, and that's when I realized it was real. It was going to happen. That may be my best Stanley Cup memory. That feeling of, I don't want to call it relief, but joy and pride. It's a great trophy. For years, out of all the major championships in North America, it was the only trophy that was presented to the players themselves. When a trophy was won in other sports, it was handed to the owner. But when the Stanley Cup is won, it's handed to the players, and it's always been that way.

I picked it up and hoisted it. I didn't realize how heavy it was and it started to roll forward, but the guys had my back.

We made it our goal at the start of the 1984–85 season to win the Cup again—and to prove that beating the Islanders hadn't been a fluke. And it wasn't. We were on a roll. We swept the Kings and the Jets, and closed out the Black Hawks in six. We met the Flyers in the final.

Philadelphia was a great team, full of guys who just didn't give up. Brian Propp was one of their top scorers. Brian and I are good friends today, but back then he'd just started this thing called the "guffaw," which he'd learned from watching comic Howie Mandel. After a goal, Brian would go down on one knee, take his glove off, and flip his hand in the air. It drove us nuts. We wanted to chop his hand off every time he did it.

They also had the Sutter brothers, Richie and his twin, Ronnie, along with Dave Poulin, Mark Howe, Derrick Smith, Brad Marsh, Dave Brown, Tim Kerr, Peter Zezel, Brad McCrimmon, and a great young Swedish goalie named Pelle Lindbergh.

The Flyers dictated the first game and beat us 4–1. Glen Sather was so steamed by the way we played that he burned the game tapes after he watched them. We got the message and took the next three games. In Game Five, we were ready to bring the series to an end.

Grant Fuhr played phenomenally well. He'd kept us in through the first round against L.A., and in the finals against Philadelphia he made some critical saves. Paul Coffey had an incredible series too. In the final game he scored back-to-back goals, which took us into the second period with a huge advantage, up 4–1. What most people didn't know was that Paul had injured his foot and his hip in the division finals against Winnipeg. And yet he wound up with twelve goals (thirty-seven points) in the playoffs, breaking Bobby Orr's and Brad Park's records of nine playoff goals for a defenseman, along with Denis Potvin's record of twenty-five points. I won the Conn Smythe, but both Paul and Grant could have easily been picked instead. I remember Peter Pocklington saying that winning the Cup again was like having a second child.

We didn't make it to the final the next year, though. Calgary had our number, and went on to meet Montreal in the final. The Habs rode a young Patrick Roy to victory in the first all-Canadian Stanley Cup matchup since the 1967 expansion. We came back in 1986–87 determined to bring the Cup home to Edmonton.

We ran into the Flyers in the final, and that meant a showdown with a hot—and hotheaded—goalie. Ron Hextall was standing on his head in his rookie season. Sadly, the reason Hextall really got the opportunity to play in Philadelphia was that in November the season before, goalie Pelle Lindbergh died in a car crash. Philadelphia's young team was just devastated by his death. It took them a year to recover. Hextall's outstanding performance was part of that.

He was a big guy—6'3"—and he was an outstanding puckhandler. In fact, he became just the second NHL goalie ever to score a goal. But it was Hextall's intensity that really carried the

Flyers. He was the first goalie to rack up more than 100 penalty minutes in a season.

The thing is, his chippiness also helped us. I can't say we went into the finals complacent, but we *were* a little laid-back, and it was Ron's fire that made us hate them and get us into the series. Hate can be a great motivator. For example, in Game Four we were ahead 4–1. Glenn Anderson used his stick on Ron's pad to free up a puck, and seconds later, when Kent Nilsson skated by the net, Ron got him in the back of the leg with a two-hander that cost him eight games at the start of the next season. Ron's fiery temper helped the Flyers over-achieve and take us to seven games. But we used it to win the Cup.

Hextall won the Conn Smythe that year. Not to take anything away from him—he played tremendously and kept them in the series—but when the losing goalie wins the MVP, it tells you that his team was pretty badly outplayed. That was something people never said about Grant Fuhr. He was incredible in net. To me, Grant was the greatest goalie who ever played.

But in 1987, something that seems to happen to all dynasties began happening to us. We started losing players. When Paul Coffey and Glen couldn't come to terms on a new contract, Paul sat out for the first twenty-one games of the season and was traded to Pittsburgh.

We also lost Andy Moog. Andy was tired of being Grant Fuhr's automatic backup. He wanted to play. He decided to sit out, and took the opportunity to play for the Canadian Olympic team. He eventually played five seasons for Boston and four for Dallas and a final season with Montreal.

We'd come off three Cups in four years. We knew we were a good team. Meanwhile, Boston was coming off a very good series, having beaten the Montreal Canadiens in the Stanley Cup playoffs for the first time in forty-five years. The Canadiens won eighteen straight series between 1946 and 1987. To me, that's still one of the most shocking stats in the history of hockey. I mean, think of the great teams with Milt Schmidt and Johnny Bucyk, and then of course with Esposito and Orr.

We had fully expected to meet either Boston or Montreal in the final. The good news was that we knew our experience would be a big advantage—the Bruins were going to be in the same situation we were in '83 against the Islanders. The bad news was that our record as a team and as individuals was just absolutely horrible in the Boston Garden.

Look at our stats. From '79 to '88, we had only two wins over a nine-year period. Part of that was the effect of the small ice surface there—we were a skating team, and the Bruins were experts at using their rink to take away time and space. But the other thing to keep in mind was that every time we played Boston during the season, we'd be on the tail end of a five- or six-game road trip. We might play Buffalo Thursday night, Philly Saturday, and Boston Sunday. We were professionals, so we couldn't make excuses. But it was a factor.

So we were thinking, "Hey, they haven't seen the real Edmonton Oilers. We're gonna play the first two games at home and then fly to Boston, where we're going to have a nice skate and a practice. We'll be comfortable and rested and ready to play." Not that we took them lightly. They had Ray Bourque, Craig Janney, and Cam Neely, who was a lot like Clark Gillies. And speaking of guys who were no fun to play against, Ken Linseman was now with the Bruins. And in net for the Bruins? Andy Moog.

We played really well in the first two games in Edmonton. The hockey world had anticipated that Boston would be better than us at defense—it was their strength, after all—and so everyone was surprised at how strong we were in our own end. In Game One we held them to fourteen shots and won 2–1. Game Two we held them to twelve shots and won 4–2.

Now we were heading to Boston for Game Three, and because of our record there, everyone figured that the tide would turn. What people didn't know was that Glen and John Muckler had us watching videos of their games so we could see what we needed to do on a smaller ice surface—how we were going to break out of a smaller neutral zone, how the wingers had to be more tentative and stay back instead of getting ahead of the play. In those days, you couldn't make a two-line pass out of your zone, so the Garden's small neutral zone meant that we had to be more patient as a group and come up together. But the biggest factor was what to do with Ray Bourque.

Ray Bourque was the key on defense. Everybody in the National Hockey League said one thing: "When you play Boston, don't dump it to Ray Bourque. Keep the puck away from Ray Bourque." Glen and John said, "Let's do the opposite. Go ahead and dump the puck to Ray Bourque, because he's going to move it to his partner and we can get on that guy."

So for five days, at every practice one of our young defensemen would come out in a number 7 jersey (someone even put it on his helmet), and we'd practice dumping the puck to Ray. We had it down to a science.

We went into Game Three and started working our strategy—and I think it caught them off guard. For years and years teams had dumped the puck to the other corner, and now all of a sudden they had to figure out how to handle our new system. Physically, our guys simply wore Ray down. They just dumped it into his corner and pounded him—and we had a big team. Meanwhile, we played

Steve Smith against Cam Neely—every shift. Cam was becoming the best player in the Eastern Conference. A bull. He was fearless and could score sixty goals. But Steve Smith was a big strong guy too. Steve and Cam battled toe to toe for four and a half games. Steve did a great job on him.

My good friend Ace Bailey had a buddy who owned a restaurant bar in Boston called Three Cheers. I said, "Ace, let's set up a party after Game Four. Food, hors d'oeuvres, champagne. We've got about eighty people." (During the playoffs, we'd normally have a team meal back at the hotel, where they'd set up a buffet. Our families would be there because, as I've said, Glen was really good about that. Looking back, I understand why he did it. It put the players at ease. When you play and your family comes out, you can't help worrying, "Okay, where's my mom and dad gonna go eat tonight? Where are we going to go after the game?" Glen took away that worry.)

In Game Four, with about three and a half minutes left in the second period, Craig Simpson scored to tie it 3–3. And then all the lights went out.

It was pitch black on the ice. After about ten minutes one of the older guys, I can't remember who, said, "Power isn't coming back on. This game is over."

I thought, "Over? How can it be over?"

We went back to the locker room, and everyone was quiet. When we got on the bus I said, "Well, we have to go to Three Cheers. We've got all this stuff!" And so the whole team went over to Congress Street by Boston Harbor. We were still in disbelief. We ate the Buffalo wings and onion rings and potato skins and everyone had a few beers and some wine, but no one was celebrating. It wasn't as if we'd lost, so no one was upset. It was more like, "Okay, now what?"

I've been through a lot of things in professional sports and amateur sports, and I've never seen anything like it. What was even more amazing was that while we were still sitting in the locker room wondering what to do, we watched NHL president John Ziegler on CBC. He was standing in a corner of Boston Garden holding the rule book. There were a ton of reporters surrounding him. Ziegler had found a bylaw on the books from the 1920s that said if the lights go off and they can't come back on, the game will be replayed in its entirety. There was to be a Game Five, Six, Seven, and Eight if necessary. And all the individual statistics from the game would count. It was all mapped out.

I turned to Mark and said, "Is this really happening? They kept that rule in for all these years?" Here's the funny thing about it. Somebody said, "Well, what would Glen Sather have done?"

I said "Glen wants to win." If there was no rule and they said "We're starting at 3–3," Glen would have said "We're starting over." If they'd said "We're starting over," Glen would have said "We're starting at 3–3!" He'd look for any advantage he could get.

The next morning we flew to Edmonton at nine a.m. We had a great practice. In the locker room our attitude was, "Okay, we got one more game. Let's win."

We took the game 6–3, but it turned out to be a wild one. The Bruins had no intention of rolling over, and they scored first. But once we had fought our way back into it, the fight started to leave them. I knew what that felt like. By the end, Andy Moog was left alone a little. The lopsided score wasn't his fault. It just goes to show how important desire and the will to win are to the game of hockey. If you come to the conclusion that you can't win, it's game over. In the end, we became the only team in NHL history to accomplish a four-game sweep in five games.

When we won the first Cup in '84 it was chaotic. People were jumping on the ice, you couldn't move, it was out of control. By the fourth one, the fans wanted to sit back and take it all in. In those days, when you got the Cup you skated around the ice in a group. We didn't do what they do today—give it to one guy who skates up and down and then passes it to the next guy. We just sort of passed it to each other in a pile.

So when we were done skating with it, I looked around and saw that no one was left on the ice except the people from our team, the PR guys, the scouts, the extra players, the trainers, and the coaches. I thought, "Wow, we gotta get a picture."

We pulled everyone together and I said, "Do you remember in the 60s when the Leafs and the Canadiens won the Cup and they got a picture on the ice?" And everyone said, "Yeah, yeah! We gotta do this picture!"

The fans were great: they stayed in the stands cheering and taking pictures while we piled together on the ice and got a team picture. It's become a bit of a tradition. Every team that wins a Cup now does a team picture on the ice. It's a pretty special picture for me, as it was my last time in an Oilers sweater.

People always say the same thing: "Oh, you had it planned. You knew you were getting traded." I had no idea. My dad did, but he didn't tell me until later that night when he said, "You know what, you're gonna get traded."

I was traded to the L.A. Kings that August, but Edmonton still had a strong core of players led by Mess and Kevin Lowe. Your best players, the core group, usually sort of carry the load. Normally the core group is at their best somewhere between the ages of twenty-three and twenty-nine. In 1988, Mark was twenty-seven and Kevin was twenty-nine. Edmonton was on top for a twelve-year stretch because over that period Glen would tinker, as did Serge Savard or Scotty Bowman, with a couple of players to incorporate some new energy, new blood, and new excitement—but you can't switch up all your core players. Look at the success of, say, the Flyers or the Canadiens in the 70s—they didn't really mess with the core. Gordie Howe's GM in Detroit, Jack Adams, always said that a team can stay on top in hockey for five years and then things fall apart. I don't agree. I believe that you can go a good, solid ten years with a core group of players.

In 1989–90, the Oilers made some changes in the lineup. Grant Fuhr missed the first ten games with appendicitis, then hurt his shoulder. That opened the door for Bill Ranford. Glen Sather traded Jimmy Carson, who had come to Edmonton in my trade, to Detroit along with Kevin McClelland for Peter Klima, Adam Graves, Joe Murphy, and Jeff Sharples. The Oilers finished fifth overall and Mess was second in scoring in the league with 129 points.

In the playoffs, the Oilers fell behind against the Jets but won three in a row to move on. They swept us and knocked off Chicago, and then met the Bruins in the final. Game One of that series was the longest in the history of the Stanley Cup finals. Peter Klima had been benched most of the game, so by the third overtime, he was about the only player on either side not exhausted. He scored and the Oilers took the series four games to one for their fifth Cup. Bill Ranford won the Conn Smythe for his outstanding goaltending through the playoffs.

In 1990–91, the Oilers started to slip just a bit. Jari Kurri couldn't get the contract he wanted from Edmonton, so he played for HC Devils Milano in Italy for a year, and Grant Fuhr was out for fifty-nine games. They were still good enough to beat the Flames in seven games and us in six, but then they lost to Minnesota. Minnesota had a great Cinderella run that year until they ran into Mario, Jagr, and Ron Francis with the Penguins.

Prior to the next season, 1991–92, the Oilers traded Glenn Anderson and Grant Fuhr to Toronto. Steve Smith was traded to Chicago. Jari's rights were traded to Philadelphia. Charlie Huddy was claimed by Minnesota in the expansion draft. And Mess was traded to the Rangers, where he would eventually lead them to their first Stanley Cup in fifty-four years. The days of the Oilers' dynasty were over.

Thirty-Five

YESTERDAY, TODAY, AND TOMORROW

I don't know if we will ever see another dynasty like those Oilers teams. That's not boasting. I just think it is harder to build a roster like that today than it was in 1979. There have definitely been some special teams since then, and the Detroit Red Wings came close, but the league is different now. It is harder to win in today's NHL, if only because it's harder to make the playoffs. You see teams win the Cup one year, then not even qualify the next. And when you have finally put together a winner, it's so much harder to keep that team together.

The team that may be closest to dynasty status today is the Chicago Blackhawks. The Hawks have won three Cups in six years, and even though they were out of the 2016 playoffs in the first round, they still have potential for more. Every time they lose a veteran due to salary cap pressures, they seem to find new stars. They lose goaltender Antti Niemi, they find Corey Crawford. They lose Patrick Sharp, they find Artemi Panarin. They lose Brandon Saad, they trade for Artem Anisimov and Andrew Ladd. With one of the strongest core groups ever—Jonathan Toews, Patrick Kane,

Duncan Keith, and Brent Seabrook—they just keep winning, and all this under a salary cap.

Chicago's general manager, Stan Bowman, is Scotty's son. He was always intrigued by Scotty's work, and when he was a kid he'd sit close by and listen when Scotty was on the phone. Afterward he'd say, "Why is this happening? What did that mean? Why did you say this?" Even before he went to college at Notre Dame to study finance and computer applications, he had a summer job as an assistant stock analyst. He'd sit in a room all day analyzing stuff.

Stan really wanted a job in sports. So he sent his résumé around to teams and players and got a response from the Blackhawks. GM Mike Smith had been a computer guy himself, and so in 2001 he brought Stan in to learn the ropes. Stan ran around getting coffee, doing anything he could for Mike.

Mike was fired in 2003 and replaced by Dale Tallon, who came to the team as a player in the 70s and had worked in the front office for years. Stan started working for Dale, advising him on regulations and bylaws. In July 2009, Dale was fired and Stan was promoted to GM.

Some people want to get to the chase right away, but Stan likes to take his time. Knee-jerk mid-season trades aren't his style. But in February 2015, Chicago's star right-winger, Patrick Kane, had sixty-four points in sixty-one games and then broke his clavicle after Florida's Alex Petrovic cross-checked him into the boards. It put him out for the rest of the season. Stan put Patrick on the long-term reserve list, which doesn't count against the cap. That gave him a couple of million dollars. Then he made a trade with the Coyotes: first-round draft pick and defenseman Klas Dahlbeck for center Antoine Vermette. Vermette helped the Hawks win a Cup and then went back to Arizona as a free agent. It was a win-win deal and a lot like something Sam Pollock might do.

There's so much more parity now because of the salary cap. The cap was the result of the 2004–05 NHL lockout: NHL commissioner Gary Bettman—and this is what I admire about him—wanted every team, whether it's Ottawa or Arizona, to be able to compete with Philadelphia, the Rangers, and Toronto. If you had thirty teams but only sixteen of them could make a lot of money, that would eliminate fourteen teams. How would that grow the game? But now, thanks to the cap, you've got a chance to win a Stanley Cup no matter how big your market is.

Before the cap, teams could spend as much as they wanted to keep a dynasty franchise together forever, but obviously that didn't happen. Going all the way back to the glory days of the Toronto Maple Leafs in the 60s, great teams were torn apart not necessarily over money but over personalities. The Leafs had great players like Dave Keon, Tim Horton, Carl Brewer, and Johnny Bower in net. They also had Frank Mahovlich, one of the most gifted players of that era. Mahovlich was good enough to beat out Bobby Hull for rookie of the year. He scored forty-eight goals in his fourth season—the most ever for a Leaf at that time—and a record that stood for twenty-one years. The Leafs won the Stanley Cup in 1962, and then before training camp that fall, Mahovlich's contract came up for renewal. But he and Punch Imlach couldn't come to terms, and so Mahovlich walked out of training camp.

The Chicago Blackhawks heard about the dispute and offered the Leafs a million dollars for Mahovlich, which made headlines. At first, Leafs co-owner Harold Ballard accepted the deal and ten one-hundred-dollar bills as a deposit. But the next morning owner-ship had second thoughts and Ballard canceled it. The Leafs gave Mahovlich the contract he was looking for.

But Punch Imlach never forgot what he saw as Mahovlich's act of disloyalty and disobedience. Imlach would constantly rag on him, telling him that he wasn't playing up to his potential. He'd mispro-nounce "Mahovlich" and put him down. He made Mahovlich's life miserable. Things got so bad that in 1964 Mahovlich missed a month due to depression. His doctor told him that his depression had a name: it was called Punch Imlach.

Mahovlich led the Leafs in playoff scoring when they won the Cup in 1964, and he was among the scoring leaders when they won again in 1967, but just before playoffs, on March 3, 1968, Imlach traded him to Detroit along with Peter Stemkowski and Garry Unger for Norm Ullman, Paul Henderson, and Floyd Smith. The deal also included rights to defenseman Carl Brewer, who didn't get along with Imlach either. He had been sitting out since 1965.

In 1968–69 Mahovlich played on a line with Gordie Howe and Alex Delvecchio and scored forty-nine goals. He played a year and a half more in Detroit, and then was traded to Montreal, where he won two more Stanley Cups.

Stafford Smythe fired Imlach at the end of the 1968–69 season, blaming him for depleting the team of player strength. Imlach said that someday he'd make Smythe eat his words. The next year, 1970, when Buffalo and Vancouver finally got expansion teams, Imlach was hired as the Sabres' coach and GM. His first draft pick was future superstar Gil Perreault. In 1975, Buffalo won the Prince of Wales Conference in their final game of the season—by beating the Leafs.

The Calgary Flames had a similar scenario in the 1980s. They were an incredibly strong team. GM Cliff Fletcher had started signing U.S. college players who'd slipped past the draft. He used some of those players to trade for Joey Mullen and Doug Gilmour out of St. Louis. Then he made some excellent draft picks—Joe Nieuwendyk, Gary Roberts, Hakan Loob, Mike Vernon, defensemen Al MacInnis and Gary Suter, and Theo Fleury, who was 166th overall. They were so loaded that they traded Brett Hull for depth on defense. With size, toughness, and character, Calgary went to the Cup final in '86 and won the Cup in '89.

If that team had stayed together they would have continued to be contenders, maybe even a dynasty. But just like Frank Mahovlich in the 60s, Dougie Gilmour's contract was up and he was looking for fair compensation. Even though Al MacInnis had won the Conn Smythe in their Stanley Cup year using his slap shot from the point to score thirty-one points, Dougie had made huge contributions as well. He scored two goals in the third period of the deciding game in the '89 final, helping the Flames become the first opposing team ever to win the Cup in the Montreal Forum against the Canadiens.

But Cliff Fletcher didn't want a big pay gap between players: he thought it was divisive. In the mid-1980s the Flames' payroll was $5 million. It didn't matter if you were Kent Nilsson or Tim Hunter. Fletcher's philosophy was, "I don't want to pay my top guys too high, and I don't want to pay my bottom guys too low." Then, in 1991, Fletcher moved to the Leafs and Doug Risebrough replaced him as Calgary's GM. Risebrough had played with Yvan Cournoyer through four Stanley Cups, 1976–79, and so he kept telling Dougie Gilmour that he wanted him to be his Cournoyer. Gilmour told him that that was fine as long as he paid him like Cournoyer. Negotiations were stalled. They were fighting over a $100,000 difference. After scoring a goal and an assist in an overtime win on New Year's Eve against Montreal, Dougie walked out the next day, January 1, 1992.

Risebrough had grown up in the Montreal Canadiens organization, and he was all about team loyalty. So he got on the phone with Cliff, and in the heat of the moment they worked out a deal— Doug Gilmour, experienced defensemen Jamie Macoun and Ric Nattress, goaltender Rick Wamsley, and prospect Kent Manderville would be traded for Gary Leeman, Craig Berube, defensemen Alexander Godynyuk and Michel Petit, and goalie Jeff Reese.

Leeman, who'd scored fifty-one goals two seasons earlier with the Leafs, struggled in Calgary. He scored just two goals in the rest of the '92 season and then only nine before being dealt to Montreal in January 1993. Eleven goals in two seasons—for Doug Gilmour, who had back-to-back hundred-point seasons for the Leafs.

That trade marked the beginning of a long decline for the Flames. Risebrough continued having trouble coming to terms with many of his players, including Al MacInnis, who went on to several great years in St. Louis and won an Olympic gold medal; Gary Suter, who was on the World Cup of Hockey winning team in 1996 and two U.S. Olympic teams; and Mike Vernon, who won another Stanley Cup with Detroit in 1997. Risebrough's estimation of their market value was very low. It got so bad negotiating with Vernon that the coach at the time, Dave King, went up to Doug's office and said, "Leave him alone. This is going to affect his play."

The Flames didn't really turn it around until their 2004 Cinderella run to the Stanley Cup finals. Meanwhile, Gilmour's arrival in Toronto had moved them from a team that missed the playoffs to a legitimate Cup contender right away.

One or two guys like Gilmour, the character guys, can change a franchise. Chicago found that in Jonathan Toews. Toews is the leader, the glue. Everyone knows his history and reputation for taking responsibility, how he plays, and what a good team guy he is. When he became captain of the Hawks at twenty years old, he was the third-youngest captain in NHL history behind the Penguins' Sid Crosby and Tampa Bay's Vincent Lecavalier, who were both nineteen.

Around Toews are guys like Brent Seabrook and Duncan Keith, who's a horse. He reminds me so much of Brian Leetch, who was one of the best players I ever played with. Brian was a guy who had the heart of a champion, and that's how Duncan plays. There's also Patrick Kane. We play in an era where everyone says you have to be big and fast. It's not that Kane isn't fast, but he's not the fastest guy out there and he's not the biggest. What he's got is unique hockey sense. It's very special—I don't know if there's anything comparable. He's his own man. He can slow the game down to his pace, with all five opposing players skating his game, and then he'll shift to another gear. He's also got possibly the softest hands in the game. He does things with the puck I've never seen anybody do.

Edmonton has Connor McDavid. He's already started to drive the bus and take all the pressure off the other guys. Teams can be great only if they have guys who allow them to be great. A great player can pioneer the trail—Orr, Howe, Béliveau, Richard, and hopefully McDavid.

If you look at the Oilers trying to find their way, as they have for the last number of years, you see a lot of changes—change the coach, change this, change that—all because there hasn't been growth. But I think we'll see more success now with McDavid at the center, along with guys like Darnell Nurse, who's a Kevin Lowe type; Oscar

Klefbom, a solid d-man, their Charlie Huddy; and Jordan Eberle, who might be like Craig Simpson. In terms of his role and importance on the team, Ryan Nugent-Hopkins would be like any of our era's third-line centers, Mark Lamb or Kenny Linseman.

McDavid makes everybody around him better. He's a really bright kid. I'm told that players already look to him and that he deflects it in a humble way, which is all the more reason for his team to want to follow him. Players around a guy like that will evolve. A core player won't make them—after all, people are who they are—but that player's strengths will come out in those around him, and you build on that.

The draft really is everything, it really is. It's so important—that's how you build the foundation of the team. Look at the 1980s Oilers' draft picks: Messier, Anderson, Kurri, Fuhr, Coffey. Montreal's 1975–76 Stanley Cup–winning team was pretty much all developed within the Habs' system. They were so deep they basically had two teams.

Today, because of the cap, a player's true value as a draft pick is maximized during development. That way a team can supplement their roster with players on entry-level contracts. If they're drafted high, your top six players have to be part of your overall roster because the veteran guys who are carrying the majority of the baggage are seven-, eight-, or nine-million-dollar players.

Drafting Patrick Kane, Connor McDavid, Steven Stamkos, and Taylor Hall—those aren't the hard picks. You know what you're getting. What really becomes important for a franchise is your second-, third-, and fourth-round picks. Chris Chelios was a 1981 Montreal second-rounder; Chicago picked up Duncan Keith second round in 2002; and Colorado picked up Paul Stastny second round in 2005. Third-rounders include Kris Letang (2005) and Brad Marchand (2006). Fourth- and fifth-rounders like Braden Holtby (2008) and Kevin Biekesa (2001) have to be able to jump in and be a big part of the success of their team.

And then of course you get your steals. Dougie Gilmour was 134th in 1982; Luc Robitaille was 171st overall when Los Angeles picked him up in 1984; Jamie Benn was 129th for Dallas in 2007; Calgary's Johnny Gaudreau was 104th in 2011; and in the same year Chicago's Andrew Shaw was 139th.

I'll tell you a funny story about the draft. Pittsburgh Penguins GM Craig Patrick drafted Jaromir Jagr fifth overall at the 1990 draft in Vancouver. Four teams had passed on him before Patrick grabbed him because Jagr had said he wasn't going to leave Czechoslovakia. He'd told the four teams who picked ahead that he was playing for his father's team in Kladno and didn't want to play in the NHL. But when the Penguins interviewed him he said, "If you draft me, I'll come tomorrow." That was because he idolized Mario Lemieux and secretly wanted to play with him.

That's another reason it's hard to build a dynasty today. Pittsburgh picked Jagr, but Jagr also picked Pittsburgh. And that is even more true with free agency. Guys want to go where they are going to have the most success, and who can blame them? Some teams just know how to win, and if I were a developing player I would want to go where my hard work was going to be maximized. But the other side of that is some franchises are going to find it hard to hold on to guys they have drafted and developed if they can't convince them it's in their best interest to stay.

Thirty-Six

"I JUST LOVE TO PLAY"

I n my early years in the NHL I'd often sit with Bobby Hull, Gordie Howe, Phil Esposito, Guy Lafleur, and Jean Béliveau. They were very good to me. And I wanted to spend as much time as I could with them—socially, at the rink, in a restaurant, anywhere—so that they could pass on to me their beliefs about the road to personal success and to winning as a team.

As a leader, Jean Béliveau was calm and focused, and he preached by example. A couple of years before he died in 2014, someone asked him how he wanted to be remembered and he said, "I want to be remembered as a team player." That tells you a lot. He didn't say, "I want to be remembered as the guy who scored over five hundred goals." There was no mention of his records. He wanted to be thought of as a team player. That's who he was.

When I was in New York in '98, I got a message saying that the Rocket wanted to come see me before the game that night. At around four-thirty that afternoon the trainer came in the room and said, "The Rocket's here."

When I went out to meet him, he handed me a replica of the beautiful Maurice Richard Trophy, which features a gold figure of the Rocket with his stick on the ice. That year the NHL had donated the trophy to be awarded annually to the leading scorer. Maurice said, "Wayne, I know you're never going to win this trophy, but I want you to have one. You should have won it."

To this day it's the only trophy I have in my home. It sits on a bookshelf in our study next to the kitchen. You can't go anywhere in the house without seeing it.

I recently had a wonderful dinner with Alex Ovechkin, who reminded me of me when I first met Gordie Howe. I'd asked Gordie a thousand questions, just as Alex did. "How do you get ready? What do you eat before a game? What do you think of this guy? How many days a week do you practice?"

In the old days they used to say that if you don't win a Stanley Cup, you're not a Hall of Famer. Now it's tougher to win a Cup. There are more teams, for one, and because of the salary cap there's more parity. So in this day and age you can make it into the Hall without a Cup, but it's an extra notch if you win it. Alex desperately wants to win a Stanley Cup. That's all he thinks about, that's all he cares about. I think that when most kids come into the NHL they're in a sort of survival mode, just wanting to stay in the league. Then, as they start succeeding, their mindset changes to wanting to make a difference on their team, and from there it goes to wanting to win a championship. That's where Alex is now.

We talked about what it takes to win, how special it is when you do, and how important it is to lift the Stanley Cup. Alex is a nice young man, and I have a great deal of fondness for him. I told him that when he gets to the final game and the chance to win the Stanley Cup, Janet and I will be there.

I've had the opportunity for some quiet, one-on-one sit-downs with other guys from the next generation. Hockey has changed—the game is different from what it was in the 80s, and in the 80s it was different from what it was in the 50s—but the players themselves haven't changed a whole lot. I still see the will to win, the intensity, the unselfishness, the sacrifices they make, and the best players playing at a higher level when it counts. None of that has changed.

I've always carried with me something Gordie Howe told me at the '79 series against Moscow Dynamo. We were talking about what to expect, and Gordie said, "All you gotta do is just play the way you've always played. Get the puck to Mark and me and we'll be fine." Not even two minutes into the game, Gordie got the puck and sent it to me. I gave it to Mark, Mark gave it to Gordie, and Gordie gave it back to me, and I scored. After the game I said, "Gordie, oh my God, you really are that good."

He said, "You know, Wayne, I just love to play, and if you love to play good things happen."

Mark Messier used to say, "There's not one thing about the game I don't love." I felt the same way—going to practice, being in the locker room, sitting on the bench, playing big matchups. There were years when I played more than 130 games—preseason, the Canada Cup, the playoffs, and another fourteen exhibition games. We played in Houston, San Antonio, Dallas, Cincinnati. Places where they were trying to promote hockey. Mark Messier and I played every one of them because people were paying to come and see us. Someone might have saved up for a whole year or driven for hours to see us play. You had to put your best foot forward. What if it was some kid's first time at a game?

My dad's mother, my grandmother Mary, took me to my first NHL game at Maple Leaf Gardens. I was seven, about to turn eight, and the Leafs were playing the Oakland Seals. On January 1, 1969, my dad drove us down from Brantford to the Gardens in Toronto. He had a light-blue Pontiac that chugged so much my stomach was in a knot the whole way. Would the car make it to the game or would we break down and miss it altogether?

He dropped us off in front and said, "I'll pick you guys up right here when it's over." I think he was nervous because I was so young and my grandmother was older. She would have been only fifty-nine. That's not very old to me now, but I remember looking up at her and thinking she was an old, old lady, which is funny because I'm in my mid-fifties now and have a grandson of my own.

We were at the very top row in the gray seats, right across from the Seals' bench, between the red line and the blue line on the side where the TV cameras shoot *Hockey Night in Canada*. When the Leafs came on the ice for warm-up, I couldn't believe how blue their uniforms were. I'd only seen the games on black-and-white TV.

Toronto had just won the Cup two years earlier. They had Dave Keon, Ron Ellis, Norm Ullman, Paul Henderson, Murray Oliver, Bob Pulford, and Tim Horton. The Seals were in just their second year after expansion. So Toronto's shots on goal were almost double theirs, but to me it was incredibly exciting.

The final score was 7–3. My grandmother stood up to go and I said, "We can't leave, I gotta see the three stars." On TV you just saw them skate up to the announcer, but in real life they sat on the bench and skated out when their names were called.

I think Ron Ellis was the first star, if I remember correctly. On the way out I said to my grandmother, "That was the best night ever. I want to play hockey here someday." It was the first time I'd ever told anyone about wanting to be an NHL player. She looked down at me and nodded. "You're going to make it, Wayne. You'll see."

ACKNOWLEDGMENTS

This book is dedicated to my amazing wife of nearly thirty years, Janet Jones Gretzky. Without her nothing would be possible, especially our wonderful children—Paulina, Ty, Trevor, Tristan, Emma, and our more recent additions, Dustin and Tatum.

I want to thank all our extended family for being there for the highs and lows of this amazing journey tougher. My mom and dad have been there from the very beginning, and I would not be the son, brother, father, or husband I am today without their love, support, and guidance every step of the way. Also my grandparents, Harold and Betty Hockin, and Tony and Mary Gretzky, who were always there for our family, and my mother-in-law, Jean, who has always been a shoulder to lean on and the most wonderful grandmother to all of our children. My brother Glen has been a constant at my side, always there to bounce an idea off of or provide another way to look at things—as have my brothers Brent and Keith.

I would like to thank my partner through this process, Kirstie Day, who shepherded this idea from just an idea to a book that I am really proud of. Kirstie and I would like to thank the following people for all of their help with the elaborate, sometimes grueling, but incredibly rewarding process of getting a book produced and written:

Clara Gerzon, my right hand and chief financial officer at WDG Enterprises, my agent Ira Stahlberger from WME | IMG and his wonderful associate Janelle Miller, Jay Mandel from WME's literary division, Alicia Glekas Everett of WME Business Affairs, and Lauren Shonkoff, Jay's terrific assistant. Kirstie's content team: contributing writer and editor Larry Day, chief researcher Kaitlyn Kanygin, hockey expert and fact checker Ron Wight, Julie Sinclair, Steve McLellan, and Max Sinclair, as well as Len Glickman from Cassels Brock Lawyers.

From Penguin, Nick Garrison, our editor, who worked so tirelessly on this book and whose boundless determination brought the initial idea to life, publisher Nicole Winstanley, who stepped up for us at crucial moments, president Kristin Cochrane, and David Ross, Justin Stoller, and Liz Lee, all of whom threw themselves into the painstaking work of ensuring that it all came together.

Special thanks go out to good friend Kevin Lowe, Eddie Mio and Bob Nicholson, Don Metz and Tom Braid with Oilers Entertainment Group. Thanks to my friend and confidant Mike Barnett, too. Also Bruce Bennett, Andy Moog, Craig Patrick, Scotty Bowman, Ernie Hicke, Lee Fogolin, Bill Torrey, Morris Lukowich, Serge Savard, Joe Pelletier, and Tom Webster, as well as:

Kathy Bailey	Craig Campbell and	Steve Carlson
Charles Barkley	the Hockey Hall	Dana Carvey
Red Berenson	of Fame	Ron Chipperfield

ACKNOWLEDGMENTS

Kim Clackson
Bobby Clarke
Cam Connor
Ronald Corey
Jimmy Craig
Joe Daley
Shane Doan
Peter Driscoll
Dave Dryden
Theoren Fleury
Kerry Fraser
Mike Gartner
Blake Geoffrion
Danny Geoffrion
Marlene Geoffrion
Tony Granato
Randy Gregg
Glenn Hall
Al Hamilton
Craig Hartsburg
Kelly Hrudey
Pat Hughes
Dick Irvin Jr.

Curtis Joseph
Red Kelly
Ed Kirrane
Jack Kirrane
Paula Kirrane
Adam Kostis
Mike Krushelnyski
Jari Kurri
Brian Leetch
Claude Lemieux
Ken Linseman
Ron and Cari MacLean
Kevin McClelland
Wendy McCreary and
	the NHL Alumni
Bill McCreary Jr.
Bruce McNall
Marty McSorley
Barry Melrose
John Mio
Rennie Mio
Larry Murphy
Bearcat Murray

John Muckler
Lou Nanne
Bernie Nicholls
Jim Nill
Terry O'Malley
Willie O'Ree
Dean Patrick
Jamie Belo Patrick
Carey and Jerry Price
Brian Propp
Doug Risebrough
Jerry Rollins
Terry Ruskowski
Joe Sakic
Glen Sather
Fred Sasakamoose
Ken Schinkel
Eddie Shack
Dave Semenko
Jay Sinclair
Brent Sutter
Mike Vernon
Julie Folk Woldu

PHOTO CREDITS

Lake Placid victory, 1980: AP Photo

Tex Rickard: Library of Congress, Prints & Photographs Division, LC-DIG-ggbain-20962

Lester Patrick: Courtesy of Jamie Patrick

Jack Kent Cooke: Herald Examiner Collection/Los Angeles Public Library

With Peter Pocklington at trade press conference: Edmonton Sun/Post Media

Jacques Plante: Library and Archives Canada, Acc. no. 1987-129, PA-195211

Howie Morenz receiving stitches: Courtesy of the Boston Public Library, Leslie Jones Collection

Brendan Shanahan: AP Photo/Karl B. DeBlaker

Boston Bruins in practice sweaters: Courtesy of the Boston Public Library, Leslie Jones Collection

Dick Irvin: Hockey Hall of Fame

Punch Imlach: Richard Holborn, Archives of Ontario, I0005427

Gordie Howe with the Red Wings: Courtesy of the Ernie Harwell Sports Collection, Detroit Public Library

Gordie Howe with his sons, Marty and Mark: Dick Darrell/Toronto Star via Getty Images

With Gordie Howe: B. Bennett/Getty Images

Lou Fontinato: B. Bennett/Getty Images

Glenn Hall: Frank Lennon/Getty Images

Ted Lindsay: Bettmann/Getty Images

Marcel Dionne: Paul Chinn, Herald Examiner Collection/Los Angeles Public Library

Jean Béliveau: B. Bennett/Getty Images

Young Gretzky with Jean Béliveau: ©Archives/Journal de Québec

Playing with Gordie Howe: Bill London/Hockey Hall of Fame

Mario Lemieux and Jaromir Jagr: Chris Relke/Hockey Hall of Fame

The Soviets' KLM Line: B. Bennett/Getty Images

Willie O'Ree: Post Media

Fred Sasakamoose: Hockey Hall of Fame

California Golden Seals: Portnoy/Hockey Hall of Fame

Kim Clackson with the Pittsburgh Penguins: Portnoy/Hockey Hall of Fame

Bill Goldsworthy with the Minnesota North Stars: Portnoy/Hockey Hall of Fame

Bobby Clarke: B. Bennett/Getty Images

"In the office": Edmonton Sun/Post Media

In Vaughan Nationals sweater, 1975: CP Photo/The Globe and Mail

Bobby Hull with $1,000,000 check: CP Archive Photo

Flying to Edmonton: Edmonton Sun/Post Media

First game in Edmonton: Edmonton Journal/Post Media

Bobby Clarke celebrates with Bobby Hull, 1976 Canada Cup: Frank Prazak/Hockey Hall of Fame

With Guy Lafleur: Doug Griffin/Getty Images

Habs celebrating 1979 Stanley Cup victory: CP Photo/Charlie Palmer

Steve Yzerman raises the Stanley Cup with the Wings: Dave Sandford/Hockey Hall of Fame

With Dave Dryden and Brett Callighen: Edmonton Sun/Post Media

Mark Messier playing ping-pong: Edmonton Sun/Post Media

Kurri and Anderson with Campbell Bowl: Oilers Entertainment Group

With Dave Babych: Phil Hossack/Winnipeg Free Press

Playing against the Flames: David E. Klutho/Getty Images

Playing against the Islanders: Paul Bereswill/ Hockey Hall of Fame

Mark Messier and Joel Otto: David E. Klutho/Getty Images

1988 Oilers fourth Cup win: Edmonton Sun/Post Media

Michel Goulet, 1984 Canada Cup: B. Bennett/Getty Images

Glenn Anderson and Igor Larionov, 1987 Canada Cup: B. Bennett/Getty Images

Mario Lemieux, 1987 Canada Cup: B. Bennett/Getty Images

With Brian Leetch, 1991 Canada Cup: B. Bennett/Getty Images

Keith Tkachuk and Claude Lemieux, 1996 World Cup: J Giamundo/
    Getty Images

With Dave Semenko: Edmonton Sun/Post Media

With Marty McSorley: B. Bennett/Getty Images

Jarome Iginla: B. Bennett/Getty Images

Doug Gilmour: David E. Klutho/Getty Images

Wendel Clark and Marty McSorley: B. Bennett/Getty Images

Playing against the Canadiens: Paul Bereswill/Hockey Hall of Fame

The Chicago Blackhawks: B. Bennett/Getty Images

Sidney Crosby: Damon Tarver/CSM/REX/Shutterstock

With Connor McDavid: Andy Devlin/Getty Images

Gordie Howe: B. Bennett/Getty Images

With Walter Gretzky: Dennis Robinson/The Globe and Mail

Wayne and Janet: Edmonton Sun/Post Media

INDEX

INDEX

INDEX

INDEX

INDEX